DONALD A. YATES
324 Morrill Hall
Mich. State Univ
E. Lansing, Mich.

SOTILEZA

José María de Pereda

By Glenn Barr

EDITOR

A Cara o Cruz, Macmillan, 1932.
Selections From A. Palacio Valdes (with H. J. Russell), American Book Co., 1935.
Revista de America, II (with Amner and Staubach), Ginn and Co., 1946.
Anaconda (with W. K. Jones), D. C. Heath, 1948.
Cuatro Cuentos Rioplatenses, D. C. Heath, 1950.

AUTHOR

Un Verano en Mexico (with W. K. Jones), D. C. Heath, 1942.
Resumen Gramatical (with W. K. Jones), D. C. Heath, 1942.
Our Friends in South America (with W. K. Jones, et al.), Macmillan, 1950.
Translation of *Sotileza*.

SOTILEZA

A Novel by José María de Pereda

Translated by

GLENN BARR, Ph.D.
*Professor of Romanic Languages
Miami University, Oxford, Ohio*

An Exposition–Banner Book

EXPOSITION PRESS   NEW YORK

Exposition Press Inc., 386 Park Avenue So., New York 16, N.Y.

FIRST EDITION

© 1959 by Glenn Barr. *All rights reserved, including the right of reproduction in whole or in part in any form, except for brief quotations in critical essays and reviews.* Manufactured in the United States of America.

to
MARCELLE

PREFACE

In this translation of *Sotileza* I have used the Suárez edition, Madrid, 1923 and the Aguilar edition, Madrid, 1950. I have also had the opportunity of consulting the French translation (Paris, 1899), and the Italian translation (Milan, 1935).

I am most grateful to my friend and former colleague at the Ohio State University, Professor Demetrio Cabarga, whose M.A. thesis, *Notes on the Vocabulary of Sotileza,* was most helpful. I would also like to thank many friends and colleagues for helpful suggestions. Chief among these helpers is Padre Antonio Gómez L. Hoyos, of Santander, who was of constant help to me during my visit to that city in 1957.

G. B.

Oxford, Ohio
July 4, 1959

CONTENTS

Introduction   11

PART ONE

1. Cocoons   19
2. From the Maruca Beach to San Martín Hill   32
3. Where the Mullet Girl Had Landed   42
4. Where She Was Wanted   53
5. How and Why She Was Given Shelter   68
6. A Meeting of the Fisherman's Guild   77
7. The Sailors of That Day   80
8. Venancio Liencres, Owner of *La Montañesa*   91
9. The Interests and Enthusiasm of Andrés   97
10. The *Patache* and Other Particulars   104
11. Don Venancio's Family, a Button and a Nickname   112

PART TWO

12. Butterflies   123
13. Andrés' Orbit   134
14. The Tempter on Stage   143
15. The Old Stand-By   154
16. A Day's Fishing   164
17. The Night of That Same Day   176
18. Getting Fleeced   185
19. How About the Moat in Your Own Eye?   197
20. Cleto's Love Affair   207
21. Various Matters; and Muergo All Dressed Up   217
22. The Upper Town and the Lower Town   226
23. The Females of the Mocejón Family   232
24. Some Results of That Scandal   252
25. Other Consequences   260
26. Further Consequences   272
27. Another Result That Was to Be Expected   280
28. The Most Serious Consequence of All   290
29. In Which Everything Comes to an End   307

INTRODUCTION

The two great masters of the novel in nineteenth-century Spain were Benito Pérez Galdós (1843-1920) and José María de Pereda (1833-1906). Galdós came from the Canary Islands and wrote about Spain as a whole. He was liberal and progressive in his attitude and tried to give Spaniards a new national conscience. Many of his works have been translated into English and several have been edited with notes and vocabulary for the study of Spanish in the United States. He and Pereda were good friends.

Pereda was born in Polanco, near the city of Santander in northern Spain. This area, with the sea and mountains, became almost a passion with him. He wrote mostly about this region, known as La Montaña. His family was aristocratic, wealthy, patrician; consequently he was conservative and in favor of tradition, with a firm, honest faith and almost a hostile attitude toward modernism.

This edition of *Sotileza* is the first of his novels translated into English. Doubtless no one ever tried to do any of them before because of the richness of his vocabulary and the difficulty of finding the meaning of many of his popular expressions. The difficulty of fully understanding *Sotileza*, for instance, is best illustrated by the fact that an eight-page glossary is included in Spanish editions of this novel. The richness of Pereda's vocabulary is demonstrated by the relatively large number of pages of notes and vocabulary in an American classroom edition of his *Pedro Sanchez*,[1] a novel whose action takes place in Madrid, and whose language is void of regional terminology.

Pereda went to school in Santander from 1844 to 1850 and came to love its people and customs. During this time he made

---

[1] Ralph Emerson Basset, *Pedro Sanchez*, Ginn and Co., New York, 1907.

the observations which later became the novel *Sotileza*. In his introduction to this work he states that he is the chronicler of the old traditions, of the old Santander that was fast disappearing because of modern improvements such as railroads and breakwaters.

Other great novels by him dealing with La Montaña are *El Sabor de la Tierruca* (1882) and *Peñas Arriba* (1889). *Sotileza* (1884) is considered his masterpiece, and his most popular novel. It has been translated into French (Paris, 1899), German (date not known), and Italian (Milan, 1935).

Pereda excels in description and in portrayal of character. He is a realist who paints life as he sees it, but not with the sordidness and moroseness of some of his European contemporaries. *Sotileza* appeared at the time when extreme scientific realism and naturalism were in vogue in Europe. But even the unfavorable environment in which the heroine is placed cannot overcome her strength of character and her moral fiber.

Padre Apolinar, affectionately known as Pa'e 'Polinar, is the best-drawn character in the book. The first chapter, in which he is trying to teach something to a group of young wharf rats, has been immortalized in bronze as part of a large monument to Pereda on the Paseo de Pereda in Santander. The next to the last chapter, which describes a storm at sea, is one of the greatest in all Spanish literature.

Pereda's language is of the people. His art is not the art of the cities, penetrated with conflicts of ideas and sentiments; his art is regional, dealing with picturesque customs and manners of the people. His characters speak with living dialogue.

Silda, nicknamed Sotileza, is a woman who seems to have little or no feelings, and has difficulty in expressing any she might have, but in all cases she is complete master of herself. She is quite enigmatic; both attractive and repellent. She seems to believe that actions speak louder than words.

Translation is a difficult art. The translation of any novel by Pereda is complicated by its vocabulary, especially *Sotileza*, whose talk of the fisherfolk requires a glossary even for his own

Introduction

countrymen. Efforts to maintain the original word order would only complicate the pages for English readers. In the present translation an attempt is made to translate ideas and meaning rather than words. To me, translation is interpretation, or transposition. To get any sense in English out of some of Pereda's sentences that are ten and twelve lines long, certain unimportant parts must be deleted. Likewise some of his long descriptions that have nothing to do with plot or characters have been omitted, especially in Chapters VI, VII, X and the end of Chapter I.

The title of the novel, *Sotileza*, is a double pun in Spanish. By the end of the first part of the novel the little girl Silda (Casilda) has been given the nickname of Sotileza both because of her skill (*sutileza*) with the needle, and because she is strong and fine like the wire leader or *sutileza* close to the fishhook.

Both the French and Italian translators, uncertain what dialect to employ, made the Santander wharf rats and fishermen speak academic French and Italian. I have tried to keep the original flavor of the novel by using mistakes in grammar, mispronunciations, etc. The nicknames have been kept in Spanish with an English equivalent the first time used. The author explains the fondness for nicknames around Santander in Chapter I. Spaniards, using interjections, are inclined to use dirty, filthy words; I have substituted the kind of swear words that are more familiar to American usage. (It might be observed that Pereda, alive at the time of the French translation, insisted that some of the interjections used by Pa'e 'Polinar be kept in Spanish because the French equivalents suggested did not meet with his approval.)

The search for English equivalents of many words and expressions used in *Sotileza* proved long. During the summer of 1957 I spent four very delightful weeks in the lovely city of Santander working in the Menéndez y Pelayo Library, and talking with sailors, fishermen, teachers and priests trying to learn the meaning of some words and expressions. Fishermen frequently replied that their grandfathers could have told me but they couldn't because the sailboats and the hand lines used in Pereda's time were now replaced by motorized boats and nets.

In spite of this and a new housing project for sailors and fishermen, called appropriately enough Sotileza, the lot of the sailor-fisherman in Santander is still hard and fraught with danger. Many of them still live on Calle Alta (High Street), and the ascent is just as steep as ever, and the houses just as crowded. The balconies, too, continue draped with drying nets and gear. The fisherfolk of today still have many of the brutal vicissitudes, the strife, the sorrows, the sullen resignation and the sense of fatality of those of Pereda's day.

Typical of critical opinion of Pereda and his work is what Professor Northup says in his *Introduction to Spanish Literature:*[2] "Pereda is the sympathetic historian of the Santander fisherfolk and the primitive farmers of the hilly hinterland. *Sotileza*, his most popular novel, is the finest novel of the sea written by a Spaniard.

"The richness of vocabulary and the frequent use of dialect make him a difficult author for foreigners, and even for Spaniards. He is king of regional novelists, classic in his prose."

The *History of Spanish Literature*[3] by Mérimée and Morley states: "Pereda drew his creations from within; from his plastic and powerful imagination; from his heart, overflowing with noble passion; from his extraordinary tenacious love of his native soil; from his unusual powers of observation and natural talent for expression. Some of his works are pure masterpieces. I do not hesitate so to class *Sotileza*, which evokes old Santander, her men and things, with such extraordinary power.

"In every line he wrote, the reader can sniff the salt breezes from the Cantabrian shore or the fortifying odors of the mountain. It is evident that his studies were conceived and executed in the open air, from living models, amid familiar landscapes. Many of his types have been caught by surprise and fixed alive

---

[2] G. T. Northup, *Introduction to Spanish Literature,* Chicago, 1925.
[3] Mérimée and Morley, *The History of Spanish Literature,* New York, 1930.

on paper, with their manner of being, hobbies and tricks of speech."

James Fitzmaurice-Kelley (1857-1923), dean of British Hispanists, makes the following statement about Pereda in volume 17 of the *Encyclopedia Britannica*: "Pereda's masterpiece is *Sotileza* (1884), a vigorous rendering of marine life by an artist who perceives and admires the daily heroisms of his fisherfolk. He belongs to the native realistic school of Spain. His realism is purely Spanish, as remote from Zola's moroseness as from the graceful sentimentality of Pierre Loti. Few 19th century writers possessed the virile temperament of Pereda, and with the exception of Tolstoy, none kept a moral end more steadily in view. He saw, knew, understood character; he created not only types, but living personages. His descriptive powers were of the highest order, and his style, pure of all affectations and embellishments, is of singular force and suppleness. He was as original a genius as Spain produced during the 19th century."

Dr. William Lamonte, professor of English literature at Rutgers University, included *Sotileza* in his list of the one hundred greatest world novels.

A WORD OR TWO ABOUT SANTANDER

Much of the action of *Sotileza* takes place on High Street (Calle Alta) in Santander about 1850. It is a rather steep hill which starts not very far from the Cathedral, near which were plazas and market places. At the time of the action of the novel the richer people lived on the level ground near the waterfront, and the poorer sailors and fishermen lived on the hills. In those days a ramp, now called Rampa de Sotileza, gave access to the harbor area from High Street. During the years much land has been reclaimed from the bay to make room for the railroad station and yards, as well as a large area with trees and gardens called the Paseo de Pereda. Hospital Hill connected the level business section with High Street.

From San Martín Hill, toward the entrance of the bay, there

is a magnificent panorama of the large bay and the lovely mountains that surround it. Viewers from here could see ships approaching from the open ocean (Bay of Biscay), and watch them make the turn at the Point (Magdalena Peninsula) to enter the harbor area and drop anchor. Winds from the nearby mountains, tides, and a large sand bar not far from the Magdalena Peninsula make navigation difficult at times.

The boat race in Chapter XXII, between guilds of the Lower Town and the Upper Town, was held in the harbor area where the water would be relatively calm. Andrés' feat of bringing the fishing boat safely into port during the storm in Chapter XXVIII required a lot of skill and strength. At the Point he had to manipulate the boat to make practically a right-angle turn in order to avoid the sand bar and destruction.

The picnic in Chapter XVI was held on the opposite side of the bay. Sardinero Beach, out near the Smaller Cape (Cabo Menor) is now lined with apartment houses and summer hotels. Beyond Smaller Cape is Larger Cape (Cabo Mayor) which forms the west side of the entrance to the Bay of Santander, a truly beautiful bay and harbor.

SOTILEZA

PART ONE

1 ~ COCOONS

The room was narrow, with a low ceiling and little light. The walls which once had been white were blackened in spots. A heavy layer of dirt, almost hardened, covered the worn floor boards. It contained a pine table, a twisted leather armchair and three other broken chairs. On the walls were two pictures of the Crucifixion, a crucifix with a wreath of dry Palm Sunday laurel around it and a rosary from Jerusalem. An inkwell, made out of a cow's horn, with a quill pen in it, a badly worn old prayer book, a black leather bag, a calendar and a tin candleholder rested on top of the table. A blue cotton umbrella, with a curved horn handle, was standing in one of the darkest corners. The room also had a sleeping alcove. Through the chintz curtain, too small to cover the small door, one could see a bed that seemed rather hard. On it was a long black cloak and a black shovel hat, worn by priests.

Dressed in a patched cloak, black slippers and a worn velvet cap, a priest was trying, with great difficulty, to walk between the umbrella, the chairs and the table, which filled most of the room, and a half dozen ragged children who were either leaning against the wall or flattening their noses against the windowpanes or sitting, somewhat disjointedly, on the chairs quite a distance from the table. The curate was tall and somewhat stooped. His eyes were weak and sensitive to the light. Because of this, he held his head slightly forward. He had quite a large reddish nose, rather thick lips and a rough darkened skin and blackened teeth.

Among all these urchins there was not a sign of a shoe or a whole shirt. All six of them were barefooted, and half of them had no shirt at all. One of them covered his nakedness with a heavy patched jacket belonging to his father. Only a couple of them had pants in good condition. The only thing that they all had in common was a dirty face, tousled hair and dirty legs covered with scabs. The oldest of them was probably not more than ten years old. All of them smelled worse than a doghouse.

"Let's see. Who made the creed?" asked the priest as he slapped with a long ruler the boy wearing the coat. He was cross-eyed, thick-lipped, tanned a copper color and had an unusually large head. Up to this moment, he had been amusing himself by rubbing his nose against the window.

The urchin turned around after squirting a thin stream of saliva between two of his front teeth and replied, shrugging his shoulders:

"How do I know?"

"And why don't you know, you young whelp? Why are you coming here to my house? How many times have I told you that it was the Apostles? But it is not possible to make a silk purse out of a sow's ear. Now tell me, how many gods are there?"

"Gods?" repeated the boy questioned, crossing his arms behind him so that his nakedness was exposed in front because the coat had no buttons, nor any buttonholes in which to put them even if there had been any.

The good priest noticed this and said, grabbing the lapels and crossing one over the other:

"Cover up this filth, you dirty pig! And where are the buttons for your coat?"

"I ain't got none."

"You probably lost them in some gambling game."

"I did have a piece of sail rope, but I lost that this morning."

The priest went to the table and took a piece of string from the drawer. With great difficulty he succeeded in fastening the two patched sides of the coat together in order to cover up the boy's nakedness. Then he repeated the question:

"How many gods are there?"

"Well, there must be at the most eight or nine," said the boy, crossing his hands behind him again.

"Out of the depths of ignorance! Blessed Virgin, what an animal! And the persons of the Trinity, how many are there?"

The cross-eyed boy looked the priest over from head to toe, and with the greatest of curiosity answered the priest, who was looking at him as best he could with his scant vision:

"Persons! What are persons, sir?"

"Blessed Saint Apolinaris!" exclaimed the simple priest, making the sign of the cross. "So—you don't know what persons are, or what a person is? Well, then, what are you?"

"Who, me? I'm Muergo" (a razor clam, ugly and almost inedible).

"You're not even that, because there are lots of them on the beach with more brains than you've got. What are persons?" repeated the priest, facing the boy on Muergo's right, also shirtless, but wearing a pair of trousers which were small and not much good. All in all he was less ugly than Muergo.

This boy, not knowing what to answer, looked at the fellow closest to him, who looked at the next one in line. Soon all were looking at each other with the same doubt painted on their faces.

"So!" exclaimed the priest, again facing the boy next to Muergo. "You don't know what you are either?"

"Oh, sure thing, I do," replied the boy, believing that he saw a way out of his difficulties.

"Well, what are you?"

"I'm Survia" (poison).

"That's exactly what I should give you now so that you could die, you jackass. And you, what are you?" added the curate, turning to another boy who was wearing no coat, half a shirt and not much that could be called trousers.

"I'm Sula," (sardine) replied the urchin, who was blond and thin, a combination that made the dirt on his body more noticeable than on the tanned background of his companions.

In this same way, trying to answer the same questions, the other three boys gave their nicknames, which were Cole (head-first dive), Guarín (suckling pig) and Toletes (oarlock pin). Probably none of them knew his baptismal name.

The priest, who had looked them over well, did not lose his patience. He uttered a few unpleasant expressions that they could understand, and another half dozen in Latin. Then he said to them with saintly calmness:

"It's all my fault. I'm to blame for all this, because I keep shaking the tree when I know very well that there is no fruit on it to come down. The least that any of you has been coming to me is two months. And for what good, by the holy name of God? And why, by the Blessed Virgin? Just because Padre Apolinar is so easily influenced and is such an easy mark and is so very good. Women say to him: 'Pa'e 'Polinar, this kid is driving me crazy because I can't do anything with him. In school they do not pay a bit of attention to him. . . . This fellow, and that one and the boy upstairs or the boy downstairs . . . you, who understand all this, that's why you were born. . . . I wish you'd teach him. . . . You tame him. . . . You instruct him in proper behavior.' And with three of you who offer to come, and three that I have to go after, you see the house full of kids, and I endure this smell, and explain, and hammer away at them . . . and then give them some bit of bait so that they will come back for another nibble another day, because I know well what would happen otherwise . . . and do it all good-naturedly because it is your duty, because you are what you are, a priest of our Lord and Master Jesus Christ . . . in whose name I repeat His words: 'Suffer little children to come unto me.' And they all laugh at the neighbor downstairs, and at the father of that fellow, and at the mother of another farther down the street. And they all talk and gossip and say that you kids leave my hands more like jackasses than when you first came to me, just as many others did who came here long before you. . . . Vile tongues, miserable, lustful flesh!

"You laugh at that just as I do, because I should laugh. . . . But you blockheads, worse than blockheads, what do you do to help the efforts of Padre Apolinar? How are you coming with your letters at the end of two months? You don't even recognize the letter O in this classroom if I paint it on the wall for you. And the Christian Doctrine . . . it is evident what you know about that. . . . As I do not want to get angry with you, although I really have reasons to throw each one of you headfirst out the window. . . . Let's get to something else, and praised be the Lord for ever and ever, because there is nothing else that matters. . . ."

After this outburst he walked around with his hands clasped behind him and passed to what he called his plain, everyday duty: to ask these urchins the usual simple prayers so that they would not forget them, because this was the only thing that he had succeeded in getting into their heads, even partially. Muergo didn't need help more than three times in the Ave Maria, Cole said the Lord's Prayer only so-so and the one who knew the Creed best didn't get beyond "his only begotten son" without some prompting.

In view of all this Padre Apolinar did not give Sula more than half a cooky, a button from an officer's uniform to Toletes and a dried fig to Guarin.

"This isn't very much, boys," the poor priest said to them at once. "Another time it may be less and worse. Now, make sail, you rascals . . . but wait a minute, Muergo."

They all stopped. The curate said to Muergo, lifting up the ends of his coat:

"You can't go on this way, without a shirt. When you have a coat it is all right, but not without pants. Where are your pants?"

"Mum put them out on the grass to dry day before yesterday," replied Muergo haltingly.

"And haven't they dried out yet, man alive?"

"A cow ate 'em up while Mum was takin' the insides out of a fish that smelt pretty bad."

"Punishment from God, Muergo. Punishment from God!" said Padre Apolinar, scratching the back of his neck. "The fish that smell bad are old and rotten and should be thrown back into the sea and not secretly cleaned to be sold later at half price to poor people like me who are so very gullible. But wasn't there anything left of the pants, boy?"

"Just the patch on the seat," replied Muergo, "and that was in ribbons."

"That's very little," said the priest, squirming inside his clothes—a movement that was very habitual with him. "And aren't there any other pants in the house?"

"No, sir."

"Nor any guess about where some might come from?"

"No, sir."

"Great heavens! In any case you can't go on this way. You have more than enough cloth in that coat to cover your body, but it does not fit you at all and that rope might break any minute. You don't notice it, and even if you did, it wouldn't make any difference, so it's the same old thing, the same old thing. You can't do anything, but you can still say: 'Carry me on your back, Padre Apolinar.' Isn't that it? Isn't that the pure truth? It surely is, I swear!"

Muergo shrugged his shoulders and Padre Apolinar went into his bedroom. There was the sound of something being moved and muttered Latin expressions. He was not long in reappearing. In his hands he carried a black bundle which he placed at once in Muergo's hands.

"These are not much," he said to him, "but at least they are trousers. You tell your mother to fix them for you as best she can. And tell her not to put them out to dry on the grass, as she did with the last pair, whenever she has to wash them. If they do not seem like much to her, she can be consoled by the fact that right now not even Padre Apolinar has a pair as good. So start moving, you rascals. Set your sails and get going with the breeze."

Again the group started to move, grunting and squealing like a drove of pigs that smell the swill when it leaves the hogpen. All their faces showed the eagerness of wanting to reach Padre Apolinar's stairway in order to examine the gift given to Muergo, who was surprised that the gift was warm when the priest gave it to him.

Just then the door opened and two new personages came into the room. One was a ruddy-faced, fat little boy about twelve years of age with black eyes, shiny messed up hair, a pleasing mouth and a round chin. He was dressed like the children of the better-class families and seemed to be in good health. He was leading by the hand a poor little girl, considerably shorter, thin, pale and somewhat sharp-nosed. She had blond hair, a smooth forehead and a rather brave, bold look. Her feet and legs were bare. The portion of her skin that could be seen was white and clean. All that she had on was a short serge petticoat, already old and worn, held up by a flexible belt over an old blouse, which was not torn or greasy. The same could be said for the petticoat. There are children who by nature are clean without realizing it, just the same as cats. This comparison is not inapt because there was something of the feline in the graciousness, in the sure, gentle step, in the wild, distrustful countenance of this shy little girl.

As soon as he saw her Muergo began to laugh like a fool, Cole let out a loud snort and Sula also let out one, but not quite so loud. The little girl imitated Muergo with pretended laughter, making her face rather ugly, without paying the slightest attention to the other urchins or to Padre Apolinar, who gave a blow with his knuckles to each of the three boys.

"Why this laughter, you pigs?"

"She's a Highstreeter . . . ho, ho, ho," replied Muergo, rubbing his head, which had just been hammered by Padre Apolinar's knuckles.

"We know her," explained Cole, rubbing his matted hair. "She just about drowned, and if it hadn't been for Muergo . . ." added Sula.

Muergo started to laugh again in the same foolish manner, and the little girl continued to make faces at him.

"And why are you laughing, you goose?" asked the priest, giving him another blow. "That certainly is something to laugh at!"

"She's a Highstreeter," replied Cole, "and was playing on a log in the water makin' it go up and down at Maruca Beach. Me and Sula was there throwin' stones at her from the shore. Then Muergo came and he hit her with a rock, and splash, into the water headfirst."

"Who?" asked the priest.

"She did," replied Cole. "I thought she was drownin', 'cause she was goin' down, and Muergo was laughin'."

"Me too," volunteered Sula. "I yelled to him: 'Dive in after her, Muergo, you swim well. Get her out 'cause she's drownin'.' And then he jumped in and pulled her out. Then we put her on the ground with her keel up and hit her on the back and she spit out the water she'd swallowed."

"Is that true, girl?" asked the priest.

"Yes, sir," she replied, without ceasing to imitate Muergo, who was now laughing like an idiot.

"All right," replied the priest. "But what did you come here for; and you, Andrés, why did you come? And why are you holding her by the hand? In what café did you just eat together? And what tune do I play in all this?"

"She's a Highstreeter," the boy named Andrés replied very seriously.

"Yes, yes, I'm finding that out. They've told me that already three times. And what's so funny about that?"

"I have known her for quite a while at the boat dock," continued Andrés. "She comes down there about every day. I didn't know about what happened at Maruca, but if I had known about it"—and he made a defiant gesture at Muergo—"because I know these fellows too."

"At the boat dock?" asked Padre Apolinar without a trace of astonishment.

"Yes, sir," answered Andrés. "They go there often."

"And he goes to Maruca Beach," added Guarín.

"The devil take you! What a place for you to go! You are surely showing your true colors. But let's get down to cases. It turns out so far that this girl is a Highstreeter, and that you and all these rascals, in spite of different social standings, are pretty much alike. And what more?"

"This morning the lookout sent word to my mother that the *Montañesa* had been sighted, and I left the house to go to San Martín Hill to watch it come in . . . and I reached the boat dock . . . and . . ."

"The boat dock? Don't you live on San Francisco Street?"

"Yes, sir."

"Well, you certainly took a good road to get to San Martín Hill!"

"I was going to see if Cuco was there and whether he wanted to go along with me."

"Cuco! So . . . you are also a friend of Cuco's? That discourteous tough wharf rat who sings indecent songs whenever he sees me. . . . To the devil with all these kids."

"I never heard him sing those songs. Maybe he is a bad boy, but he never hurts anybody. He works on Castrejo's boat and is teaching me how to row and how to dive headfirst and how to tread water and how to float on my back and . . ."

"Yes, and to steal cigars from your father to give to him, and to play hooky, and to get into fights . . . and a lot of other things I won't mention now. Your dad will get stomach ulcers when he gets into the harbor with his ship and sees you on San Martín Hill in company with such an illustrious comrade! Holy heavens!"

Andrés blushed a deep red. Then he said, with lowered head:

"No, sir . . . I'm not doing any of those things, father."

"Well, are you going to confess to me now?" replied the priest very slowly. "But you are trying to tell me these things, Andrés. In short, we'll talk about them on a better occasion. Now, to get on with your story. What did Cuco tell you at the boat dock?"

"I didn't get to see Cuco because he was out rowing in the bay with some men. But this girl was eating a piece of bread that some workmen had given her out of pure pity, and she told me that she had slept last night on a little boat because they had thrown her out of the house."

"And why?"

"Because she likes to wander around like a little tramp, and they beat her."

"Lovely, lovely. That is what you call an excellent training school for a woman! What's your name, child?"

"My name is Silda," the little girl answered dryly.

"She's a Highstreeter," added Andrés.

"Well, well. That makes four times!" exclaimed the padre.

"She ain't got no father . . . ho, ho, ho," cackled the brutish Muergo. The girl as usual imitated his laughter.

"He got drowned on the last sea bream run," said Cole.

"She ain't got no mother, neither," added Sula.

"A Highstreeter named Mocejón took her in out of pity," explained Andrés.

"Tut, tut, tut," exclaimed Padre Apolinar on hearing that. "Then this girl is the daughter of the late Mullet, a widower for a couple of years who died this last winter along with several other unfortunate fellows. Well, I took a few steps myself, by the divine grace of the Blessed Virgin, to have them take you into that house! My child, I did not recognize you now. The truth is that I don't remember seeing you more than a couple of times, and at that rather poorly as I see everything with these rascally eyes of mine that aren't very much good. But, what is the matter now, Andrés?"

"Well," replied the latter turning his Basque cap around in his hands, "I said to her when I heard what she told me: 'Go back home,' and she said to me: 'If I go back they'll beat me and I don't wanta go back for that,' and I said: 'What are you going to do here all alone?' and she said: 'The same thing the others do,' and I said: 'Maybe they won't beat you,' and she said: 'They have whipped me so many times . . . they are all bad up there, and that's why I have run away and I'm not going back.' Then I remembered you and I said to her: 'I'll take you to a man that will fix everything if you want to come along with me.' And she said: 'All right. Let's go.' And that's why I brought her here."

During all this time, when she was not making faces at Muergo the little girl was looking at the furniture, the floor or the walls just as calm and unconcerned as if she had nothing to do with what Padre Apolinar was discussing with Andrés, the son of the captain of the *Montañesa*.

"That is to say," exclaimed the priest, crossing his arms in front of Andrés and Silda, "that there weren't enough of us so grandmother had a baby. That is just about the last straw. The devil with all the nice little bargains that come Padre Apolinar's way! Families can break up, marriages can go smash, kids can run away from home, the two different town councils can claw at each other, shirtless Johnny can fall in love with the rich girl Janie, mountains can slide into the sea and close off the entrance to the harbor, and here is Padre Apolinar who gets the job of fixing everything! As if Padre Apolinar didn't already have anything else to do than to straighten out other people's messes and to try to make human beings out of brutes like you kids listening to me now. And who told you, my dear little Andrés, that all it takes is for me to want this little girl to be taken into a good home and it can be considered done? And how do you know that I want to do it even if it were possible? Didn't I do it once? Has it done any good? Has anybody ever thanked me for it? Well, you should know that getting mixed up in other people's business kills the soul. I'm fed up all the way to the top of my head, my boy, and even higher than that. The devil take my sins!"

Here the priest paced around the room while the eight children looked at each other. Some of them stretched, others seemed bored. After wiggling around inside his clothes, the curate stopped in front of Silda and Andrés and said:

"So . . . what you want me to do is to accompany you right now to Mocejón's house and have a heart-to-heart talk with him and say: 'Here is the prodigal son who is returning to his father's house repentant.'"

"No, not me," interrupted Andrés quickly. "She's the one that you have to take along. I'm going right now to San Martín Hill to see my father bring in his ship, which ought to be arriving any time now."

"And I'm going with you," said Silda with great calmness. "I like very much to see the big boats come in."

"Well then, you devilish goat," said Padre Apolinar as he assumed a serious attitude in front of her, "for whom am I going to work? What am I going to get out of this? If it does not make any difference to you what results from the step you are making me take, what the devil does it matter to me? I'm not going, so that's that!"

"Yes you are, Pa'e 'Polinar," said Andrés smiling very confidently at him.

"I bet I'm not!" yelled the priest, trying to be stubborn.

"I bet you are!" insisted Andrés.

"The devil," answered Padre Apolinar, almost infuriated. "I'm betting both ears that I am not, and that I am not, and not!"

Then, as if the eight children who surrounded him all came to an agreement at the same time, they shouted as one with all the noise they could get out of their throats:

"I bet you are!"

When they saw the priest scratch his head nervously and hit Muergo on the head again, they all started down the worn narrow stairway, which shook and creaked. They did not stop till they reached the street door, where they started to examine Padre Apolinar's gift to Muergo.

After they all agreed that it was not anything wonderful, Andrés said to Silda:

"By the time we get back from San Martín Hill, Pa'e 'Polinar will already have been to Mocejón's house or to some other house. In one jump I'll go up the stairs to his house to ask him how it turned out. You wait for me here and I'll come down and tell you. Don't worry, because among all of us, we'll fix it up for you. Now, let's go."

The little girl shrugged her shoulders. Muergo tightened the string that held the top of his coat together and said, while showing his teeth and rolling his eyes:

"I'm goin' too as soon as I leave these pants with my mother."

"Me too," added Sula.

Silda called Muergo a jackass. One of the others said that he was going to the boat dock. Others said that they had something else to do. They separated from each other quickly.

All this happened on a beautiful morning in the month of June, quite a few years ago . . . many years ago . . . in a house on Ocean Street in Santander; in that Santander that had no breakwater and fewer people, no railroad, no streetcars, or before there were stained-glass windows in the cloister of the Cathedral, or any summer hotels on the Sardinero Beach. It was the old Santander with an inner harbor and tenders and lighters stretched out for a long way in the bay; the Santander with the Maruca Dock and Beach; the Santander of the good old days; the Santander that I, the author, have here inside in my heart and sculptured in my memory in such a way that I can see it all with my eyes closed. In fact, I could make a drawing of its streets, the color of the cobblestones, the number and names and even the faces of many of its inhabitants. It was that Santander of the fisherfolk, which is disappearing among the motheaten, insipid confusion of present-day customs.

2   FROM THE MARUCA BEACH TO SAN MARTIN HILL

Maruca Beach was tempting when the four children who were going to San Martín Hill passed near it. The water was making clouds of spray on the side of the dock and the foam marked the rising tide on the wall of the small breakwater.

The tide, at most two-thirds of its height—and the tides were very high at this time—and all the floating pieces of wood attracted their attention. Besides the usual spars there were two big beams that had not been there the day before; two beams held together by a four-pointed anchor.

"There would be nothing to it!" as Andrés expressed it, wincing with pleasure when he saw them. "I could take off my shoes, roll up my pants to my thighs and in a jiffy bring the beams alongside by pulling on the end of the anchor, jump on top of them, and with a stick that I got hidden in a place that only I know where it is, right near here—gosh, what a beautiful boat that would make, and what a tide!"

Sula and Muergo thought the same and they tempted him not to go any farther, but his urge to go to San Martín was more powerful than his desire to stay at La Maruca. Also on account of Silda, who perhaps was remembering the previous soaking she had had when she saw the log that Muergo had already stupidly pointed out to her with his crossed eyes, Andrés wanted to move on, and was deaf to the attractive suggestions of his ragged companions and blind to the attractions that such a "boat" offered.

So it was that their stop there was brief, and soon they were climbing the meadows going toward San Martín Hill. Although Andrés had already noticed that the yellow quarantine flag had not yet been hoisted above the blue flag of the Port Authority, proof that the ship had not yet entered the port, he was still in a hurry because, having resolved that San Martín was the place from which to see his father's boat come in, he believed that the boat would be going faster than his thoughts and was afraid of arriving too late.

While he was walking along in front of the others, they were bothering him with many questions or one of them stopped him to make him look at Muergo turning somersaults in the grass, or to see some other kid swimming near the rocks at the entrance of the cave, or the tacking movements of a lugger attempting to leave port against the wind, or Silda imitating the cross-eyed look and the stupid laughter of Muergo.

"Will your father probably bring some nice things?" she asked Andrés.

"He brings some pretty nice ones once in a while," answered Andrés, without turning his head toward her.

"For you, too?"

"And for everybody. Once he brought me a parrot."

"The cigars and cigarettes was better," suggested Sula.

"Or the jelly," added Muergo.

"For himself he brings hundreds of triple Corona cigars," said Andrés, replying to Sula.

"Boy, I know well what that jelly is like, by darn," insisted Muergo, licking his lips. "Once I tasted it. Ha! ha! ha! ha! A woman at the dock gave it to my mother. I think she stole it. Ha! ha! ha! And then I stole it from her one night and ate half a box. Damn, what a beatin' I got later when she found it out!"

"Maybe he'll bring you some silk shawls, too," suggested Silda as she tightened the tucks of her skirt about her waist. "If he brings you several of 'em, you'll keep one for me, won't you, Andrés."

The latter turned toward her, surprised at the order she had just given him, and he saw Sula trying to stand on his hands in the grass, throwing one leg into the air and then the other, but never both at the same time. This art of standing on his hands quickly and well was one of Andrés' greatest abilities. His pride was hurt on seeing Sula's awkwardness. Then he gave him a kick in the pants, knocking him over, and said loud enough for everyone to hear:

"This is the way to do that."

And in a jiffy he made a perfect handstand, moving his feet and legs, forming the letter Y and almost the letter T, without disjointing himself in that uncomfortable position. Urged on by the applause of Silda and Muergo he nearly wore himself out. In the process most of what he had in his pockets, which wasn't much, fell out on the grass. This included a few copper coins, a cigarette, a penknife with a broken blade and some bits of paper.

As soon as Muergo saw the cigarette, he grabbed it and went quite a distance away. Before Andrés had got on his feet and picked up the money, the paper and the knife, Muergo had already taken a match from a box that he had in the deep pocket of his jacket, struck the match on a stone, lit the cigarette and taken three big puffs without letting any smoke out his mouth. When Andrés jumped on him, reclaiming with blows of the fist what was properly his, Muergo let all the smoke out at once. His monstrous head seemed surrounded by smoke which was coming out all the openings of it, so much so that it even seemed to come out of his matted hair. By that time he gave back to Andrés only the dirty, badly chewed butt. Even in this state, Andrés finished it up in a few puffs. Even if he could beat Sula at handstands, he couldn't beat Muergo at inhaling a cigarette. How could he when Muergo had been taught to smoke by Cuco, the biggest smoker of the docks, which is equivalent to saying the greatest smoker in the world? When Andrés threw the useless butt away, Sula picked it up and got a couple of good puffs from it.

At the fountain they climbed over the edge of the big bowl and drank water, not because any of them was thirsty, but just to drink. Silda washed her hands and smoothed out her hair with her hands. Then they started up the steep alley by the sardine cannery and came out on the Molnedo meadows.

There Muergo tried to do a handstand and lagged behind

a little so that the others wouldn't see him if he failed. In the effort to straighten only his body above his head—because he couldn't even get one foot off the ground—his jacket fell around his head and covered his eyes, exposing his bare buttocks. Silda was the first to notice that he wasn't with the group and she motioned for them all to return to where Muergo was in such a picturesque position. One of them got a nettle plant, another a stick and Silda an old shoe sole full of nails, and they swatted his copper-colored buttocks enough to make the sparks fly.

"That's my payment for knockin' me into the water," shouted Silda as she left the imprint of the shoe nails on his hide, when she had a chance to do so between Andrés' blows with the club and Sula's with the nettles.

Muergo let out roars of anger and even some swear words after being whipped so barbarously. But only when he pleaded for mercy did his executioners leave him in peace to scratch at his leisure the blisters that hurt him so.

Sula wanted to go along the shore of the bay. But Andrés said that they had had too many stops already considering how much in a hurry he was. But Sula didn't pay any attention to Andrés' objection and ran to the shore. Right away he began to holler:

"By devil, it's beautiful here. Boy, what a tide. Holy Virgin, what big crabs. Come on, you guys!"

And there was nothing else to do but to go to the place where Sula was. In fact, the tide was good, but not to be exaggerated. And as far as the few crabs they found were concerned, they were just ordinary. But Sula was in his element, and he couldn't help saying what he did. The sun was quite warm, and the water was a transparent green. At this place, it was about twice as deep as their height, but the big pebbles on the bottom could be counted one by one.

"Throw in your money, Andrés," the wharf rat said, pawing impatiently, "and I'll bring them up for you with a dive."

"I don't have any money," answered Andrés, who wanted to continue on his way without losing a minute.

"You don't have no money?" exclaimed Sula in mocking surprise. "Of course you don't, because I picked most of it up when it fell out of your pockets back there."

Andrés insisted and Sula continued:

"The devil. At least throw in a copper. Come on, just a copper, 'cause I know you got one. Come on, man! Lookee. Wrap it up in one of those crumpled pieces of paper that I put in your pocket."

And Andrés said no and no. But Silda backed up the pleas of Sula, and finally the dirty coin was wrapped in a piece of white paper and thrown into the water. The four other kids watched with fixed attention how it went down in rapid zigzags to the bottom, and how it shifted till it got almost under a big boulder, but without being entirely hidden from sight.

"The devil!" said Sula, scratching his head and postponing the task of removing the half shirt he was wearing, without tearing it into pieces. "Golly, there might be an octopus in there!"

This didn't bother Muergo in the least, because in a twinkling of the eye, he undid the rope that served as a belt, threw off the long jacket that reached nearly to his ankles and jumped into the water headfirst with his hands joined in front. It was such a clean dive that he made scarcely a sound, and only the few bubbles and a little ripple on the surface indicated that this bronzed, shiny animal had dived like a dolphin, moving in and around the big rock, among the floating algae as if it were just a handful of seaweed. Then they saw how he moved the stone while his legs continued kicking slowly, caught the wrapped up coin, put it in his mouth and then changed position with the agility of a tuna, and with a couple of kicks and strokes of his arms appeared on the surface with the coin between his teeth, puffing like a baby hippopotamus.

"Ain't you goin' to throw in the two-cent piece too?" he asked Andrés, after he removed the cent from his mouth and remained straight up in the water by treading.

"Not the cent nor nothing, damn you," replied Andrés impatiently. "And I am not waiting any longer for you."

No sooner said than done, he started off up the road without turning back.

Later, when he did turn around, he was near the San Martín meadows. He saw that not one of his three companions was following him. Then he suspected, not without good reason, that perhaps the money acquired by Muergo was the cause of the desertion, because Sula and Silda would want him to spend it on them.

Andrés was not too grieved to be alone because he didn't like the idea of being seen in public places with pals of such a sort.

And he was less grieved to see that there were many people who had got there before he did with the same idea of watching the *Montañesa* come into port. He knew most of these people well. Among them were some sailor friends of his father's and some harbor pilots, off duty that day, that he had seen a thousand times, not only on the dock, but even in his own home. Also there were the wives of some of the crew members, and even Fernando Montalvo, professor of navigation, who had taught his father and all the other captains and young pilots of that day, a man of proverbial strictness in his subject. This individual induced fear in Andrés because he knew that some day, not too far away, he would be studying under him. Another was Montalvo's friend, "Count Turnip," with his jacket embroidered with silver, the glorious remnant of God only knows what employment during his youth. Another was Don Lorenzo, the mad priest of High Street, uncle of Andrés' friend Colo (Nick), destined to study Latin at the request and under the protection of that insane priest. Another was Ligo, a young man who was soon to make his second sea voyage as a pilot, who had generously given Andrés a couple of handfuls of cut tobacco—and also a few blows on the head. In those days the arrival of a ship like the *Montañesa*, registered from Santander, belonging to a merchant of Santander, manned and officered by captain, pilots and crew from Santander, was an event of great importance in the capital of the province, where few bigger things happened. Furthermore, the *Montañesa* was coming from Havana and everybody expected a lot of things from there, such as a letter from an absent son, cheap cigars, a box of candied fruits, a Panama hat, a bank draft for fifty pesos, a survey of the market situation, news of such and such a person whose address was not known for sure or at least regards and greetings for half the town. On board there might even be some friends who were returning after making their pile in Cuba. Other boats of that day such as *La Perla* and the *Santander* and others aroused the same curiosity for the same reasons. Everybody in the city knew when they left, what cargo they were carrying, where they were going and all that could be known. Their captains and pilots were very popular men and their sayings and their deeds were engraved on the memory of all like the glories of a family.

In spite of the fact that there were many people on San Martín, they talked very little among themselves, which always happens when expecting an event of equal interest to all, or people are in the open air, face to face with nature, which speaks a great deal, without letting anyone else butt into the conversation. And how eloquent nature was that day. The sea, greenish and phosphorescent, was whipped by a slight breeze that could almost be called playful, if the word were not so discredited by insipid poets and ordinary impressionists who perhaps have never left their little corn patch in the hills; the sun, gaily wasting its beams of light, reflected on the waves in the bay, and on the treacherous reddish sands of the shoals.

There, in the background of this landscape, the bluish peaks of Matienzo and Arredondo, and closer the high curved points of the mountain range which were outlined in the view from Quintres Point and the Galizano Hills to the ports of Alisas and La Cavada (on the opposite side of the bay), standing out in a subtle shining fog like a piece of cloth woven by fairies with intangible threads of dew; and there, almost within arm's length, were the Puntal Hills, receiving on their sandy bases the salty kisses of the rising tide. And for noise, there was the incessant murmur of the waves as they spread out lazily on the nearby beach, or splashed the rocks with their spray, moved by the wind. In that salty atmosphere one never saw a set of lungs that could breathe enough of it, nor anyone's gaze that could be satisfied by that shimmering light, which seemed talkative and mischievous as it danced on the fog, the water and the flowers.

I do not know whether precisely these thoughts were going through the minds of all those persons as they moved from one place to another on the esplanade of the castle, or as they climbed the small walls of the parapet, or stretched out on the grass in the meadow outside, without saying any more than two or three words in succession, with their gaze wandering over all parts of the landscape; but you can bet that, if by some magic art one could have placed them in front of the greatest wonders of human industry, or the marvels of Aladdin's palaces instead of in front of this miserable old castle, they would have looked at them without the slightest astonishment; evidence, without their realizing it, that in their eyes, the marvels of nature were worth much more.

Andrés was thinking about the arrival of his father, and his father's ship, and at the most about all those people who were there to see the very thing that interested him so much because he was the son of the man who was the hero of the occasion. How vain and glad and worried he must have been! His friend Ligo had joined him for a while. They had gone from one place to another making each other laugh or blush with the things that they asked Count Turnip about the weakness of his knees, or Caral about his tall silk hat. Then they had gone together to the highest and farthest part of the promontory.

Finally they heard voices shouting together: "There she is!"

And, in fact, there was the *Montañesa* luffing in, with full sail, even to the topmast head, with its flag waving on the end of the boom, and the harbor pilot already on board, because his rowboat was tied alongside. She had scarcely reached Harbor Point when you could see her pass near La Horadada, a small island, and immediately take, like a well-driven, docile colt, the proper course in the channel. The wind was pushing her along affectionately, and her heavy beams seemed to rock on the soft whitecaps. Each movement of the ship brought forth a round of applause from skilled observers at San Martín and produced a flutter in the heart of Andrés, who was the most interested of all in the feats of the corvette and in the arrival of her captain.

Thus she was gradually approaching, following her course like one who is on familiar ground and who is furthermore on the way home. So skillfully was she brought alongside the coast where the spectators were that anyone with an expert eye in these matters would have known that the harbor pilot who was steering her had proposed to demonstrate to these shore pilots that he did not do things clumsily but easily and well.

And you may be sure that old Cudon, the harbor pilot who had boarded and taken control of the corvette at the Sardinero Beach, knew as well as anyone how to bring in the most important ship!

And thus she continued approaching with a speed of about seven knots. The rumble of her wake could be heard and the creaking of her rigging when the sails filled, and the clatter of her anchor chains taken from the hold, with a sufficient length of it on the deck near the bow in order to drop anchor at the proper time. Some spectator believed that he could make out familiar faces on the ship's bridge; the first mate Sama could be seen clearly and distinctly on the forecastle with his gum boots, his dark jacket and his gold-braided cap, and Andrés exclaimed: "Look at him," pointed with his arm extended at his father, who was standing on the poop deck near the wheel with his right hand on the flag's halyard. Moments later, when the corvette was almost directly opposite the spectators on San Martín, he replied to their shouts and greetings by hoisting the flag three different times, while the starboard side of the ship was filled with crewmen and passengers who waved their caps and straw hats in the air. Then the spectators could enjoy in full view all the details of the ship. The presumptive thing! How she had taken care, before entering port, to clean up and to arrange all her adornments. Her brass shone like polished gold. Her yardarms were clear and no canvas covers were on the backstays or outer edges of the platforms. At the rail there fluttered feather weather vanes, displayed only in port, and from the tops of the masts there waved the blue streamer with the name of the ship in white letters, the flag of the shipping company and the red and white flag indicating Santander registry.

Again the colors of the *Montañesa* saluted, and again the shouts, the hurrahs and waving of hats were repeated between those on board and those on land. Then it seemed that the ship itself had participated in the sentiment which moved so many minds by making her whole rigging creak and plunging the beams of her prow into the water so much that spray got on the anchors, which were all ready with rope and chain. Then she listed to port, and showed on her starboard side, above the water line, more than one row of shining copper.

In this graceful position, rocking playfully on her bed of foaming spray which she herself stirred up and produced, she slipped along the length of the rocky ledge below San Martín, sailed past the Three Sisters' Reef in a jiffy, her mainsail was lowered, her jibs, topsails and topgallant sails slackened, and a little farther on at the resounding, manly command of "Drop anchor," which was heard clearly on the bridge, the anchor fell into the water. The harsh noise of the links of more than forty fathoms of chain passing could be heard going through the hawsepipe. With this the graceful corvette, after a tremendous shudder, remained motionless on the tranquil waters of the anchorage area in the middle of the channel, like a spirited steed stopped still by its rider after going full speed.

3   WHERE THE MULLET ORPHAN GIRL HAD LANDED

Mocejón (mussel), the one that lived on High Street—because there was also another younger Mocejón in the Lower Town—was a short, heavy-set sailor bordering on sixty years of age, liver-colored, with chapped skin, small greenish eyes and a heavy beard, almost white. It was heavy, like the hair on his head, which was never combed and very rarely trimmed. His gait was like that of all seamen, awkward and uneven, as were his words, his voice and his conversation. His gaze, on land dark and disdainful, at sea, where he was at home, was another matter because everything that was on it or around it attracted his attention. The vile interest and the instinctive fondness for his miserable hide awakened worries in his spirit, and there is nothing like the light of worry to make even listless eyes sparkle. As for his disposition, it was much worse than his chapped hide, his beard, his tangled mop of hair, his gait and his gaze. Not because it was exactly fierce, but because he was grumpy, indifferent, harsh and disagreeable. Brown trousers, gradually becoming petrified with grime, salt water and tar from his fishing boat, had taken on the shape of his stiff legs. He wore some low shoes, without heels or any sign of polish, on his swollen feet. A loose, woolen garment over his heavy shirt, and a stocking cap, placed some way or other on his unkempt hair, like a dirty rag stuck to the wall, composed the constant covering of that body, a propitious place for mange, and even capable of making alliances with leprosy, but nevertheless an object that would never be touched by any water not from the sea.

Well, that's the way Mocejón was, but at that he was not the worst of the household because his wife, Sargüeta (sheephead's fish), excelled him in everything. Her sour disposition, vile tongue and lacerating, reputation-wrecking voice were the

Where the Mullet Girl Had Landed

terror of the streets, where there were so many quarrelsome women of the first magnitude. She was taller than her husband, but quite thin and bleary-eyed. She had a sharp nose like a hake and black teeth which were sharp-pointed and not very numerous. The color of her cheeks was a hardened red, and the rest of her face looked like an old piece of parchment. Her chest was flat, her arms long. The tendons and even the bones in her bare legs were visible enough to count. The odor of sardines that came from her was strong enough to reach half a league. She was never known to wear any other outfit than a dark scarf tied under her chin and sticking out over her forehead, falling over her eyes because they were sensitive to light; a woolen shawl, also dark, dirty and darned, with the ends crossed over her chest and tied at her back; a skirt of heavy, glossy wool, and on her feet she had some slippers full of holes.

Nevertheless, there are those who affirm that this unbearable woman was more tolerable than her daughter Carpia (Policarpia), a girl just past nineteen, as unkempt and piggish as her mother but smaller in stature, darker, stockier, with just as shrill a voice and harsh a tongue, more squatty and, in addition, pockmarked from smallpox. Her work was that of a sardine seller. Many people covered their ears in order not to hear her swear, their eyes not to see her messy appearance and others held their nose in order not to smell her whenever she passed with a basketful of wet fish on her head, with water and grease dripping from the basket over her head and shoulders. All the while she would be moving her short dirty skirt in rhythm with the vulgar rolling movement of her hips and shouting the price of her merchandise. No sardine seller could hold the last syllable as long as she or hit such a high note. Some listeners even lost hope at times that her harsh, penetrating shout would ever come to an end. But should any passerby let her know of such a suspicion with the slightest gesture or express his displeasure with the slightest word, or should any inexperienced servant, after having asked her from a balcony "how much?" not reply to her answer, or reply in a disagreeable manner, or after having replied, for example, that she was willing to pay three cents, and the seller told her to come down and the servant didn't come down, or delayed in coming down—that was when you should have seen and heard Carpia with her basket on the ground, in the middle of the street with her eyes fixed sometimes on her aggressor, or the place where she had been if the latter withdrew discreetly to hide in fear from the hail of sounds. At other times Carpia fixed her gaze on the first passerby who happened to be near, or on all those in the street or on all the balconies of the street! Looking at her in such a state, one wondered what was most astonishing about her. Was it her words, her ideas, her gestures, her voice or attitudes? It seemed impossible that all of that could be found in one human being, especially in a representative of the same sex in which are found cleanliness and shame. And nevertheless, Carpia was not really angry. That was no more than a slight impudence which was half joking and half spite. Because when she really got angry, that is to say, when she quarreled with all the ceremony of the members of her profession, which has formed a school, prospering at the present moment—God of goodness! In short she was almost as terrible as her mother, from whom she got her method either by listening to her in the neighborhood or learning with her to sell sardines when the two of them carried a basketful between them.

Carpia had a younger brother named Cleto. He resembled his father more than his mother. He was gloomy and silent, but already a good worker. As could be expected, he did not get along well with his sister. In their quarrels he used to kick her in the belly, or anyplace he could reach. He did not know how to "talk to her" in any other way.

This nice family lived near the south end of High Street on the fifth floor of a seven-story house whose front was not much wider than the series of wooden balconies in front of each story. I say that it had seven floors distinguishable from the outside because by counting the cellar, all the mezzanines and other subdivisions of floors and attic rooms, the total was fourteen habitations, or if you wish to be more exact, fourteen families had shelter there, each one in his corresponding hole, with his fishing gear, his raincoats, his buckets full of sand and fish gills (for a combination bait and sinker), his shabby clothing used every day, and all the grease and all the smells that these things and these people necessarily have with them. Certainly the tenants who had a balcony used it for cleaning fish, hanging old rags, nets of all kinds and fishing lines. They also had the neatness of throwing into the street, or on the first person who passed along, the useless scraps, as if the drippings from the nets and wet clothes were not filthy enough rain to make the use of the street feared by landlubbers who unfortunately had to use it. As for those dens inside that had no balconies on the street, the inhabitants got along very nicely being born and brought up in that rotten atmosphere whose very stench seemed to make them fat! But how could it be helped? The renters in the houses next door and on down the street, or those on the other side, or in any part of the Upper Town fared no better. The same can be said about those of the Lower Town.

Coming back to Mocejón, I may add that he was the owner and captain of a small fishing boat from which he collected two and one-half shares—one and a half as owner, and one as captain, or what is the same for the readers not too accustomed to this lingo, he got two and one-half shares of all the profits from all the fish divided equally among the whole crew. This wealth came from an inheritance, decreased by one half in Mocejón's hands, because what he inherited was the boat. No one knows the importance that this wealth gave him in all the Upper Town, where it was very rare for a sailor to own any part of the boat on which he worked. Nor does anyone know how much it influenced Sargüeta and their daughter Carpia to become the most shameful and feared among the quarrelsome women of the Upper Town.

As Mocejón was quite slow with numbers and got seasick

when he had to count more than his ten fingers close together, it was his wife who collected each Saturday for the amount of fish sold during the week over the side of the boat when it came back to port. This produced quarrels in which Sargüeta made use principally of her poisonous tongue, the loudness of her voice, the threat of her gestures, the sharpness of her fingernails and the strength of her fingers when entangled in the hair of anyone at the fishmarket. For that reason a wholesale fish seller would prefer to steal the money from the alms box in the church if she didn't have it ready for her on Friday night rather than ask Sargüeta to wait ten hours more for payment of her debt. Although the wives of all boat captains are called "the captain's wife" whether or not she collected for the sales during the week, when anyone mentioned the "captain's wife from the Upper Town," everyone knew that Sargüeta was meant! Because that is what she was!

By now it can be understood why the little girl Silda did not lack motives for refusing to return to the house from which she had fled. The reason they had to protect her when she was an abandoned orphan was none other than the fact that Mocejón was a sailor of some means, and besides Mullet was the godfather of his only son, Cleto. It need not be said that it took all the persuasive power imaginable to make Mocejón and his family take charge of the little orphan; nor that Padre Apolinar and all those concerned with him in this same charitable undertaking heard horrible things about Carpia and her mother before they succeeded in what they were attempting to do. And this did not come about until the Town Council offered Mocejón some help from time to time in the cost of her maintenance, provided that the orphan girl was treated and kept as was to be expected. At the advice of his wife, Mocejón wanted the promise of the Council to be "in writing by someone who knew how to draw up legal agreements." But the Council opposed this condition. As there was more than one family inclined to take Silda in for the amount of help offered without an agreement in writing, greed tempted Sargüeta and she convinced

Where the Mullet Girl Had Landed

the rest of the family that if it came to the worst they could "take it out on the child's hide," and they gave her shelter in their hovel. What they gave her was not much more than just shelter—and plenty of work.

Temporarily, there was no bed for her. It was also true that there was none for Carpia or Cleto. There was no other bed in that place, properly speaking—and as far as shape is concerned, neither in comfort nor in cleanliness—than the double cot used by Mocejón and Sargüeta, which was in a very small space, with light from the bay, which was called the parlor, because it also had a pine table, a reed-bottom chair, a leather-covered stool and a picture of St. Peter—the patron saint of the Upper Council—stuck to the wall with masticated bread. Carpia slept on a half-rotted mattress in a dark alcove with an entrance through the corridor, and her brother on top of a big box in which everything from bread to Sunday shoes was kept. Silda was accommodated in a corner formed by a partition of the kitchen and the corridor, that is to say at the very end of the corridor and in front of the door leading to the stairs, on a pile of worn-out fishing nets and under a remnant of an old blanket. If the poor kid had been able to take along with her the bed, mattress, the two half sheets and threadbare coverlet to which she had been accustomed in her own house! But all that, and all else that there was inside the house, was not enough to pay her father's debts. After all, even if Silda had taken her bed to the house of Mocejón, Carpia or her brother would have taken possession of it and she would have had the same result as not having a bed of her own. I do not know whether Silda reflected this way when she went to bed on the pile of old nets in the corner of the kitchen, but it is a known fact that to stretch out there, cover herself as far as the half blanket reached and go to sleep like a log were one and the same thing.

She missed the food from her home even more than the bed. What she used to get was not wedding cake, but what there was, good or bad, was at least abundant, because when things are divided between only two people, regardless of how little it is, each gets a great deal. Then, as the only daughter of a man who did not resemble Mocejón in temperament or cunning, she was relatively speaking a pampered daughter. As a result, her father used to give her part of his share of the food. Ever since she had come to live with the family of Sargüeta she never had enough to eat to calm her hunger, and the little she did eat was poor and usually given to her between growls and swear words or pinches and slaps. She was always the last to get her spoon into the common casserole of cabbage and green beans. All the rest in the house had teeth that made the sparks fly, so that by the time they got once around, it was almost useless for her to try to take her turn. They had such skill in filling a spoon! Each spoonful of Mocejón's seemed like a load of hay. Only his wife could do better, not so much in filling it, but in emptying it in her mouth, which seemed to come to meet the spoon with the lips doubled over the angular open jaws, showing her buck teeth like points of rusty nails; then nothing, because Silda could never figure out what happened, even though she was quite observant. She couldn't tell whether the mouth closed in on the spoon, or the spoon threw its contents inside the mouth from halfway there. So rapid was the motion, so great the opening of the mouth, so dexterous the bite and so enormous the gullet where what she had seen just a second before disappeared! Carpia and her brother were not so clever at eating, even if they were just as voracious. But the children and the parents had this pleasant custom: after eating a spoonful, they would rub it, or whack it a couple of times, against their trousers or shirt, before putting it back in the pot. This was done to remove any scruples of cleanliness others might have who were waiting their turn.

Because Silda didn't "clean" her spoon that way the first day she ate there, Sargüeta called her a dirty pig and Carpia gave her a blow on the head. When there was no stew, as occurred quite often, there were many sardines. Silda appeased her hunger with a couple of them, broiled, with a little salt.

Where the Mullet Girl Had Landed

If there were no sardines or needlefish or sea bream or ray or any other kind of fish of little value in the market, there might be a couple of little raw fish or a strip of cod or herring, the only thing to go with a piece of bread three days old, or a piece of corn bread, according to times and circumstances. Such was her dinner. It is easy to guess what her lunches and breakfasts must have been.

In the meantime she had to be on the go for everything they commanded of her if she wanted to eat that poor food in quiet. And what they ordered her to do was certainly too much for a girl her age. For a while she helped the women of the house, inside or out of it, with the gear for the boat, that is to say, mend the nets, dry them, mend the sails, prepare the fishing tackle, etc. When the whole family, men and women, went fishing in the rivers flowing into the bay, or looking for mollusks at low tide, especially the ox-eyed cockerel—a fish that was very abundant in those days—Silda had to go along too and work as much or more than the women, or at least more than Carpia because Sargüeta rarely went to the bay with her husband. They gave her the troublesome task of getting the worms. This she did by sinking her two hands into the sticky mud with fingers extended like a hayfork, scoop up a handful and drop it in order to find the worms, which she tossed into an old pan or tin pot with sand in the bottom. Other times she was there with a little basket on her arm, jabbing into the mud with a knife at low tide to find the well-hidden clams, or on the sandy beaches pulling out razor clams with a wire hook. But in any case, these tasks and others like them, although burdensome, especially in the winter, gave her a certain amount of liberty and frequently she spent some very happy moments with boys and girls of her own age who also were looking for clams, for worms or for broken pieces of rope. This was what she always preferred: to take her little basket and set out for the dock collecting pieces of rope, nails, copper or anything usable that was washed ashore to be sold for junk. It was there that she met Muergo and Sula and other wharf rats who lived on Ocean Street, but especially the famous Cafetera (coffeepot) who, although he was from High Street, never put in an appearance there.

She met a lot of the town characters and all the young girls who went with them in everything they did. Going along with this gang of kids she became fond of the boat docks and the independent life enjoyed in that district in which everyone was his own boss, as if he were a hundred leagues from the city or any civilized country. Without realizing it she was gradually postponing the time to return home, and she usually came back with an empty basket. Sometimes she did not get back till night. Because they whipped her as much for being a little late as for being very late, she calmly chose the latter. She went almost daily to the docks although they had ordered her to go to Rock Cave, and with the wharf rats she learned about La Maruca. There she became acquainted with Andrés.

It should be noted that Silda, although she was present at all the undertakings and games of the wharf rats, only rarely took part in them except with her attention. This was not out of virtue certainly, but because that was her cold nature, concerned only with herself.

She knew where copper or chocolate or sugar could be stolen and how and where it could be sold with no questions asked about the source, and at what price; she knew where the money thus received could be spent for coffee and rum and just how much you got for coins of different value; she knew how to gamble with cards, and many, many more things taught in such a school where vices take root in children who have never had any more education; but nothing ever went into her basket that couldn't be seen honestly by everybody; she never sold even an old nail or a piece of rope in Olivero's cheap shop; she never took cards in her hand to gamble nor a stone to throw in the gang wars at low tide between the wharf rats and the landlubbers, or between kids from High Street and Ocean Street. She was satisfied to be present at everything and to find out all

Where the Mullet Girl Had Landed

the little rascals were doing, but was dauntless and without feeling by nature, not by virtue.

Neither did Andrés take part in these enterprises of the wharf rats. However, he did take part in their stone throwing, their diving and games to show agility, in their attempts, almost always successful, to catch a stray dog and throw him into the water with a stone around his neck. His preferred amusements were to row with Cuco in his boat and to fish from the steps of the dock with a little pole that he had. Silda also liked this, and whenever Andrés would wet his line she was there at his side, very quiet, with her eyes fixed on the bobbin.

"You've got a bite," she would say from time to time in a low voice when she saw the line moving.

"It's just a nibble," Andrés would reply, without pulling in his line.

And thus the two of them used to spend long periods of time together. Whenever he was fishing for sea bream, Silda would help him bait the hook, and if he caught two of them at the same time, she would take one of them off the hook.

And during all the time she remained very quiet and impassive, and her face, her hands and her feet were always clean. She was like a dainty young lady in that group of savages. For that reason, she seemed quite cute to Andrés, who had courtesies and considerations for her that he never had for the other ragged girls who used to come around there. On the other hand, she did not show any greater appreciation of the good clothes and manners of Andrés than she did for the rubbish and barbarity of the wharf rats. On the contrary, the object of her visible preferences seemed to be the monster Muergo, the most stupid, the ugliest and most piggish of all her companions. But these preferences were not revealed by going near him frequently—because she went near others, too, whenever she wished to—but by the fact that she was not as affectionate with anyone as she was with Muergo.

"Clean the snot from your nose and wash your face, you pig," she used to say to him, or, "Why don't you cut off some of that tangled mop of hair," or, "Tell your mother to put a shirt on you!"

Among all the dirty, shirtless kids that were there on the docks, she was grieved only by the filth and nakedness of Muergo. And Muergo responded to these indications of relative delicacy on the part of Silda by laughing at her, kicking her or knocking her into the water as he had done that day at La Maruca. And this preference continued on the part of Silda. And why? Goodness only knows! Perhaps it was the force of contrast or the very monstrosity of Muergo; or an unconscious anxiety—the product of human vanity—to dominate and make submissive someone who seems uncontrollable and rebellious, and to beautify the horrible; to do with Muergo what some women, called elegant in the world, do with certain wooly, ugly dogs: to get pleasure out of seeing them stretched out at their feet growling with affection, very clean and well combed, precisely because they are horrible and loathsome and should not be there at all.

It is easier to explain the inclination of Andrés for the boat docks and the gang of scallawags that held sway there. As the son of a sailor and headed to be one himself, the happenings in and around the bay tempted him, and the smell of salt water and the smell of ships seduced him. He selected that area in order to satisfy his sailor desires, because there were boats to rent and abandoned launches, and ships on the ways being cleaned and calked, and the opportunity of swimming easily in the nude at any time of the day, to play hooky from school, to smoke with no fear of being caught and principally because other kids of his social class were often there too! All these were advantages that couldn't be found except at the docks and in the area known as La Maruca. For that reason he went frequently to La Maruca.

As for his friendship with these wharf rats, there was nothing else to do than to choose between it and the fatigue of getting into their territory by force of arms, which was too hard and hazardous to be done daily. Generally, that was done the first time. Afterwards a peace agreement was made, and he lived handsomely, taking care to keep the makers of the peace well supplied with cigarettes and other tidbits from the city, especially for Cuco, who with his corpulence and barbarity was the most feared because of his jokes, although in his way he was sociable and affectionate.

Silda was becoming more fond of this give-and-take life of the boat docks and her absences from home were longer and longer every day. The Council did not seem to remember about giving the monetary help promised for her keep, and the Mocejón family was resolved not to keep, without recompense, such a useless, rebellious girl. As a result of all this came that terrible whipping one night that made Silda, who had suffered so much already, run away and sleep on a fishing boat. On the way out of the house the sailor Mechelín (Mike), who with his wife Sidora (Isidora) occupied the ground floor of the same building, offered her shelter, but she did not want to accept it.

4 WHERE SHE WAS WANTED

Mechelín and his wife Sidora were the exact opposites of Mocejón and Sargüeta physically and morally. Mechelín was smiling, rather tall, of regular stature and very communicative. Frequently he could be seen smoking a cigarette all alone at the street door of his home, telling of some happening which he considered funny, talking and looking at the doorways or at the empty balconies on the other side of the street, or at the people who were passing along the street, for lack of anyone to listen to him close by. And he would talk and laugh and even reply to himself with intonation and convenient gestures. He was also somewhat short-necked and stoop-shouldered, but he was relatively neat and clean, with his face quite well shaven.

His side whiskers and hair were gray, but not precisely a thatched mess. He was so active a talker and so gay in his glance that those humps on his back only seemed what they were, namely, the result of the rigors of his occupation, not any defect of mind or body. He sang not too badly, almost in a whisper, some songs of his youth, and he knew many stories. His wife, Sidora, ordinarily showed very good humor. She was short and chubby, always used good shoes and good stockings, dressed neatly although cheaply and wore on her head a neckerchief tied at the nape of the neck. No one boasted as much as she about the witty remarks of her husband, and when she started to laugh she laughed with her whole body, but no part of her shook as much during the laughter as her bosom and her stomach, which, besides being large in their own right, were made more projecting in such cases when she put her hands on her hips and threw her head back. She had the reputation of being a pretty good healer of ills, and almost dared to consider herself a good midwife.

This exemplary and agreeable couple had never had any children. Mechelín was a member of the crew on one of the five launches that there were in the Upper Town, the citizens of which always had smaller boats (for eight men) rather than launches, and Sidora was devoted principally to the care of her husband and her home; and to selling his share of the fish when he didn't want to sell them at the ship's side, and to accompanying, at day wages, some fish wholesaler at the market who would solicit her help in weighing, collecting, etc.

Any time left over was divided in the neighborhood of her street prescribing concoctions of herbs for household remedies one place, stopping the flow of blood at another, helping to cut a dress for her neighbor Nisia or making pleated sleeves for Conce or acting as midwife at the birth of some unfortunate child.

As neither she nor her husband had any vices, nor many mouths to feed, they took care of themselves quite well, and even had saved some gold coins, well wrapped up in more than three folds of paper, in a safe place, just in case. On Sundays they were rejuvenated. She wore her dark blue cotton dress, blue stockings, high-top shoes fastened with buckles, a fringed shawl of black silk over her jacket and another small dark scarf on her head. He had his bell-bottom trousers, coat and vest, all of fine black cloth, a middy tie, a sash of black silk and a Basque cap of blue wool with a long, black tassel; his face well shaven and his hair well combed, at least in the places where it could be combed.

All these articles of clothing, plus a mantilla with strips of velvet, which women used to use for funerals and solemn religious services, were worn up to a few years ago by fisherfolk of Santander as characteristic, traditional garb.

A brother of Mechelín, who was also a Highstreeter, like all the family, married a girl from the Lower Town, a rare occurrence. His relatives, friends and women of his acquaintance teased him greatly: "This is going against custom and can lead to no good!" "She is not much good, and surely didn't attract you because of her chastity." "In the Upper Town you get women like yourself in conformity with the law of God which says that every fish has to stay on its own beach."

And it turned out, as time went on, that she turned out as had been suggested by the Upper Town. This was not, as I understand it, because the bride was from the Lower Town, but because she really was no good by her own nature. She gave herself to drink and to laziness until the poor husband, burdened with grief and misery, died very suddenly leaving his widow with nothing but a two-year-old boy, who seemed like a black poodle dog. Mechelín and his wife helped these unfortunate survivors as much as they could; but when they noticed that their help, whether in goods or money, was traded for alcohol by the widow, leaving her naked baby to crawl around the floor, half starved, and that, aside from fuming at her brother-in-law and sister-in-law for being stingy and meddlesome and that the boy, as he continued to grow, was becoming as wild and even more vile than his mother, they cut off all communication with their ungrateful relatives. Thus four years passed, during which the young boy grew and became the Muergo we already know. Muergo, then, was a nephew of Mechelín, in whose house he could not remember ever setting foot. His mother, La Chumacera (oarlock), fish seller at times, had obtained out of charity, from the men who had been companions of her late husband, a wage of a peseta a day, which a woman makes by getting up early to buy bait of various kinds, such as squid, for the launch from the fishermen and boatmen along the bay. The fear of losing this bargain of a peseta a day obliged her to be faithful and punctual in the performance of this task, the only one that she knew to make an honest living.

Mechelín and his wife would have gladly taken in the child, orphan of such a good father, if they had believed that they could have made something, even halfway, out of that savage, untamed stripe of his, and quite particularly without the risks to which this continual point of contact with the shameless mother exposed them! They were anxious to have a child about the age of this wild nephew in order that it might fill a need in their home, like one's own children do, children that are anxiously desired by those who do not have any. Thus it is that when the negotiations on the part of Pa'e 'Polinar with Mocejón to take Silda into his home were going on, the eyes of the tenants of the ground floor followed this little girl playing in the street; and they were tempted, more than once, on seeing the priest come down the stairs in bad humor, to pull his robe in order to get him inside their house and to tell him in a whisper, "Bring her here, Pa'e 'Polinar, and we will take her free of cost and still be very grateful for the opportunity." But the final agreement was a question for the decision of the Council, which had studied the matter well; and, furthermore, the members of the Mocejón family would believe that the attempt to steal the offer of help for her maintenance was what moved them to take in the orphan.

"You may be sure," Mechelín said to Sidora, "that not even painted on a piece of paper could she be more according to

Where She Was Wanted   57

specifications! She is fine and clean as the king's canoe!"

"It is true," added Sidora, "that it hurts to consider what kind of life is waiting for her up there if God does not place himself on her side."

"Right," added her husband, who always used this interjection whenever he thought that someone's statement had no reply.

When Silda was taken in by the family on the fifth floor, Mechelín saw her go up and said:

"Unhappy child! You won't be so plump and well looking when you come down! And that in spite of the fact that you will be leaving there soon!"

"I think the same thing," his wife replied thoughtfully with her hands on her hips. "But you and I let matters alone that are none of our concern and we'll keep quiet about it, because I am more afraid of those people on the fifth floor than I am of a storm in March!"

"Right," concluded Mechelín with an expressive shake of his head and a wink of his eye, turning half around and humming a tune as if he had not said anything or feared that the people upstairs might hear him.

But from that moment they did not lose sight of the orphan, who, to judge by her impassive countenance, seemed to be the one least interested of all in the life which she was dragging out in the prison to which she had been condemned by people who thought that they were doing her a favor. They felt sorry for her during the first months of her stay to see her enter the house during the winter with her teeth chattering, purple with cold, with the basket of clams on her arm or with a pan of worms in her hand; or coming down the stairs with welts on her face or with her neckerchief around her forehead like a bandage. They never saw her cry nor any signs that she had been crying, nor did they hear any complaint come from her lips. On the other hand, Sidora was very anxious to talk with the girl to draw out details of what was happening up there; but the fear that she had for the scandalous Mocejón family made her restrain herself. On occasions, when they heard Silda coming downstairs, either Mechelín or Sidora went to the street door with a crust of bread, acting as if they were eating it, but in reality for the sake of having a pretext to offer it to her.

"You just came in time, girl," they would say in feigned surprise. "I was just goin' to put this bread back in the box because I do not feel like eatin' it now. If you want it, you are welcome."

And it was left in her hands. At the same time they would whisper in her ear:

"How is your appetite today?"

"Just so-so," she would say, revealing by the zeal with which she held the crust of bread the desire she had to devour it.

But they couldn't get her to stop there an instant, nor to say a word in passing about what they wanted to hear. Was it fear of revenge on the part of her protectors? Was it hardness and coldness of character?

They attributed her reserve to the first of these reasons, and this consideration doubled in their eyes the value of the moral qualities of that innocent little martyr.

They saw, after a time, how she was returning late to the house, and learned about the life that she was leading away from there and the punishments the Mocejóns gave her for her conduct, and the times that she had slept in the open, in a doorway, or on the floor boards of a boat.

"They will kill the unfortunate kid after ruinin' her," Mechelín used to exclaim when he talked about the matter. "She is so tender and clean, but give her a naggin' in the mornin', some blows at noon and a beatin' at night, with little to eat, and I'm sayin' that she, or even a three-masted boat treated the same way, will break. If I was in her place, I would leave and never come back!"

"That's bound to happen," added his wife. "That's what happens when you put meat in a shark's mouth."

"Right."

One night when they could hear the horrible things that

Sargüeta and Carpia on the fifth floor were vomiting forth against the little girl, who had just arrived at the house, and two "ouches" uttered by a child's voice, penetrating, sharp, lamenting as if unexpectedly a brutal hand had yanked at one pull all the roots of life from a little body full of health. Afterwards some inhabitant of each room in the building leaned out the door in spite of the fact that such beatings and disturbances were frequent in that neighborhood. About that time Mechelín and Sidora saw Silda coming down the last flight of stairs with the same speed as if wolves were chasing her. They went out to meet her in the doorway. Sidora was holding a candle and observed that her clothes were in disorder, her hair all tangled, her eyes moist, her look showing half fear and half anger. She was panting.

"Let me pass, Sidora," she said on seeing that the sailor's wife was blocking her exit to the street.

"But, where are you goin', unhappy child, at this time of day?" exclaimed Sidora trying to stop her.

"I'm goin'," replied Silda, slipping toward the open door, "never to return. Everybody is bad in that house."

"Come into mine then, my dear, at least until tomorrow," said Mechelín, stopping the girl with great difficulty.

"No, no," she insisted, breaking away from the hand that gently held her. "It is too close to that other one!"

And she went out the door like a rocket.

"But listen, child! Wait, poor thing!"

That is what Sidora exclaimed when she saw Silda disappear into the shadows in the street, without making up her mind to follow the fugitive. Mechelín himself, who had good eyesight, couldn't find out, regardless of how fast he went, whether the girl had gone straight down the street in the direction of Rua Mayor or toward the Big Wall, or Hospital Hill.

The reader knows what happened to her that night and the morning following, because he has heard Andrés tell about it, and has seen her so carefree and proud in the home of Padre Apolinar, near La Maruca, and at the fountain.

She probably had not arrived at La Maruca with Andrés and his following of wharf rats when Padre Apolinar had crossed the Dock Market in the direction of High Street. He had his priest's hat low over his eyes, and his head down because of the bright light. The ends of his worn cloak were held between his hands. He coughed frequently and occasionally wiggled his body inside his shirt (that is if he hasn't given that away also since we left his house with our story).

Without being seen by Sidora—rare event—although the door of her home was wide open, he reached the fifth floor and knocked with his knuckles on the door, saying at the same time, "Ave Maria."

A woman's voice from within replied with some indecent remark, but in such a tone that the priest, without relaxing his grasp on the ends of his robe, wiggled a couple of times inside his shirt to scratch his back, and murmured after clearing his throat:

"Sounds like stormy weather inside."

Immediately he cleared his throat again, wiggled his body inside his clothes, shoved open the door as the voice had commanded him to do and went in.

Mocejón was at sea, but Sargüeta and her daughter were at home, unraveling pieces of old rope. Although they were not expecting the visit of the priest, as soon as they saw him they suspected the motive that brought him there. They still had in mind the happening of the night before and remembered the insistence of Padre Apolinar that the wishes of the Council be fulfilled with respect to the orphan girl as well as the promises of piles of money offered in exchange for the help asked of them and the times that they themselves had unsuccessfully asked for the fulfillment of those offers. In short, they knew right away that he had come on account of Silda, and before he had finished saying good morning to them, the house was already trembling.

Mechelín had not gone to sea that day because he had spent the night with a hot brick wrapped in yellow flannel on his starboard side in order to try to kill a pain that started a few minutes before he went to bed. In the opinion of his wife, this had resulted from the displeasure that he had had so soon after eating from what had happened to Silda. The pain was better by daybreak, but he was in some doubt about getting up when he heard the wake boy call in the street. However, his wife decided that he should not work that day, and he had stayed in bed till quite late.

Then he dressed and ate a small bowl of cocoa bean husks in milk and then, in order not to be bored by idleness, started to twist some fishlines by using a piece of tile. This process did not completely satisfy him because it was better to twist the lines on the leg, that is to say, the thigh, with the palm of the hand, instead of tieing a piece of tile to the end of the line and make it turn around in the air. But Mechelín noticed when he started to do this task that the continuous massaging of the string with the palm of the hand on the thigh made his pain greater than by the other method; hence his decision to use the piece of tile. He was working thus till about noon.

While he was finishing off the last fathom of the ninety that he thought of making the line he was working on, his wife placed a big hook, the only one that a hake line has, at one end of the leader, or fine wire that should be on every line, and had ready the sinker, or lead weight that is fastened to the place where the line and leader meet, so that the tackle will sink when put into the water.

The work had reached this stage when they heard the voices of Sargüeta and Carpia on the stair landing shouting:

"Sponger."

"Trickster."

And at the same time they heard the buzzing of another harsh, mannish voice and the loud noise on the creaking stairs as someone made awkward steps coming down three at a time.

The couple on the ground floor came out to the doorway terrified. Padre Apolinar did not delay long in arriving, making the sign of the cross with one hand and holding onto the dirty handrail with the other, muttering Latin expressions and hurling forth pleas and entreaties:

"Deliver me, O Lord, deliver me from perverse wrath and from the iniquities of these women! Hear my prayer! Lord, Lord, Jesus, Mary and Joseph; furies of hell. Wow! Flee, flee, corrupt flesh! Your cruel word will scandalize the earth, but the Lord will confound you. He will confound you. Blessed be his holy name! Praised be the Lord!"

The bewildered priest had come down the stairs exclaiming these things and had reached the last step without failing to hear the other words that were being thrown at him from above with threats and insults.

"Deceiver."

"Lousy."

This was the least harsh and also the last which was said to the poor man from the top of the stairs. When their voices became quiet, the women appeared in the balcony more insulting and shameful than ever because they planned to keep up the barrage against the priest as long as he was in the street. The poor fellow stood frightened in the doorway looking up at them and hearing them again from there. The next Latin expression stuck in his half-opened mouth. Go out into the street then! Who could make him?

But he couldn't have gone out in any case, because Sidora and her husband had got in front of him so that he couldn't leave without talking to them. They made signs for him to keep quiet and each took hold of one side of his cloak and led him into their home and closed the door behind them.

This home had a small living room with a bedroom on the south side, a barred window which filled it with light, some of which even reached the second bedroom, separated from the first by a partition with a small window at the top. The light also entered a passageway that led to the room from the doorway. When this door was opened a little light entered the kitchen and two small additions under the stairway. When this door was closed all was dark inside and Sidora had no other

Where She Was Wanted

remedy than lighting a candle, although it was about noon. The doors of the bedrooms had curtains of flowered percale, and the walls were well whitewashed. On the walls of the living room there were three pictures: one of the Virgin of Carmen, the patron saint of Spanish sailors and fishermen; another of Saint Peter the Apostle, the patron saint of the Upper Town, and the Archangel Saint Michael, in veneered mahogany frames. Underneath the picture of the Virgin was a chest of drawers with a mirror on top. It had the appearance of much use and the varnish was faded but clean, like the four reed chairs and the two pine stools and the leather trunk with crosspieces of wood studded with nails. Even the basket full of fishing tackle, which was on top of one of the wooden stools, and the flagstone floor were spotlessly clean. The bed—which could be seen through the curtains, which were folded over a fancy square-topped nail, somewhat worn and bent—filled about two-thirds of the room and was quite fluffy to judge by the size of the percale mattress that covered it. The mattress was stuffed with cut up twigs, rooster feathers and other picturesque flying things. The smell that one noticed in the house was a sort of mixture of that of sardines and smoke; but with all that, the house seemed like a silver vase full of roses compared with each and all of the other living quarters up the stairway.

Padre Apolinar was led into the small living room. There he fell into a chair which Mechelín offered him very solicitously. After removing his hat, which he put on another chair, and wiping his face with his large, coarse handkerchief of unbleached muslin, he continued his interrupted lamentations:

"Flesh, miserable flesh, fragile, sinful flesh. Wow! What shameless women! Not even any consideration for a good man, nor any respect for a priest, nor any fear of God! And the insults will continue in broad daylight! Serpentlike tongues! Certainly I don't owe them anything and will pay them nothing. Trickster, eh! All right; the most honest of men may be that, as I am, and she is the devil! Because she certainly is a trickster and a deceiver! Because I offer, in the name of someone else, what that other one refuses to give—because he ought not give it. Is the name deserved? Well then, we'll call it stingy, stingy! Why? With whom? Certainly no one would believe that of Padre Apolinar but those that do not know him. See here, man! And may God confound me if I do any boasting!" And he raised his cloak higher than his knees, letting it be seen that only some cotton underwear and some black stockings darned with yarn covered his legs. "And excuse this way of showing you, Sidora, but an hour ago I had a pair of pants, although not much good. See whether I have prospered any since then, if I am stingy! Flesh, lustful, corrupted flesh. But, in short, Christ endured more than that for us because He was who He was! Shameless things! Forgive us our debts as we forgive our debtors. Because I forgive you with all my heart, and if I have any other feeling I hope I bust with it. Rascals! Does that hell keep on vomiting out more dregs, Mechelín? Do you hear their perverse voices on the balcony, Sidora? You hear so well."

"And what difference does it make to you whether they are shouting or quiet?" Sidora answered him, wishing to make a joke out of what was happening, which was like the prologue of a tragedy. "Make the sign of the cross at them like you do to the devil and calm your nerves, because the more poison those women throw out now, the less they will have inside their bodies for the next time."

"Right," added Mechelín, who looked constantly at the priest and did not lose a word of the few, but good ones, that reached his ears from the balcony of the fifth floor in spite of the fact that the door of his house was closed. "This is one sure thing: make a tack and change course."

"The fact is, if I am saying the truth, that I do not feel safe against such hurricanes even in this safe harbor. If they sense that I am here, the devil! It is not that my weak flesh trembles, but I fear an evil tongue more than I do a charge of grapeshot."

"If they sense that you are here, Pa'e 'Polinar," replied Mechelín in a solemn tone, getting ready to say something big, "if they sense that you are here, it will be just the same as if they didn't; because no one can get into my home when I put the bar on my door."

"Bah," added Sidora with a great deal of scorn, "all they have to do is to want to put their noses in somebody else's business to have their own way. But forget about them, Pa'e 'Polinar, and tell us what the devil you have had to do with them, confound them! What ill wind brought you here today, good man, to fall into the clutches of such people?"

"Right. That is what we want to know."

"Well, my dears," said the priest after gently wiping the bloody edges of his eyelids with a piece of fine linen that he had for that purpose, "with a couple of words I'll satisfy your curiosity. . . . The girl presents herself in my house."

"What girl?"

"Dead Mullet's girl."

"Silda?"

"I think that's what her name is."

"When did she come?"

"I don't think that it was an hour ago."

"Where did she come from? Where is she?"

"Keep quiet, man; that will all come out in due time. And then, Pa'e 'Polinar, what happened?"

"I say that the girl presents herself to me, or in order that the devil won't laugh at my lie, they present her to me and say to me: 'Padre Apolinar, last night they beat and mistreated her in her home and she ran away from there and slept in a small boat; now she doesn't have any other home than the street, with the sky for a roof . . . and see how you can fix up this matter.' Because, as you know well, Padre Apolinar gets everything from both the Upper Town and the Lower that can't be fixed. . . . That is my lot. It is nothing much, but there are worse ones . . . and especially since I can't choose. Padre Apolinar hears this, and on behalf of the abandoned girl he thinks of going to the home of Mocejón, to hear, find out, implore if necessary. . . . And I come, I knock, they tell me to come in, and I enter, and instead of listening to me, they insult me, they vilify me, because I interceded to have them take in the girl and the Council hasn't given them what it offered through other spokesmen besides myself, and that they will do this and that to me. And, by the devil, I had to leave fast to keep those furies from devouring me. And now you know as much about the case as I do."

Sidora and her husband exchanged a knowing glance, and no sooner had Padre Apolinar finished his story than she said:

"So at the present time Silda is without shelter."

"Except the protection of God," replied the friar.

"No one lacks that," replied Sidora. "The Lord helps them that helps themselves. And what about her now, the unfortunate girl?"

"I can't tell you. She left my house to go to see the *Montañesa* come in, with the son of the captain. And is she grieved about what is happening to her? No, and double devil with such kids."

"Just innocent children, Pa'e 'Polinar. God makes them. And you, what course do you intend to take?"

"Back to my house as soon as I get out of here."

"I mean with respect to the girl."

"Well, with respect to the girl, I mean, too. Afterwards I shall give a complete account to the president of the Council in order that he may know what is going on; and may they rack their brains well there. . . . I wash my hands of these innocents."

"And if in the meantime a good home could be found for the abandoned girl," asked Sidora, while her husband confirmed her words with expressive gestures and glances, "why shouldn't she take advantage of it?"

"Right," concluded Mechelín accenting his interjection with a swing of his fist in the air.

"A good refuge," exclaimed the friar. "What more would she want! What more would she want! But where is there one, my dear Sidora?"

"Right here," she replied with very cordial vehemence, sticking her chest and her hips out more than usual. "Right here in this very house."

"Here!" exclaimed the astonished friar. "But, are you crazy? You have peace and you are looking for war?"

"Why war?"

"Don't you know that this kid is like a wild goat?"

"Because she ain't had no good shepherds; now she will have."

"And the women up there on the fifth floor? Do you think that they will give you any peace?"

"We already understand those people; for good, if they are good, and if they are bad; everything isn't perfect even in the ocean, you know that well."

"Well, my dears," exclaimed the friar, getting up from his chair and pulling his shovel hat well down over his eyes, "with such good will, the help of God will not fail us. My duty was to inform you, and now that I have and you are not frightened, I say that I am glad for the good of this innocent girl; and as I do not say anything more than I feel, right now I am leaving to find her trail, with no more fear of those she-devils up on the balcony than I have of mosquitoes in the air. Christ suffered beatings, insults and the cross for us. Courage, and suffer something for Him."

Then he went out accompanied by this honorable couple. When they passed along the corridor in front of one of the bedrooms, Sidora raised the little curtains on the door and said, detaining the priest:

"Looky, and pardon me, Pa'e 'Polinar. This is where we intend to put her. We'll take out all these raincoats and all that fishing gear which take up a lot of room and don't smell good, and put them in a corner next to the kitchen; the bed will be fixed up like it ought to be, because right now it has only a mattress on it; and we can even hear her breathing from our bedroom. You will see how nice it is going to be. Just as it would have been the bed for my nephew if he had deserved it."

"What nephew?" asked the priest, walking toward the street door.

"The son of Chumacera, from down below."

"Oh, yes—Muergo! Little rascal. If he keeps on the way he is going he will outdo his mother. Flesh, flesh, already gnawed by the corruptive worm. Little rascal! All right, all right! So, until later, well, good-by, Mechelín, good-by, Sidora."

They clearly heard him mumble these words as soon as he set foot in the doorway:

"Lord, hear my prayer."

No doubt he was asking the Almighty to free him from the insults which the women of the fifth floor wished to hurl at him from the balcony.

If he had left a few minutes before and gone, as he did, from that point of the street to the corner of the next without hearing an insult, it would have been a real miracle; because then Sargüeta and her daughter Carpia were still there, leaning on their elbows and letting forth insults from their mouths.

5 HOW AND WHY SHE WAS GIVEN SHELTER

With all the excitement of the arrival of his father's boat, Andrés did not forget. He had promised Silda to see Padre Apolinar when he came back from San Martín and, in order to keep his promise, he left the road that he was taking to his home, a little after noon, and went to Ocean Street, crossing part of the market in New Plaza.

He found Silda seated on the first step of Padre Apolinar's house entertaining herself by tying a piece of red silk to the end of one of her braids of blond hair. The braid was still so short that after passing over the left shoulder there was scarcely

How and Why She Was Given Shelter

enough of it for her eyes to oversee the operations of the hands; so it was that they and the braid and the ribbon and the chin, contracted in order not to hinder the vision of the half-closed eyes, formed such a confused jumble that Andrés did not learn at once what was going on.

"What are you doin'?" he asked Silda as soon as he saw her.

"Puttin' this ribbon in my hair," the girl replied.

"Who gave it to you?"

"We bought it with the money you threw to Muergo. He wanted cigarettes and Sula wanted caramels, but I wanted this ribbon that was in one of the shops and I bought it. Then I came here to wait for you in order to find out about that."

"Is Pa'e 'Polinar at home?"

"I haven't taken the trouble to ask," replied Silda with the greatest calmness.

"Well, gee!" said Andrés, standing in front of her with arms akimbo, kicking the ground and moving his body from one side to the other. "Well, who should be more interested in it than you?"

"Didn't we agree that you would climb the stairs to see Pa'e 'Polinar and that I would wait for you in the doorway? Well, here I am waitin'; so go up as soon as you can."

Andrés began to climb the stairs two steps at a time. When he was near the first landing, Silda called him and said,

"If Pa'e 'Polinar wants me to go back to Sargüeta's house, tell him that I'll jump into the ocean first."

"My gosh," shouted Andrés from where he was, "why didn't you tell him that when we were in his house before?"

"'Cause I didn't remember," replied Silda unwillingly, engrossed in the task of putting the ribbon on her hair braid.

A quarter of an hour had not passed when Andrés was already back at the street door.

"He was at the home of Mocejón," he told Silda while still panting, "and those women nearly killed him."

"Don't you see?" exclaimed Silda, looking at him firmly. "They sure are bad; very bad!"

"They are going to take you to a good home," continued Andrés in a very pondering tone.

"Which one?" asked Silda.

"To an aunt and uncle of Muergo."

"What's their name?"

"Mechelín and Sidora."

"You mean the ones that live on the ground floor?"

"I think so."

"And they are Muergo's aunt and uncle?"

"Apparently."

"They are good people, but they live too close to those others."

"Pa'e 'Polinar says that doesn't make any difference."

"And when am I goin'?"

"He'll come right down to take you. I'm going home now to wait for my father, who will soon be disembarking, if he hasn't already—gee, what a beautiful entrance the *Montañesa* made! You missed that! More than a thousand persons were there looking at it from San Martín. Good-by, Silda; I'll be seeing you."

"Good-by," she replied dryly, while Andrés left the doorway and went down the street as fast as he could run.

Padre Apolinar came down soon; but before Silda saw him she had already heard him murmur between the sounds of his wide shoes on the stair steps:

"The devil take such a girl. Carelessly capsized, and doesn't give a darn about something that makes me sweat blood! You run over half the town looking for her, to find out that she didn't go to San Martín, but people had seen her at the Point with two wharf rats. Then you go back home, and you can't eat your daily bread, and report at best that you couldn't find what you were looking for, and you get excited because you can't, and then you have it right on your doorstep, not worrying or caring. Darn that snot-nosed boy! Why didn't you come up yourself, silly thing?"

"'Cause I was waitin' for Andrés, who was the one that had to go up."

How and Why She Was Given Shelter

"Had to go up! And who is the person that is in God's great outdoors and needs a crust of bread and an honest family to give her a little love? Isn't it you? And since it is you, to whom did it matter more than you to climb the stairs to my home and ask me, 'Pa'e 'Polinar, what about it?' More than snot-nosed! Come on. Let that darn ribbon alone and come along with me."

While these two were walking toward High Street, Pa'e 'Polinar was trying to inform the girl. Among other things he said:

"And now that you have found what you deserve, have lots of humility and little deceptive flattery. This business of going to La Maruca is over, and also to the docks—because if you give them any motive for kicking you out of this house, Pa'e 'Polinar is not going to tire himself looking for another one for you. You understand? Your father was a good man; your mother was no worse; both used to make confession to me. But as good as or better than they were are the people that are going to give you a home. So, if you turn out bad, it is because you want to be or that you have a bad make-up. But don't ask me to straighten out what you get twisted up because of your badness. Double darn! I am crucified enough for being a redeemer so many times. See what happened this very morning. And speaking of that: we'll go by way of Rua Menor to Hospital Hill, and as soon as we reach the top of it you look around the corner very carefully, and look without being seen, at Sargüeta's place. If there is anybody in the balcony, jump back and tell me; if there isn't anybody there, run as fast as you can to the sidewalk on the other side. I'll follow you, and sticking close to the house and walking fast we'll go to Mechelín's door. He'll be waiting there for us. You understand well? All right then, get started."

Silda did not suspect why so many precautions should be taken for what interested Pa'e 'Polinar so much, because she had had only a brief account from Andrés about what happened at Mocejón's house. But as it mattered greatly for her to pass unnoticed, she carried out his directions at the opportune moment with a scrupulousness only comparable to the terror which the women of the fifth floor instilled in her. Since she couldn't see them in the balcony or any visible part of the street, she and the friar crossed the street like two flashes of lightning and slipped into the doorway of Mechelín, whose wife was just then emptying the contents of a kettle into a dish on the table to get ready to eat, believing since it was now past one o'clock that Silda would not appear as soon as Padre Apolinar had believed.

The guest could not have arrived at a better time. She calmly ran her eye over everything she could see in the house and sat down dauntlessly on the stool that Sidora kindly offered her, in front of another on which was steaming the hot food in a deep dish, faded in color and somewhat cracked because of its years of use without a single day's interruption. Mechelín, with eyes dancing with joy, offered Silda a big piece of bread and a tin spoon, because in that house each one ate with his own spoon. The offer was accepted as the most natural thing and the meal was started without their noticing the slightest sign of strangeness or shyness on the part of the little girl. She kept her turn placing her spoon in the dish and heard, without replying anything more than a cold stare, affectionate words of encouragement which Sidora and her husband said to her.

Padre Apolinar believed the occasion right for repeating to Silda what he had said en route, and even for adding some more advice, but Sidora cut him off, saying:

"She will do all of that and more without bein' ordered on her own account, won't you, my child? Now eat calmly; fill up your little belly, because it must be pretty empty; sleep in a good bed, and afterwards there will be room for everything; time to work and time to enjoy yourself."

"Right," exclaimed Mechelín. "You can't ask the body for more strength than it's got. And you, who are able to talk convincingly and have influence everywhere, it would be a good idea for you to tell us the pros and cons of this matter."

"That's what I'm thinking, within the responsibility that's mine," replied the priest. "I know how to do that well."

"Right. Today is Saturday. Tomorrow there'll be a meeting

How and Why She Was Given Shelter 73

of the Council to take up matters of aid and other particulars."

"So much the better, then," said Padre Apolinar. "I was thinking of seeing only Sabano when he came in from fishing this afternoon; but now that you remind me, I'll come back here tomorrow and have the matter handled by the Council."

"Right! But no money involved, nor any help on the case. We don't want nothin' more than the authority and a hand against anyone opposed to what we are doin' gladly."

"That's understood, Mechelín. It's no little interest I have in it myself. And when they flay you for what you are doing, they'll get after me too. Has it been such a long time since you saw what happened to me? Have you forgotten already? Well, I'm still quivering and my ears still buzz. Tongues, serpent tongues, and lost souls!"

"Well," Sidora said half jesting, "you ain't as tough as I thought you was, Pa'e 'Polinar. Who remembers about what happened today except to make the sign of the cross and think about something else?"

"Surely, Sidora, surely," he replied quickly. "For what they are and for what I am, we shouldn't even mention them again. But we are weak clay, miserable flesh, and we make a hundred mistakes every hour. I should set a strong example, and I do, Sidora, as a funny looking thing, because really, I am not worth a darn. Lord, remember not my sins. And with this, if you have nothing else to say, I'm getting back to my work. Silda, remember what I said. You've been pretty lucky; you've landed on your feet. If you throw all this out the window you will not deserve God's pardon, nor can you count on me regardless how bad off you are. So Mechelín, and Sidora, peace be with you. I think that I can leave without running into too much trouble, can't I? What do you think?"

Sidora got up, smiling maliciously, went out to the street door, looked, listened and returned to the living room, saying:

"I don't see a soul and I don't even hear a mosquito."

"Don't take my question so seriously, woman," said the priest, somewhat regretful for having asked it. "Because you know when it comes down to cases Apolinar has a tough hide for insults; but by all means a little precaution is well taken, and may God repay you for it."

He said good-by and left.

A few moments later Sidora asked Silda:

"And how are you set for baggage, child? Don't you have anything more than what you have on?"

"This and another clean blouse that's still up there."

"Well, we won't think about gettin' it, even if it was made of satin. There will be another one, won't there, Mechelín?"

"And whatever else is necessary," replied Mechelín. "For necessary things we have our savings."

Suddenly Silda said:

"The one who hasn't a sign of a shirt is Muergo."

"He would surely have one if he deserved one," replied Sidora.

"This morning," added Silda, "he didn't have any pants either, and Pa'e 'Polinar gave him his."

"He certainly had them to spare," said Sidora with visible anger toward her nephew.

The girl replied right away:

"He gave him the pair he had on, and I don't think he had any others."

Sidora and her husband looked at each other remembering that Padre Apolinar had on only underwear.

"All right, and so what?" asked Sidora.

"Muergo needs a shirt more than I do."

Mechelín and Sidora looked at each other again. And Mechelín asked the girl: "And when this one is bein' washed, you'll need one, won't you?"

"I'll stay in bed till it dries," she answered, shrugging her shoulders.

"But where did you get acquainted with that pig Muergo?" asked Sidora.

"Down there."

"And why are you tellin' me that he doesn't have a shirt or pants?"

"Because Andrés told me he was a nephew of yours."

"Who is Andrés?"

"The son of a gentleman, the son of the captain of the *Montañesa*."

"Do you know him?"

"He's the one who took me to Pa'e 'Polinar's house when I was alone on the dock this morning."

"Why did he take you there?"

"So they would do for me what has now been done. That gentleman's son is a good boy."

"Does he know Muergo?"

"He knows him very well."

"And why doesn't he give him a shirt since he is rich?"

"He's mad at him because he threw me into the water."

"Who threw you in?"

"Muergo."

"And how did you get out?"

"Muergo got me out 'cause Sula and another boy named Cole told him to."

"So if they hadn't told him to do that you would have drowned?"

"Maybe."

"And in spite of all that, you are askin' for a shirt for him? The devil take him!"

"It turns your stomach to see how he is. But if you give him a shirt here, it shouldn't be taken to him unless he cuts his hair and washes his feet. He's like a pig! Or even a donkey! And very bad!"

"Then why in the devil are you so worried about him?"

"Just because, 'cause it turns your stomach just to look at him. And his mother is a shameless woman."

When Silda got that far with her answer, a voice that was suddenly heard at one end of the passageway, as if it had the material strength of a catapult, hurled itself against the innermost part of the bedroom. The voice was vibrant, shameless, with tones that indicated too much alcohol, half provocative and half cruel, with rising and falling inflections and tones that were asking for a fight. It was saying:

"There it is. So that they can change her lousy clothing tomorrow, which is Sunday, or make some ring-shaped pads which abound in my house, or use it for a party dress the day you marry her to a marquis with gold watch chains, the little devil. Because all the wealth of the West Indies will come to the ground floor with that brat that we swept out yesterday with the rubbish. Zowie! Take that for her and the bleary-eyed cheat that came to you with the little princess and her story! Indecent things!"

When the voice continued down the street, Sidora came out from her hiding place very cautiously and found in the middle of the passageway a white bundle. She picked it up, unwrapped it and saw that it was a child's blouse, doubtless Silda's. Then being bold enough to go to the street door and put her head out, she saw Carpia going down the middle of the street, her arms akimbo, barefoot and barelegged, her skirt swishing, carrying two empty baskets on her head.

"They know it now," Sidora said to herself. "So much the better. We have passed that part of it! It bothers them and they are beginnin' to bite. Well, let them bite. They will get tired. The big rascals! Drunks! Shameless things!"

6 ☙ A MEETING OF THE FISHERMEN'S GUILD

What used to be called the Big Wall, near High Street, still exists with the same name, between the first house on the south side of this street and the last house on Rua Mayor. However, the old railing which protected the little plaza from the cliff and the wide stone steps which went down to the left to low tide level are lacking. At the foot of the steps was a landing for the boats of the sailors of that day. (Today it is part of a built-up area, with the railroad station in the center. The Z-shaped ramp leading to High Street and Rua Mayor is called Sotileza Ramp.)

There on the Big Wall Plaza, the Upper Town guild meetings were held in the open air if the weather permitted. If not, they were held in the Seville Bar which was the sailors' hangout, store, bank, inn, tribunal, and sooner or later the bottomless pit of their economics.

It was already known, because Mechelín told it in his house, that the following day there would be a meeting of the guild "to take up matters of aid and other particulars." And in fact it was very well attended. Not a single sailor eligible to have a voice and a vote was absent when the clock on the hospital tower struck 9:30. Sobano, the presiding officer, set the example by being one of the first to arrive. He was a man of few words and very serious; he had already been an alderman for two terms, representing the sailors, but was still working as a fisherman and didn't have anything more than the rest of them, although he had acquired that flippancy or air of sufficiency which comes, among ignorant, penniless persons such as he, from frequent contact with persons of brilliance and money. It is certain that when the fishermen's guilds named him for such a high position, they had already seen in him qualities of understanding, judgment and manners that were not common among seafaring people. But what about what he had learned during his two terms of two years each? Who failed to see him in the religious procession of Corpus Christi or Holy Week or in the pews reserved for guild members in the church, with his black suit and medallion of office around his neck, and his white cotton gloves—because there was no way of getting his big calloused hands in kid gloves?

The Town Meeting of the Upper Town met.

The principal items of business had to do with an approaching selection for military service, payment of help to seamen's widows, to sick seamen, selection of another "contract" doctor to care for the needs of the sailors and the planning for the celebration of St. Peter's Day, their patron saint.

The executive board occupied the most visible part of the Plaza. Others were grouped around the esplanade and paid attention only to the things that interested them.

In the meantime the incessant mumbling of whispered conversations could be heard, and above this the buzzing of Mocejón which seemed like a tenacious, bothersome horsefly. Everything that was said or agreed on at the meeting produced growls from him. He held his short, stubby pipe in his teeth and stood there with his arms crossed, his head lowered, making gestures of anger or boredom, dirty and unshaven.

There were many like Mocejón who seemed to disagree with most of the things that were going on, but today he was the worst.

For example, if the president said "white," he would say "black," and he considered himself more intelligent than the president.

After more than an hour and a half of discussion and arguments most of their business was performed and the meeting was about to adjourn when the president raised his arm and said:

"Just a moment, gentlemen, there is one other matter to be arranged, and it must be arranged before we leave here."

Curiosity moved all the people assembled there to close in and make a compact circle around the executive board.

A Meeting of the Fisherman's Guild

Sobano began to talk then about a certain responsibility undertaken by the Council more than seven months ago to help the family that would give a home to the Mullet orphan girl, whose father was lost in a storm at sea with all his companions during the sea bream run.

Mocejón, guessing that that matter involved him, received the words of Sobano and the looks of the people like a dog does a stick which kids poke at him from under a door.

The president added that if the Council had not fulfilled what it had promised it was because it did not feel itself obliged to because the girl had paid for her poor bed and board by the work she did and the barbarous beatings she got from the family that had taken her in.

"Right," exclaimed a voice.

"It's a lie; prove it," growled the voice of Mocejón, decidedly affected by alcohol. "Make that good."

"It will be done," replied the president, "and everything else that has to be done. But it would be better for a certain person who hears me to keep on rowing till this nor'wester passes than to put up so much sail."

"Right," repeated the voice of Mechelín.

"And that fellow who is tryin' to pick a fight with me," growled Mocejón, "is he puttin' up too much sail or not? Is the nor'wester blowin' the same for everybody here or some other way? And see here, you runt with the funny jacket, if you have anything to say to me, why don't you say it clearly to my face, and don't try to hide in the seaweed like the devilfish! Watch out!"

There was only a slight movement, like the backwash foam, among the group on hearing Mocejón talk thus. Then Sobano told in a few words what had happened to Silda in Mocejón's house until she was taken in by Mechelín.

The Town Meeting was asked if it considered that the home of Mechelín was sufficient shelter and refuge for the orphan, and the answer was yes, among the growls and oaths and gestures of the savage Mocejón.

Mechelín then started to speak and said:

"May it be known that for the help of the abandoned girl no pay nor nothin' like it is wanted. But the Council is asked for authority for doing gladly for her what should be done—things that others have not done, either because they couldn't or didn't want to. Is that statement worth anything or not? Do you understand me or don't you? Is there any assurance or not that the matter will be done as requested?"

"There is," replied many voices.

And Sobano added right away, facing Mocejón:

"The Town Meetin' helps this girl. Do you hear what I say? Well, nothin' more needs to be said because nothin' more is needed for some people to understand what is meant."

Mocejón did not cease mumbling and protesting everything when the meeting broke up. He followed some of them to the Seville Bar and said:

"Well, look at that other guy. Lousy! Softy! We'll see if it pays to be a tattlin' bootlicker like you to defame someone who is worth more than you and that mangy bitch of a wife you have and all that bunch of dirty connivers that are on your side. God damn it!"

7 ❦ THE SAILORS OF THAT DAY

The reader from the hinterlands might like to remain a while on the Big Wall near High Street after the town meeting was over in order to take in the pleasant panorama which extends from Cabarga Hill to the marshes on the west shore of the bay. Or out of curiosity he might want to ask some questions of the cabin boys, who were humming and talking below the wall while bailing out the boats or moving boats away from one another. Or he might like to stand there and look at the houses on both sides of the street, tall, close together, with balconies full of nets and rags, fishing tackle and fish strips drying in the sun; and mothers who were dirty and unkempt, trying to clean up their kids, half naked, in the doorways. Or he might move down to San Francisco Street to watch people leaving the Church of the Jesuits after eleven o'clock mass.

Among these were Don Pedro Colindres, better known among the seafaring people by his nickname Bitadura (Half Hitch), his wife and his son, Andrés.

I desire that this should be our moment of being presented to him, so that all of his qualities of a gentleman can be seen by those who have seen him on board the *Montañesa* the day it arrived, or when he disembarked the next day with his officer's clothes, with no "extras."

He was not very tall, just about average height, but, on the other hand, he was double in size when it came to shoulders, arms and hands. Begging the reader's impatience, but I need to take this personage from way back, almost from birth, in order to present him as he should be at the moment of entering the picture. I shall try to be brief; but, although I may not succeed, do not worry, because this digression, besides the immediate purpose which it serves, will save us others like it, clearing the ground that we are going to enter, because examples of this species abound, and from one example you will know all of them.

His father and grandfathers had all been sailors. As soon as he left the sixth grade he started to study navigation in the Institute with Don Fernando Montalvo; and, although he was only thirteen at the time, he already smoked anything he could get hold of, could swim on his back and stand upright in the water by treading; he could do the "dead man's float" and make a high dive from the wall and could hold his own with anyone in rowing. Because of his fighting ability, he became quite a celebrity at school and on the docks. Even at billiards in the Zanguina Bar he could beat anybody.

But at that age he still kept the landlubber way of dress, walking and speaking. As soon as he became a navigation student he took on the manners and customs of that specialized group of students, who seemed not to have been born of women, as all other descendants of Adam, but hewn out of oak on the ways at a shipyard. From them he took his rude talk, the crude insult, the bold glance, the waddling gait and gloomy appearance.

When he finished his navigation courses, he had to make two round trips to Cuba as an apprentice navigator on a boat commanded by a friend of his father. Afterwards he took an examination at Ferrol in Galicia, the nearest seat of naval jurisdiction, and was given the title of second mate. Then he embarked on a frigate from Santander for three trips, a requirement for future advancement. On occasions this tub seemed as safe as sailing in a washbowl and on others just the opposite. By the time these trips were over he was a young man, beginning to have a beard and a hoarse voice. He was quite tanned and used to take part in all sailors' sprees and gay frolics.

He got ready for his next examination by reviewing for a time with Professor Montalvo and went to Ferrol the second time. The examiners approved him in this strict examination, and his rank was raised to that of first mate and navigator. By this time he had the nickname Bitadura (Half Hitch), but the reason is not known. (I take advantage of this opportune occasion to tell landlubber readers who doubtless have the idea that it is a whim of mine that almost all the characters presented up to now in this book have nicknames, that there is no such whim nor anything like it. So frequent are nicknames among the seafolk of this port, and so accustomed are they to being called by nicknames, that there have been fishermen who did not know their own baptismal name, and many who did not learn them until they had to have a name to enroll on a ship's crew list. Nicknames for all classes of people appeared almost without knowing how or why. It generally comes from some saying or act, or any circumstance whatsoever of the person involved, who may have it applied to him more or less spontaneously; but who gave it to him and when, it is never easy to find out.)

The Sailors of That Day

Bitadura delayed quite a while in getting a position after receiving the rank of mate because openings were not always available even with the large number of sailing ships; but, finally, he found a ship and made his first trip as mate.

The return from this trip was when he was in Santander in perfect character as a mariner; he already was just like all the others. Because I do not know how in the devil it happened, but it did, be they blonds or skinny or tall or short, the cadets of the Institute, or the apprentices on their first trip, gradually were being transformed; and when they came back to port as mates they were all alike: all were broad shouldered, with big, hairy hands; all were dark, with thick, flowing sideburns; all were harsh of voice, slow in gait, frowning, plain in speech but picturesque in words, having boyish pleasures and a gay spirit. Finally, they all dressed alike: a cap with gold braid and a button with an anchor on it (but no crown, to indicate they were not officers in the Royal Navy). They wore brown jackets, waterproof boots, with their brown trousers tucked in, and a black middy tie. Perhaps this rigorous uniformity of dress and manners contributed to giving them the extraordinary similarity which was noted among them.

Bitadura was one of the most popular mariners of his day but, after having gone through storms in all the seas in both worlds, he got the idea on his return to Santander that the amusements in the Marine Café were not for him. These had included nightly sprees, disturbances of the peace, such as practical jokes, fights—some of which were rather childish. But one day he got up his nerve, brushed his hair a little, put on a clean shirt and some patent leather shoes and went to ask a retired pilot for the hand of his only daughter, a beautiful young lady. When Bitadura confessed his project to a friend, he described her as follows: "She is trim, somewhat broad abeam, graceful lines and tall of stature."

The girl came from a good family. And of course in those days there were social classes. Scarcely a half dozen families in Santander could clothe their daughters in silk. The young man was well known, and his temporary escapades were not considered sinful because many young men of good family background, good at heart and valiant at sea, did those things. The girl's father liked him and the daughter had seen him on at least three occasions literally sweep the sidewalk of rivals in a fight so that he alone remained to pay her compliments; and although he had not advanced beyond the rank of mate and was still so clumsy with fine manners and speech that he sweat blood trying to make himself understood in this matter—because it is quite evident that he didn't succeed in expressing himself—they gave him the girl, called Andrea, who had eyes like two suns and shiny black hair so abundant that there was hardly room for it on her head. Her mouth and complexion were beautiful. In short, she was a good-looking girl in every sense of the word.

As time went on they were married; and before they had been married a month he started on his last trip as mate. On his return the captain decided to go ashore for a long time, and they gave him the command of the ship, a well-known barkentine. And here you have him a captain, with a salary of sixty dollars a month and soon to be enjoying the benefits the outfitters or owners of a ship bestow on the captain who commands with zeal and intelligence. . . . But, on the other hand, how weighty were the duties imposed by this sudden promotion! It was difficult for him to mold himself to the ritual of his new rank. All at once there were no more jackets and waterproof boots and the clothes usually worn by a mate. Also, it was good-by to independence, merriment, the gay life of a carefree young man and the conventional, picturesque language! He heard direct and indirect orders such as: "Make yourself into a formal man, and talk seriously with merchants and shippers, and especially dress in fine cloth, with plenty of finery." . . . "Get that massive body into a frock coat, and those feet into patent leather shoes, and those big, hairy hands into kid gloves." And, horror of horrors! ". . . and on your head, well prepared by the barber's scissors, place a tall silk hat . . . and go out into the street with this gear, scarcely daring to walk or to turn too much for fear of popping some buttons or bursting some seams, and go to consular offices and greet the people there in the customary manner, and while you talk or they wait on you, sit down daintily in a chair, and have a doubt in your mind whether you should put your silk hat on the floor or hold it in your hands or throw it out the window, which is probably what you would prefer!"

The first time that he saw himself in a mirror dressed this way he laughed and said: "With this and a cane, I'd look like a country doctor."

"Why don't you buy one then?" asked his wife.

Bitadura looked at her with astonishment.

To tell a captain like that to carry a cane was like advising a cavalryman to carry a fan.

But, finally, he became accustomed to this outfit, although he never used it except for official functions or solemn occasions; aside from these cases, he used a comfortable suit with accessories about halfway between those of a captain and a mate: comfortable without ceasing to be serious.

When his son was three years old he was given command of the *Montañesa,* one of the best boats registered in Santander. As he was not slow, he became accustomed sooner to dealing with people than to the use of fine manners. He became one of the most popular captains as far as the passengers were concerned, and the owner of the *Montañesa* did not have any reason to regret having given him command of the ship. Furthermore, because he was an excellent mariner and zealous administrator, the owner was very generous to him. One of the first concessions granted him was permission to bring in boxes of candied tropical fruit on his own account and without paying any freight. In a few trips he made considerable money and later took more interest in the cargoes entrusted to his ship. In spite of that and the fact that he had already sailed past forty when the reader first meets him, he continued being, while off duty, the same old Bitadura, just a big boy, given to the little pleasures and interests of his home province, to picturesque speech and comfortable dress.

Andrea, who had no other children than the one we know, had gradually become more plump, and was, at the time of this story, a woman of fine appearance. Her face was pale, gay and beautiful.

She had gone to eleven o'clock mass that day wearing a dress of heavy black silk, a Spanish shawl, a white lace mantilla, a mother-of-pearl fan and silk mesh gloves. Her husband was wearing a frock coat and trousers of fine black material with straps on the bottom passing under his patent leather shoes, and a satin vest across which was festooned a heavy gold watch chain. His silk hat was resplendent. Because of the heat, the man was perspiring underneath the finery, his hands were bothered by the gray gloves, his feet by the tight shoes. His tanned face glistened, framed by his graying sideburns, the brim of his hat and the starched collar which was beginning to wrinkle because of the sweat.

He expected all that and God knows how much it bothered him, but it was necessary to appear thus in public because his wife had been dreaming about it since his last trip home. She knew no greater satisfaction, and he loved his wife too much not to please her. On the other hand, why should he refuse? If Andrea considered herself better than the wife of the town's chief magistrate when she went out on the arm of a man like hers, Bitadura thought that, in the opinion of all who passed by, there was no princess who was any prettier than his wife.

And thus the two of them walked up San Francisco Street into the Old Plaza, receiving at each step greetings, handshakes, congratulations, and "welcome home." Andrés, who walked to the right of his mother, had on his Sunday clothes, which included a tailored jacket with a silk collar, wool tweed trousers, a polkadot vest, a wide ribbon bow tie, new high shoes and a felt cap in imitation tiger skin. He proudly greeted boys of his own class, or acted as if he didn't know them when he winked at any wharf rats. They got back home as soon as they could to receive visitors and guests who had been invited to eat at one o'clock sharp. Andrea did not have much confidence in the cook hired for this occasion, whom she hoped would be better than the regular servant.

The reader and I arrive at the moment when the captain was flinging his gloves and his silk hat on the dresser. His wife, after folding her mantilla and silk shawl, put them in a drawer. She would gladly have changed to a more comfortable dress. The captain also would have exchanged his finery for clothes he wore on board, but they were expecting guests and they had to be well dressed under the circumstances. In those days a new arrival like Bitadura could not receive visitors without dressing well, especially when it was a holiday and he had such a lovely wife who was so scrupulous in these matters.

While she took a turn through the kitchen, knocks were heard at the front door. Bitadura came running to the living room, which was like that of any sea captain of that day. On the white walls there were pictures of all the ships on which he had sailed. On the mahogany corner cupboards and table there were knickknacks that he had collected from all over the world —sea shells, coral, wooden trays, music boxes, etc. The floor was made of well-rubbed pine with a small rug in front of each door. The candelabras were of silver.

The first visitors to see the captain, just back from a trip, were a married couple from the fourth floor of the same apartment building, with their oldest daughter. They were shopkeepers, having inherited a store from their parents, but somewhat insipid in their tastes as compared with Bitadura. Next came the retired Captain Arguinde, a Basque who made peculiar errors in Spanish word order. Later Sinforiana Santon, widowed quite a few years ago when her husband, a first mate, had died of fever on the coast of Africa. Others came, some because they were relatives, others because of gratitude toward him or because of business matters. He had already seen his friends and pals in a place that was convenient to talk and laugh freely.

The invited guests were Sama, his first mate, another captain and two harbor pilots named Madruga and Ligo, whom we met on San Martín with Andrés. The latter was the youngest of all and tried to be the most elegant and well informed. Madruga and he formed quite a contrast. Madruga was passive, spoke softly, and then only when spoken to. What he did say seemed to be lined with copper on his lips, with an expression that was half jest and half anger. Ligo, on the contrary, was loquacious, with great pretensions of worldly wisdom. He talked in the manner and brusqueness of what he was, with fine terms which he made up at his pleasure when necessity demanded. In this way there resulted a mixture of coarsely said fine expressions and crude things so finely expressed that it was all that one wanted to hear.

There were still some ladies there when Madruga arrived. He had gotten along quite well by removing his cap and making a small bow before sitting down. Sama had not put on any airs simply because he did not know any. He had hidden himself rather quietly in a corner where he amused himself by twirling his cap in his hands while he hummed, almost inaudibly, a tune from Cuba.

Captain Nudos, younger than Bitadura and as well dressed as he, and molded in the same pattern, did not excel him one whit in the niceties of courtesy and ceremonials of society. Really, he was almost entirely devoid of social graces, but had had dealings with people because of his employment and had heard that the lady of the house should be the one given most attention by relatives and strangers. Consequently, seeing a vacant place on the sofa where Mrs. Colindres was sitting near some other ladies, there he headed, and took anchor next to her with no more effort than that of removing something in order to enlarge the place needed for his large frame. He somewhat bothered the people next to him, but as a gentleman did not pick a quarrel with anybody.

When Ligo came in, making a lot of clatter with his heels and puffing and swinging his head and shoulders a lot, the master of the house endured those annoying moments as God

The Sailors of That Day

and his impatience gave him to understand. Andrea was talking with other ladies. Sama, tired of twirling his cap, had put his elbows on his knees and amused himself by dropping small bits of saliva at a juncture of two boards in the floor. Madruga, with his left foot resting on his right knee, with his body thrown back, with one hand between the lapels of his coat and his cap in the other, was listening, with an attention so affectedly serious that it was comical, to the few serious things that Bitadura said. Captain Nudos, judging by his face, was asking God to inspire him in some way to get out of this jam as soon as possible.

When Ligo came in and observed the setting, he was convinced that those men were no good for such a situation and even suspected that the ladies were bored. He was going to fix everything by giving a lesson in courtesy and elegant wit to his companions, and a little amenity to the gathering in order to amuse the ladies. But there he goes! An insult to one, a slap on the back to another, hints to Bitadura, compliments to Andrea, some kindness here, some gallantry there of the kind that he knew how to say. Before deciding to sit down in the chair which he was dragging from one place to another, he talked and went from one group to another until all the ladies left the room. The last one to leave was Andrea, whose cheeks were blushing, and she was biting her lips with laughter.

As soon as the five seamen were alone, Bitadura sat beside his companion on the sofa, who began to wrinkle his face and to stretch, while Bitadura said to him in a teasing manner:

"Hey, fellow! Relax a little, boy! Your face looks like an inflamed bladder."

To which Ligo added:

"If he only wouldn't get mixed up in maneuvers that he doesn't understand."

"You're the one for these maneuvers," said Madruga very seriously.

"Sure I am," replied Ligo. "I got apparatus to sail in all kinds of weather, good for big fish or small fish. If you don't think so, just remember how the ladies undid themselves laughing when I came in. Up to that time they were all bored, as if this was a prayer meetin'! Man, you are just a sea lion and nothin' more!"

And thus the battle of wits continued and the noise and the laughter. Then Sama lost what little respect the presence of Bitadura inspired in him, since after all he was his captain. He let out a Cuban dance tune, imitating with his arms and voice and looking at the other four men while dancing like the Negroes of Cuba. The only reason they didn't start to play leap frog was because Andrea arrived saying that soup was on the table, and they all went to the dining room.

Bitadura had been away for five months. For about two of these he had been at sea with no communication with the world. The first thing that would occur to such a man today when he got back home and sat down among friends would be to ask them: "Who is ruling Spain now? What's new in politics? What revolution is brewing?"

But these things were of little interest to Bitadura and all others like him in those days. What he did ask with great interest, as soon as everybody sat down at the table, was what all the town characters were doing and how they were getting along.

He uttered such expressions as: "Eat up those groceries, boy," and "bend that elbow."

By the time the dessert was served there wasn't much talking. What little there was was quite serious because the theme seemed to be what the captain was going to do about the career of his boy Andrés. As he was getting to be quite large, the father wanted him to matriculate in navigation school in about a year so that he could get in his apprenticeship with him before he retired from going to sea, or before God took away his license by having him buried at sea. Hearing these things, the poor mother became worried because it was bad enough to have a husband at sea. She could not consent to her son following the same career as his father. She tried to change the conversation.

The Sailors of That Day

With this, and because dessert was finished and gin and cordials appeared on the table, as well as the filter apparatus for making strong coffee, she and Andrés and the ladies left the dining room. The sailors remained there alone.

An hour later Madruga was dancing a jig with Ligo, and a little later, at the suggestion of his host, he was dancing a dance he learned in Cuba. The others helped provide the rhythm. They kept this up until they left to take a stroll along the Alameda.

And those grown-up boys were the men who knew how to take ships to all the ports of the world and, with a fervent prayer and a promise to the Holy Virgin, face death a hundred times with a calm face and fearless heart in the midst of the fury of storms!

Has poetry ever sung anything greater or of a more epic nature than those trifles?

8 VENANCIO LIENCRES, OWNER OF *LA MONTAÑESA*

"Exactly, Don Pedro; everything that you tell me and all the news you give me, together with the results obtained, proves again that the *Montañesa* is a good piece of property. In that the hand of her captain plays a big part because he takes her over all the seas with rare good luck. You really have the magic touch. Even the hurricanes, sometimes impelling her and other times detaining her, seem to be at her service so that the ship arrives in port at the best time for the business of her owner. May such a fortunate star continue to guide her and you for many years! And by the way—do you still intend to have your only son follow the sea?"

The speaker was Venancio Liencres, rich merchant and

owner of the *Montañesa*, talking to his captain the next day in the gloomy, dusty office which he had in the mezzanine of his house near the dock. The two had been alone for a while. The merchant, poorly dressed, was seated in a reed chair near his desk, which was loaded with bundles of unanswered letters, samples of sugar, flour and cocoa. The captain was on the dirty sofa in front of the desk, under a picture of the *Montañesa* just like the one he had at home, and a mail schedule chart which was fastened to the wall with small, yellow tacks.

While the merchant was talking in this way, he was affectionately handling the summary of accounts of the last trip, which he had ordered made in another room.

Bitadura was a little baffled by the merchant's question. It was unexpected, because it was the first time Don Venancio had ever spoken about Andrés. It was a strange question because he had never had any idea of any other career than the sea for his son. For that reason he replied:

"And if I don't make a sailor out of him, what is he going to be?"

"Almost anything. Anything is preferable to this hazardous career, in which a man of good heart and better luck cannot ever obtain that which any other man not a sailor can get with little effort, namely, family life. You know that well."

"That is certain," replied the captain swallowing a sigh and frowning, as if Liencres had hit the little corner of his heart where he kept his only secret.

"Furthermore," added Don Venancio, "you are not in the same situation as others of your profession with respect to your son. You have made money in your work, and since you have only one son, you may allow him to choose what he likes best."

"Nothing pleases him as much as a career at sea," the captain hastened to reply.

"Or you choose for him," Liencres continued, pretending not to hear the captain, "what is best for him. Because children's inclinations usually follow the whims of the moment—passing fancies of the imagination, or sharing the enthusiasm of others. You understand me?"

"Yes, I understand you, Don Venancio," said Bitadura with an attention and seriousness seldom seen in this carefree seaman, who the day before had been dancing in his home with Madruga, "but supposing that I have to choose a career for Andrés, what do I choose? Lawyer?"

"Nah!"

"Doctor?"

"No."

"Solicitor? Notary? Professor?"

"Horrors. Nothing like that, my friend. Nothing like that. All the plagues of this world, and besides they don't make much money. Lawyers, doctors, notaries, literary men! Nonsense! All they get is pomp and hunger! A father should think of something more substantial for his son. You can laugh at those who say that 'man does not live by bread alone.' The only ones who say that are the ones who never satisfied their stomachs. Bread, first and foremost, Don Pedro, that is to say, money! Much money! With that you get everything else! Just take me for an example. My father used to tend cattle in the hills and my mother used to weed corn by the day. I had no other education than I could get in a small village school: a little arithmetic, a fair handwriting and the catechism. Well, with just that and a lot of patience I started to work sweeping out a grocery store and spending a lot of time killing rats that used to eat the flour. Then I got into an office and learned to take care of the papers for the Customs House and to copy letters and deliver the mail and to endure many things in order to progress little by little. One day a clerk, later on something better and then something higher up, and here I am. I got the woman I wanted when I decided to marry. I have been president of the Chamber of Commerce I don't know how many times, and mayor whenever I wanted to be. I don't drive a carriage because I don't need one. I suppose that I am the only one in the village who doesn't go out except on holidays. And what difference in culture do you see between me and the few dozen people here who are considered important? I mean by this that business is the soul of nations, the essence of everything, the best and most worthy career for young men, and doubly so when they do not have to endure all the struggle I went through to get where I am today. You understand me, Pedro?"

The captain understood him perfectly, and because he did understand him, he allowed himself the privilege of making some observations, not without some basis, about the risk of spending one's life in a tedious office and becoming an old man, still poor, without having seen any of the world or learned anything about what it has to teach.

"Nonsense, nonsense!" Don Venancio kept saying to each objection that Bitadura made. "Business today in Santander is in good condition. There isn't much of it, but it is good, and it will get better if we are not blinded by greed, and if we don't do anything stupid, like trying to build a railroad over the mountains like the one they are building near Madrid, or a steamship line between here and Cuba. Railroads! Steamships! Crazy! Crazy ideas of people who have nothing to lose and want to play with somebody else's money and end up with an epitaph like this: 'Here lies a good Spaniard who tried to be better.' To get back to my theme. If we take care of what we've got and don't start any crazy ideas like a railroad or a steamship line, the cents we sow in business here will soon make a harvest of pesetas. You follow me, Don Pedro?"

Don Pedro did follow his ideas, but he dared to suggest that even if all that were gospel truth, there still remained the difficulty of placing Andrés in business. What did he know about it? Who could help him decide? Where could his boy start?

"We are getting to that," replied Don Venancio. "Give me your boy. I have only two children of my own. My boy is about the same age as yours, and I plan to put him in the office as soon as the summer is over. Let them work together and become good friends. The same thing can stimulate both of them, because if my son works in his father's vineyard, the father of Andrés Colindres also has quite an interest in that same vineyard. And in a few years when our sons become good businessmen, you and I can retire and rest, and your money will be making you good interest, and you could even be a partner. How about it?"

"Well, yes and no," replied the captain without concealing his lively interest in the matter. "But if it turns out that he doesn't like business after he gets started, what do I do with my son then?"

"Well, the devil," replied the merchant. "If he gets seasick after he becomes a sailor, or he drowns, or he doesn't make good, or his ship is sold, could you do any better than to make him a lazy, awkward clerk like a lot of others?"

"You are right, Don Venancio," replied Bitadura quickly.

"I should say I am," exclaimed Don Venancio, leaning back with his legs stretched out, completely satisfied with his triumph, even though he was surprised at it.

"I think that we are going to understand one another," added Bitadura, getting up. "For the present, I thank you with all my heart for the interest that you are taking in the future of my son and the offer you have made. I shall not delay long in replying with greater detail. Don't be surprised. The things that sound best to me are the ones that I want to look at objectively. One marks his route better that way than by coming alongside them."

Then he shook hands with Don Venancio. Being somewhat moved, he took leave by saying: "I am at your command, Don Venancio." Don Venancio almost saw stars and as soon as Bitadura left he blew on his red fingers, a detail which proves the danger of shaking hands with men like Bitadura when they are moved.

But why the devil was Don Venancio so much interested in the future of Andrés? Why did such a hardheaded businessman become concerned whether Andrés was successful or eaten by the sharks? When did this merchant notice that seafarers enjoy only infrequently the delights of home life? And why in his discussion did he use the same arguments as Andrea? Aha, Andrea! That name became a point of light in the darkness. "I betcha two cents," he said to himself, "that my wife has been conspiring here. Could they be her arguments that Don Venancio gave me about not making my son a sailor? In any case, and regardless of source, I should not disregard them just because they didn't occur to me."

In fact, Andrea had conspired against her husband in Don Venancio's office. All the worries she had during the long absences of her husband because of the dangers of the sea, the diseases of faraway climes, made her think more about her son. And to think that she might soon have to add worries about him to those about her husband. Both of them absent at the same time! And she all alone at home!

She had tried to talk to her husband about this but had never been able to get his attention long enough, because Bitadura, who took everything lightly, merely gave her a pat on the cheek, or kissed her. But Andrés was growing up, the hour of decision was growing near and she feared the worst. After thinking about it for a long time, she got up her courage and went to see Don Venancio three days before the arrival of her husband. In his office she explained her fears, her desires and her hopes, and the request that he keep her visit a secret from her husband.

Liencres promised to help her even though he knew Andrés only by sight.

As soon as Bitadura got home he started the conversation about Andrés' career, and as Andrea knew where he came from, she blushed a deep red at his first words. This alone accused her, and Bitadura acted angry. But she could see that it was mere pretense by the glint in his eye and the shape of his mouth. She then acted as if she had noticed nothing, and confessed the deed with all its details and with a false air of resignation.

"We'll see about that!" exclaimed Bitadura walking back and

forth in the living room with his back turned to his wife, swinging his arms and stamping his heels. "Going to the house of a neighbor with family secrets! That just isn't done!"

Andrea looked at him shyly and saw that he was too stubborn to face her. Then she started to walk close behind him and said with a tone of studied humility:

"Well, old fellow, if I have done wrong when I thought I did right, at least you know what I did. So fire away!"

"Yes, madam, I shall, and right now," said Bitadura turning suddenly. "Come here. Sit down here!" And he sat down on the sofa and made her sit on his lap.

"Look me in the eye! Let me see that nose!" And he gave her a gentle bite on the nose. "And now those ears!" and he bit them too. "And now, out the window with this armful!" He took her in his arms like a baby and stood in front of the balcony saying: "One! two! three!" swinging her back and forth at the same time. Then he turned sharply on his heels, and kissed her a half dozen times.

"Take that, for being so talkative—and because I want to do it."

Andrea laughed as if someone had tickled her, and took that sweet punishment as a good sign. Then Bitadura told her that everything that she wanted would be done. In that way the tables were turned.

9 THE INTERESTS AND ENTHUSIASM OF ANDRES

Andrés, in the meantime, was walking toward High Street, stopping to chat with all his acquaintances that he met along the way in order to tell them about his father's arrival, about what his father had told him about the trip and something about the dinner at his home the evening before, and particularly about Sama, Ligo and the other guests. How they had enjoyed themselves! He was going to High Street to see how Silda was getting along in her new home, because he considered this orphan girl as his protégée and was much interested in her lot.

When he reached the Big Wall, he saw Colo going up the hill with oars on his shoulders and carrying a bucket half full of bait. This Colo was the nephew of Don Lorenzo, the mad priest already mentioned.

Andrés asked him where Mechelín's house was and noticed that Colo was in a bad humor. Before he thought of asking what the matter was, the fisherman said, throwing down his oars:

"Man alive, that's enough to make ya sick."

"What's the matter?" asked Andrés.

"That man, damn him. My uncle, the crazy priest, damn it all. I hope he gets that idea out of his head. I hope lightning strikes him! I hope he has a stomach-ache! This morning when I was on my way to my boat, he catches up with me and, by damn, tells me that I have to matriculate at the Institute. Isn't that the way ya say it? There seems to be nothin' else to do than anchor in that school where they teach ya Latin. Damned if I know what good that'll do me!"

"That's a darn shame," said Andrés.

"Well, he insists that that's the way it's gotta be, without any delay, as soon as the summer's over. And I just flatly refused, and then the damned jackass hit me a couple of times with that big cane he carries. But why? Why do I hafta study any Latin? Wouldn't it be better ta use the money for a new pair o' pants? Well, when I told him that, he hit me again! Ain't he a brute? He says that it's sompin', sompin' about the church and a scholarship that only a member of the family can use. If I ever become a priest they'll have to knock the larnin' into my head with a club, 'cause that fella who teaches Latin uses a club more'n my crazy uncle. What do they call that fella? . . . Don . . . Don? . . ."

"Don Bernabé," prompted Andrés, who already knew about him by name.

"That's it, Don Bernabé."

"You'll get lots of whippings there," said Andrés frankly.

The two kids continued climbing the hill, and when they passed in front of Mechelín's door, Colo said to Andrés:

"That's the house."

As his own house was at the other end of the street, he said good-by to Andrés and hurried on.

About this same time Silda came out accompanied by Muergo, who was already wearing Padre Apolinar's pants. The only thing that he had done was to roll them up. At that, the best he could do was to have the seat just a little above the ankles. He was also wearing his own jacket. All this, with the tangled hair on his head, helped give the impression of a bundle of refuse capable of walking alone.

"I gotta shirt now, ho, ho!" the monsterlike child said to Andrés.

Andrés looked at him in surprise and Muergo started to run down the street. Silda pointed to him and said to Andrés:

"I wanted them to give him a shirt, but they didn't want to 'cause they said he didn't deserve one, and that his mother is a shameless thing. But I found him this morning near the Big Wall, and I brought him home so that his aunt could see him without a shirt and give him an old one of her husband's. He didn't wanta come but he did and then they didn't wanta give him the shirt, but I insisted and they gave it to him. But if he trades it for rum and they see him without it, they won't give him nothin' more and they won't let him come back here. His mother is drunk all the time and he likes alcohol a lot. He's ugly and dirty, ain't he? Come on in a little while and you'll see how nice it is here. I don't intend to go back to La Maruca Beach nor to the docks right away. You get so ragged and dirty there. Come on in so the people on the fifth floor won't see you if they come downstairs, and don't ever stop very long in that doorway 'cause they'll throw garbage at you from the balcony. They are very bad, very bad! Yesterday they made a fuss because the Council told Mocejón that they had punished me a lot, and if they don't let me alone the cops will be after them. They are very, very bad."

Sidora, who was bustling around inside the house, came out to the corridor when she heard voices, and Silda said to her, pointing to Andrés:

"This is that rich man's son that took me to the house of Pa'e 'Polinar."

Sidora was very glad to see Andrés, and praised his action to the skies. As the boy seemed good looking to her, she told him how she felt about it. This made Andrés form a good opinion of her, but her compliments made him blush. She did not personally know the captain of the *Montañesa*, but her husband did and had talked about him many times, praising his excellent qualities and good judgment. Don Pedro was a great person, and besides had High Street ancestors, another reason to be considered worthy by Sidora and for her to rejoice that his son had taken pity on this little abandoned girl and had taken her to the home of a person capable of doing for her what Pa'e 'Polinar had done. Those shameless women upstairs had treated him very badly when he went to talk to them about the girl that she and her husband had taken in later, as they would have done sooner if their wishes had only been considered. But then there were lots of other things to be considered and they had kept quiet. Now, thank God, Silda was in a safe harbor, and the Council had told those shameless women upstairs how things stood so they wouldn't try to prevent any other people from doing for the unfortunate girl what they hadn't wanted to do.

"Look at my room," said Silda to Andrés, interrupting Sidora's talk.

The room was clean and well swept. It contained a very tidy bed and a clothes rack with some of Sidora's clothes on it.

"Her clothes will be put here too," said Sidora, "as soon as they are ready. Now I am redoin' for her one of my cotton

The Interests and Enthusiasm of Andrés

dresses that's almost new. And if God wills it, we'll buy somethin' in the store when we can, 'cause we cannot always do what we wish. Later on I have cloth for two nice little shirtwaists, which is what she needs most right now 'cause the poor thing came here almost naked."

From there they moved to the living room where pieces of Sidora's cotton dress were on a chair near a pile of unraveled thread. Those scraps were the pieces of Silda's dress which Sidora had cut out and was ready to sew. Silda had watched all those operations with a great deal of attention, and Sidora hoped to arouse in her a fondness for the house, and to teach her little by little to sew and to learn the catechism, how to build a fire, at least to put things on the stove to cook and to sweep the floors. In short, she should learn what any daughter with good parents learns—a daughter who someday would be a good housewife.

In the opinion of Sidora, Silda had become rather lazy and indolent since the death of her father because those women upstairs had made their house unbearable for her. That wouldn't happen here. She would go out when she needed to and also would spend the time in the house that she needed to, but neither in the street nor in the house would she have any chores except those appropriate for her sex and her years.

While Sidora was saying all these things in her own way to Andrés, Silda was looking at both of them with an expressionless face. Andrés was very attentive and even impressed with the expansive verbosity and bigheartedness of Sidora. He scarcely took his eyes from her except for a few moments to look at the calm serene eyes of Silda as much as to say: "You hear that?" Finally he was not satisfied with what he could express in a glance and made use of words. Turning to the girl he said very seriously, and with great energy:

"I tell you that you should be ashamed if you ever go back to the docks and have anything to do with that indecent Muergo."

"She has already decided not to go back," interrupted Sidora.

"Ain't that right, daughter? As far as Muergo is concerned, we'll treat him according to the way he behaves. Ain't that right, child? But what the devil could this innocent little girl see in that scarecrow, to take such good care of him? As far as I am concerned, he is nothin' but a stupid low-down. Right, girl?"

Silda shrugged her shoulders and asked Andrés if he would be coming to High Street for the fiesta of Saint Peter, the patron saint. Andrés replied that he might, and then Sidora exaggerated a great deal what was to be seen at that time, and how well the fiesta could be seen from their doorway. There would be bonfires, where stuffed dummies of Judas would be burned, and lots of dancing in the streets. This would last for three days and nights. All the streets and balconies would be decorated with flags and colors. The altar of Saint Peter in the Church of the Consolation would be lighted, and people would be going in and coming out at all hours of the day and night. But Andrés knew as well as Sidora what the fiestas were like because he had not missed one since he could walk alone in the street.

Later he examined with much care a silk fishing line which was hanging from a nail in the wall. That was what you called a real line, and not like the cheap one that he used with just ordinary hooks. When Sidora saw him admiring that she got a basket full of the tackle which her husband had not taken to sea with him today because he was using a net to catch sardines.

Andrés had seen tackle like that many times drying on balconies or piled up in a basket, with the lines coiled around the inside. Sidora explained to him the use of each part and the way it should be handled. The lines used for catching hake were as thick as the head of a large pin and had a large, pointed hook. There was another line with several hooks, used for sea bream. It was more than eighty yards long and had many hooks hanging from short lines every four or five inches. The lines used for striped tunny were composed of three parts: the first and longest was a line twice the size of the one used for sea bream; then there was a finer line and finally the fine wire

The Interests and Enthusiasm of Andrés

leader with a big hook. The hooks for sea bream and hake were generally baited with sardines. Those for the striped tunny used any kind of lure: most of the time this was merely a corn leaf which would not be destroyed like paper by the water. To take the sea bream lines out for fishing, the men used a big cork, ring-shaped like a large mixing bowl, approximately a foot wide, with sloping sides. As the hooks on the branch lines were baited they were placed on the edge of the ring and the line coiled up in the middle. The preparation necessary to take this apparatus to sea requires considerable time because there are more than two hundred hooks in all. But sometimes more than a hundred fish are caught on it at one time. Men fish for hake with the boat adrift, at a depth of one hundred fathoms more or less. The sea bream is rather a stupid fish and can be caught quite easily merely by letting out a line with dangling hooks. The striped tunny is usually caught by trolling with the boat going at full sail. It is such a voracious fish and takes the hook with so much force that it is almost always hooked in the stomach. For all these different types of fish it is necessary to go quite a way out to sea, and there are cases where fishermen did not get back to their home port for two or three days, either because there were other ports nearer where they could spend the night, or because they were obliged to do so by some sudden storm. Sardines, which move in large schools, are caught by the gills in a net held out front. Andrés knew all this about sardines very well and could handle most of the apparatus. Consequently Sidora did not explain more to him. During all her long talk Andrés never blinked an eye, and she was enjoying the effect which her explanations were having on him.

"That's great!" he exclaimed licking his lips.

Then he confessed to Sidora that fishing had always held a fascination for him, but that he had never fished in the open ocean. Most of the time he had fished from the docks, but whether from there or from Cuco's rowboat inside the bay, he had never caught much more than the spawn of the sea bream, which seemed to be everywhere. He had never caught a haddock nor even an ordinary sea bass that weighed a quarter of a pound! For that reason he was anxious to grow up so that he could rent a boat with some friends and fish all he wanted to. He would do this until he was old enough to begin to sail, because then he would have a boat with plenty of sailor friends to help him. He would soon be enrolling in the Navigation School because his father had told him that again only the day before while they were eating dinner. In short, he knew all this, and thinking about it made him talk about it there. By so doing he was responding to the kindness of Sidora. He was also sure that both Sidora and Silda were listening to him intently, and that was the truth. A little later Sidora offered him some bread and a broiled sardine, which Andrés courteously refused. When he said good-by he promised to return there often.

When he reached home his mother devoured him with kisses and told him that he was not going to be a sailor. This news, coming so suddenly, left him stunned. But before deciding whether he was glad or sorry, and before he could ask what his father did want him to be, he wondered whether or not he should return at once to the home of Sidora to tell them the news or to leave it for another day.

Because he had told her that he was going to be a sailor!

10 THE *PATACHE* AND OTHER PARTICULARS

(A *patache* is a small coastwise vessel, described in this chapter)

The new career for Andrés was moving well along the road that his mother's scheming and Don Venancio's eloquence had started it. Bitadura was going to make another trip to Cuba in July. Andrea had proposed that during his absence Andrés should have duties, however small, in Don Venancio's office.

Bitadura had agreed to this idea wholeheartedly. As men's thoughts and ideas may change during an absence, the very day that his parents agreed that he should be in the service of Don Venancio they got a tutor for him to make a complete review of arithmetic and to learn to write script. This would take a matter of two or three months with a couple of hours' work every day. At the same time he would be learning some things at the office because Liencres believed that half a day spent at a bookkeeper's desk was worth more than courses in school.

Among a lot of other advice given to the apprentice by his mother was the particular admonition to seek the companionship of the merchant's son with whom he would be working in the office, and, as the captain and Liencres had repeated, with whom Andrés might reach the pinnacle of wealth. The mother considered this detail of great importance because an intimate friendship, at the age of these two boys, could easily become an unbreakable bond.

Andrés knew Liencres' son very well. His name was Antolín —Tolín for short—and physically speaking he was not very much. He was thin and pale, although spirited. He could not jump very far in the game of "leapfrog," and made a very poor "hump" when it was his turn to be down because of his small size and weak body. Anyone could catch him at the game of "tag" because he tired easily when running. At marbles he was a little better but not very good even at that game. He had gone a couple of times to La Maruca Beach but had not returned because each time that he went there he took off his shoes to wade in the water and that put him in bed for a couple of days with a bad cold, and to go to La Maruca without taking off one's shoes would be the same as not going. But all in all he was a pretty good fellow in the sight of the boys because he wore his heels off on one side, rumpled the visor of his cap and had lots of mud on his handkerchief! This was the best sign that Tolín was not like many other rich people's sons who never got their clothes dirty nor mingled with poorer kids, nor drank from public fountains.

Andrés knew all this because he knew all the kids his own age of all social classes in Santander. And because he did know all this Tolín was not disagreeable to him, although it never would have occurred to him to pick Tolín out as a special pal. Now that he was ordered to associate with him, he tried to do so without the slightest repugnance and soon succeeded because Andrés' friendship was one of the most desired among the boys of his time. His prestige was due in part to the fact that he was the son of a sea captain, was adept at many things, had the good appearance of the well-to-do and the strength and agility of a street urchin.

Now you see what it is to judge by appearances! Tolín's friendship gave him a pleasure that he had never enjoyed before, because Tolín had great privileges on board the patache *El Joven Antoñito de Ribadeo*, which was tied up alongside the fish factory stairway while the cargo of coal was unloaded. These favors given Tolín were in return for favors which the owner of the boat got from Don Venancio Liencres, whose many business contacts in the ports of Asturias were good. This got more cargo for the patache. Liencres never refused to lend the owner money when he needed it—which seemed to be about every other trip.

It requires a great deal of courage to work as captain of a patache, or as sailor or cabin boy, because the pay is not very good. To ship on one of them to make a living is worse than walking across Niagara Falls on a tightrope.

The patache is a small ship of about thirty tons, with square or triangular topsails. It is supposed that this type of ship was new once, but I have never actually seen any that was. Consequently one supposes that one is made up of old planking and old rigging. There are usually five men in the crew, or at the most five and a half or six. That is, the captain, four sailors and the cabin boy or cook. The captain has his special quarters aft. The rest crowd into the triangular forecastle which is small, narrow and low with two rows of bunks along the sides. The sailors sleep here using their extra clothing as bedding because there are no blankets or mattresses. The small entrance is usually covered with a piece of canvas which shuts out most of the light and air. If the canvas is in poor condition, then the rain and the sun come in. Each member of the crew buys and keeps his own supply of bread, which is generally big loaves that last about six days. The rest of the fare, poorly prepared by the cabin boy, consists of potatoes or string beans or cabbage, with a little bacon or lard or olive oil to soften them up. The sailors sit on the floor and each takes his turn with his spoon, eating from one common pot. Sometimes there is codfish, which the cook prepares in a sauce composed of fried red peppers and onions. This is done after the fish has been cleaned and washed by putting it over the side into the sea with a rope. For breakfast there may be some ground-up husks of cocoa beans served in a big tin cup. The food is always the same, even when times are good.

No member of the crew gets a fixed wage. They all go by shares, but what shares! Even when the hold and the deck are crowded with freight both directions the income is not very much, maybe not more than one hundred dollars. Of this amount the owner of the boat gets 40 per cent, the captain a share and a half, plus 5 per cent of the total amount collected. The rest is divided among the five crew members: $6.00, $8.00, $12,00 or $15.00 at the most for each of them. That amount of money would mean something in spite of its smallness if working on a patache were a cinch; but it isn't. Most of the pataches are from the Basque provinces or from Galicia or Asturias.

If there were no coal or boxes of apples or herring to haul the *Joven Antoñito* came back to Santander in ballast. In that case it was tied up to the dock and the captain went from store to store, from office to office, calling every owner by his first name, greeting them all courteously and asking them all the same question:

"Any freight for Ribadesella in Galicia?"

A morning or a whole day spent this way may get him twenty sacks of flour, two crates of sugar, eight bundles of brooms, an old bed and a couple of bundles of old rag paper. That is all the freight there is from Santander to Ribadesella. The mail may bring in other orders, but they are so few and far between that with good luck the patache gets its hold full in about a month and a half. Sometimes it has to wait two months or leave with only half a cargo. Or when it gets ready to leave a storm may come up and delay its departure for days or weeks. That means quite a long time for five or six men to live on potatoes, bread and bacon with the little money they have. That does not leave much for feeding and dressing their families ashore!

After getting out of port the patache may be becalmed and spend days reaching its destination. When that happens the crew has to eat some of the provisions carried as freight.

Once or twice a year one gets caught in a storm and is broken to pieces on the rocky shore, and the crews are rescued with great difficulty.

The miserable patache sails along the coast and has to take its chances with bad weather. The services of a steam tugboat would be more than the owners could afford.

In short, it means ceaseless work, poor food, a hard bunk for a bed, all the risks of a dangerous sea and the knowledge of never being better off. Any man who becomes a part of this legion of misery when he voluntarily joins the crew accepts all this.

Thus one understands the value of the favors which Don Venancio Liencres bestowed on the captain of the *Joven Antoñito*, relieving him of the necessity of long delays at the dock by giving him freight or by advancing him money.

Tolín knew something of all this because he got tired of meeting the captain on the stairs. As there is no patache—regardless of its condition—that does not have a good rowboat, he knew that the one belonging to the *Joven Antoñito* was a very good one. It was light and trim, not badly painted and not very dirty. Remembering all this one day, he went on board with the captain who presented him to the crew, urging them to treat him well. Guessing what the boy wanted most, he ordered the

The Patache and Other Particulars

crew to let him have the rowboat whenever he wanted it, and if necessary, someone should help him row it.

From that day on Tolín was almost more of a boss than the captain. However, he did not abuse the privilege. His only enjoyment was to get into the boat and try to maneuver it around the docks, or go here and there by holding onto the hawsers of the other vessels and launches.

Tolín spoke about these things to Andrés as soon as they became friends. Astonished at Tolín's good fortune, Andrés wanted to go on board that same day. Tolín did introduce him, not only as a friend, but as a future business partner, and also as the son of the captain of the *Montañesa*. Any one of these titles would have been sufficient to deserve all the consideration of the crew. With all three titles together, the crew almost admired him. Andrés climbed the rigging as far as the crosstrees and later went into the hold with the agility and steadiness of a cabin boy. Finally he jumped into the rowboat, took one of the oars and by standing in the stern sculled it around with one hand. That really won him the friendship of all the crew. From that time on he had a ship to loaf in and a free rowboat to row around the bay, alone or accompanied, and to dream of the adventures of a sailor or a fisherman. Tolín could not really imagine the bargain he gave his friend when he shared with him his privileges on board the *Joven Antoñito*.

In exchange for this favor Andrés tried to make Tolín a part of all his acquaintances and pleasures, some of which might almost be called contraband. But the pleasures of the dock were not for the son of Don Venancio Liencres. The merriment of Cuco frightened him, and most of the other fellows, larger than he, did not inspire much confidence. The smaller, ill-smelling kids made him sick to his stomach. He had had enough experience at La Maruca and did not want to go back. On High Street, where Andrés took him also, the people on the ground floor seemed all right, but nothing else was. Only once did he try to climb the stairs to the other levels. The rickety stairs, the smells, the sounds and the dirt made him come down again fast.

Andrés then told him that all the houses on the street were about the same in order to console him.

Tolín did not lack nerve, nor was he prudish. Physically he was weak and his strong will faltered in a sickly body. Furthermore, his education had been entirely about the land and not about the sea. The land was his element for the few feats of bravery that his physique permitted. It never would have occurred to him to do what Andrés did with the rowboat. Of course, when he tried to maneuver it near the *Joven Antoñito* he believed that he was right in front of his own house, among friends of his family.

The least maritime activity as far as amusements were concerned was his visit to La Maruca Beach, because there were plenty of landlubber kids there also. For that reason, plus the fact that it was near his home, he had attempted unsuccessfully to go there.

After the trip to High Street he had told Andrés that he could count on him for everything except visits to that area.

One day he had gone with Andrés for a row around the bay. But with both of them rowing the changing tide had rammed them against the side of a ship, upsetting their boat. They had been in danger of drowning but were rescued by some nearby fishermen. Tolín then told Andrés that he would never go rowing with him again if he left the dock area.

Andrés was surprised that any boy would not like these things, and tried to please his friend by adjusting himself to Tolín's likes and dislikes whenever he could. Consequently he went less and less to La Maruca and the docks, but he did not stop going to High Street where he had long talks with Mechelín and Sidora. He enjoyed Mechelín's stories about the sea as well as his good humor. Sidora liked to have him around. When they said good-by to him Silda never failed to say almost in a command: "Come back!"

And why shouldn't he come back if he enjoyed seeing that little girl, who previously had been half wild, seated alongside Sidora, so clean, so well combed, so well dressed, learning how to sew and knit. Furthermore Sidora had assured him that she was making good progress in learning how to cook and to take care of the house, as well as chores outside of the house. Silda did not want to talk about her experiences since the death of her father. Mechelín delighted in telling Andrés about her capabilities and in showing him the buttons that she had sewed on for him, or how she had darned his wool sweater. In short, she was a different girl now, and this modest couple was crazy about her.

Furthermore, the women on the fifth floor were as quiet as saints and tired of useless provocations and gossip from their balcony, or whenever they passed in front of Mechelín's door on entering or leaving the building. Now they were somewhat restrained because of the statement from the Town Council. They knew that if they disobeyed that statement there was the possibility of interference by the Navy, which was always tougher than the local authorities. What else could they do?

Even Muergo seemed greatly influenced by the change in the little girl. Not only had he not sold his shirt, but he had gotten another one. He also came frequently to his uncle's house as clean as was possible for such a pig. He chewed the pieces of bread which his uncle gave him somewhat begrudgingly from time to time.

Wasn't the pleasure which Andrés felt entirely justifiable on seeing such things in a poor dwelling? Wasn't the well-being which prevailed around Silda his work up to a certain point?

Who, except he, had helped this unfortunate girl along the road where she was now? Tolín should not even think of trying to get him away from High Street. That could not be done because of his fondness for things and people having to do with the sea, the stories of hearty old Mechelín and the affection which Silda showed him.

11 🖋 DON VENANCIO'S FAMILY—TWO KICKS, A BUTTON AND A NICKNAME

Andrés did not take too seriously the matter of improving his handwriting or the review of arithmetic, but he did not disregard them entirely. His mother was constantly asking the teacher about his progress and always got good reports. The father paid little attention to him because Andrea's interest in a new career for Andrés was satisfied and he himself had many things to do getting his ship ready to sail for Cuba. Don Venancio seemed very pleased to see his son become such a good friend of Andrés. Even his wife, either spontaneously or prompted by her husband, had stated that she favored Tolín's new pal. One afternoon when Tolín came running into the house to eat a snack in a hurry because Andrés was waiting for him at the door, she said:

"Tell him to come in and eat with you."

Andrés did come in after much coaxing, not because of any idea of etiquette, but because a woman like Mrs. Liencres, and a house like hers, scared him more than rowing all alone against the current in the channel. For that reason he came in quite frightened, because he had not expected such an invitation. Consequently he had no shoelaces in his shoes, his shirt was dirty, there was a hole in the knee of his trousers and his hair was a mess due to the fact that he had raced downhill from High Street without stopping.

Mrs. Liencres was one of the best examples of the newly rich in the Santander of that day. She had a snobbishly turned up nose, a haughty glance and mumbled only a few short words. When she went out of her house she was elegantly dressed, but at home she wore cheap calico clothes. Her handwriting was very poor and her spelling very bad. Let's not speak of her lineage! It was of the proudest sort, but if you looked closely you could see the hoe, the chisel or the cobbler's bench of her father's youth. She was just a pitiful woman who didn't know much about anything—either the multiplication table or the way to hurt others except by a gesture.

She received Andrés with a frown and a glance that seemed to ask him to account for his slovenliness. Certainly Tolín was not much better, but Tolín was Tolín and Andrés was the son of the captain of a ship belonging to her husband. When she went to open the glass doors of a china closet that covered half the wall at one end of the dining room, she raised her harsh voice enough so that these words could be heard in a room at the end of the hall:

"Girl, come on and eat!"

At once Tolín's younger sister appeared, very well dressed in silk, with plenty of lace at the bottom of her pantalets. Everything that she had on was the best and the most expensive, and of the latest fashion. Her mother looked at her from head to toe and then gave Andrés a look which doubtless meant: "Look at her, and be astonished, poor boy!"

The girl, whose name was Luisa, was a flimsy token of a fine lady: long hands, skinny arms, a body so thin that there was no waistline, bony shoulders, skinny legs, fine white skin, straight hair, with ordinary eyes and ordinary features. With all this and the example of her mother, she was truly unattractive, but not as much as her mother. After all she was just a girl, and the sincerity of children her age was stronger than the confused notion about her social standing inculcated in her brain by the conceit and talk of her mother.

While Mrs. Liencres was putting three plates on the table— one with dried figs for Luisa, and the other two with olives— Luisa looked at Andrés, who blushed more and more. The more he blushed, the more his hair seemed to become mussed.

"He is good looking," she said to her mother, at the same time biting into a fig.

"Come, come. Eat and keep quiet," replied the mother in a whisper while placing a chunk of bread on each plate. Then turning to the boys, she added pointing to the olives: "Eat these up and then get going. But be careful about what you do and how you play and at what you play. Let's not act like street urchins. You understand me, Tolín?"

Tolín did not pay any attention to her warning, but Andrés blushed more than ever because he caught a certain little glance that she gave him while speaking to her son. Tolín grabbed an olive and Andrés did likewise, and with heroic valor sank his teeth into it. But he could not go any farther. In his time he had eaten, without batting an eye, wild berry muffins, green cranberries and wild grapes, but he could not overcome the feeling of nausea and having his teeth on edge that the sourness of an olive produced in him.

"Mama, he doesn't like them," Tolín said as soon as he saw Andrés' face.

"Please do not pay any attention to him," Andrés hastened to correct, without knowing what to do with the olive that he had in his mouth. "I just do not feel like eating any of them."

"I don't think that he likes them either," added Luisa, attentively studying Andrés' gestures. "Maybe he wants figs, like I got."

"Ah . . . naw. . . . Thanks just the same," Andrés managed to say, blushing to his ears. "I just don't feel like it because I have already eaten some small crabs today."

Tolín's mother then gave him some dried figs instead of olives and left the three children alone in the dining room after urging Luisa to eat up her food as quickly as possible because the maid was waiting to take her for a walk.

From that day on Andrés ate frequently in Tolín's home, and spent many afternoons with him, at Tolín's expense, watching side show performers with a small traveling circus. By imitating one of these fellows Andrés learned to jump using his hands in a squatting position, with his feet off the ground, almost like a frog. Whenever the children were alone in the dining room, Luisa asked him to jump this way. Tolín could squat better than Andrés but did not have the physical strength to jump any. Andrés could jump as many as eight times to the great admiration and applause of the young girl. After eating, Luisa would usually go out for a walk with the maid; Andrés and Tolín went wherever they felt like going.

Thus the summer passed and autumn came, and Andrés and Tolín were seated facing each other at a high double desk in the office of Don Venancio Liencres. Colo entered the Institute, more to carry wood in the mornings and evenings than to study Latin. Bitadura was off on a voyage to Cuba. Other pilots and captains were also off on long voyages. Pa'e 'Polinar continued his arduous tasks of trying to teach good manners to the wild wharf rats and of reconciling opposite opinions without being cured one bit of his deep-rooted weakness of giving his shirt, when he had one, to the first man that asked him for it.

Muergo was not going any more to Padre Apolinar's home. In the middle of the summer, as the result of steps taken by the priest at the request of Sidora, Muergo was given the job of cabin boy on a fishing boat owned by Captain Reñales of the Lower Town. It took a lot of effort to teach him the daily tasks of taking the sardines from the net, bailing out the water and other similar work. But a few blows with a piece of rope and some slaps on the head applied firmly at the right time made him walk the chalk line. It was even noticed that the days that he did not go to sea with the boat were spent at the dock waiting for it to come in. Many nights he slept on the floor boards of the boat. On some cold rainy nights he would sleep in doorways near the dock, rolled up like a ball.

Because of this employment he stopped going to High Street so often, but he did go whenever it was possible. One reason he liked to go was that he always got a hunk of bread from Sidora, who treated him better now that he was subject to some discipline. Silda had succeeded in getting him to comb his hair at least once a month and to wash his face a little at least once a week. Even at that he seemed more of a monster than before. The more he was trimmed with accessories, the more his bestiality stood out. Silda did not wonder at this and did not lose her interest in him at all, because she was not trying to beautify Muergo. She merely wanted to subject him to a little discipline and cleanliness—no mean task in itself.

On the other hand, she herself was glowing with health and seemed to develop from day to day. Meals free from crying and sleep free from fear were working wonders in her. By now she was sewing without Sidora's help and could knit without counting the stitches out loud and weave a fish net quite easily. She was as clean and shiny as a new silver coin. Because she had this feeling of cleanliness, any dust or dirt in that house disappeared. The dock, La Maruca and the Big Wall were not even mentioned any more. Colo, Guarín and other companions in idleness and mischief remained only in her memory to amuse her during her present well-being, in contrast with her past troubles. She did not detest these boys because they were not to blame for the fate which had placed her in such a life, but she did everything that she could to avoid meeting them on her way to the fish factory, or when she went with Sidora at low tide to collect bait. Aside from these few occasions, she rarely set foot in the street, not because her foster parents prevented her from doing so, but because she did not show the slightest desire to leave her new home. Her well-being should be judged by these testimonies, because she never revealed it in any more eloquent way. She was obedient and docile with no apparent effort, but she was not very affable or expressive. She has already been compared to a cat because of her natural instinct for cleanliness. Also like a cat, she seemed to feel more attachment to the house than to its inhabitants, although to tell the truth it should be stated that appearances were deceiving in this case. I do not know that there was in her little heart a good quantity of gratitude for all the favors received from this good couple, but only that she never took the trouble to express it by a word, a phrase or even a gesture. Perhaps it was because she herself did not realize what she did feel, and did not trouble herself to try to find out. After all there was no real reason for such expression as her affectionate protectors were most happy with her just as she was.

Cleto, the brother of Carpia, was coming back from the sea one day carrying his oilskin coat, two oars and a basket full of fishing tackle. He found Silda stooping over the first step of the stairway cleaning the dirt from the doorway. As her back was turned to him, she did not see him come in. Being short on the use of words, instead of ordering her to get out of the way, he gave her a good kick and knocked her over.

"You jackass," she exclaimed as soon as she raised her head and recognized who it was.

Right back of Cleto came Mocejón, waddling from one side to the other, also loaded with waterproofs, bait and boat gear. Still on the floor, Silda now found herself between the huge legs of Mocejón. She had scarcely tried to sit up when she got a stronger kick which knocked her face against the stairs. The kick was accompanied by these words, which seemed more like growls:

"Get out of the way, damn you!"

Silda did not yell or cry even after she found blood on her face. She got up from the floor very calmly and went into the house where Sidora was. The latter had not seen or heard anything.

"I tripped," Silda said on entering. "I fell against the steps."

That's how she explained her bloody nose, perhaps out of horror of other more serious troubles from the same source. Sidora quickly left the work that she was doing and placed Silda with her head leaning over the first big earthenware pot she found, and put the big door key on the back of her neck—an accepted method of stopping the nosebleed. The affair had no consequences, and Silda was not at all surprised by the conduct of Mocejón. As for Cleto, that was another matter. Cleto was not a bad boy and had never struck her when she was living with his family, although he had actually never helped protect her from his mother or sister. He was very coarse and very indifferent, but did not have the badness of the rest of his family. Silda had never done anything to offend him. That is why she felt his kick more than all the other suffering she had previously endured from the rest of his family.

A few days after this, Silda was leaning against the frame of the front door while darning a hole in Mechelín's vest. She frequently worked here because she could see what was going on in the street without exposing herself to the danger of having the women from the fifth floor surprise her in the doorway. As darkness was falling she needed more light to finish what she was doing and went to the street door in order to finish up. Just then Colo came down the street with his hands under his armpits and his eyes swollen from crying. He faced Silda as soon as he saw her at the door and asked her about Andrés.

"He ain't been here for three days. What do you want him for?"

"To tell him what's happening to me, by God! And to see if he can do something for me. He's so rich and I am in a bad fix. Boy, what a beating I just got. Look here, Silda."

Then he showed her the palms of his hands and his shins crossed with welts and big black-and-blue bruises.

"What's that from?"

"From blows with a stick they used to get me to learn Latin."

"Who?"

"The teacher, damn him. Because I couldn't ship those waves of big long words in some un-Christian language. I hope lightnin' hits him! See here: these lines here are a little darker; they're from four days ago; these here are from this mornin'. Some blood came out of them other spots this afternoon when he hit me. My God! Then I couldn't stand it no more, Silda . . . 'cause I was gettin' a clubbin' every day. When I held the book in one hand, he was hittin' me on the other, so I threw the book at his head with all my strength. The barbarian! I ran away then. They can take me to jail if they wanta. I'm not goin' back for no more Latin, by damn. 'N if anybody tries to make me do it, I'll rip his head open, by damn! You see how my hands and legs are? Well, my back must be a lot worse."

"He beat you on the back, too?"

"No, he slapped my face and hit me on the back of the neck with the handle of his cane and even kicked me in the belly. What I got on my back came from my crazy uncle just now. When he saw me leavin', Silda, he hit me with his big knotty cane, which I couldn't stand no longer, by God, without rippin' a sail! So . . . look at him!"

When he said that Colo started to run down the street toward Hospital Hill because he saw his uncle, the mad priest, coming toward him with his long robe flapping in the breeze made by his fast walk. His hat was on the back of his head; his eyes were shining. They were the most attractive part of the famous Don Lorenzo.

When Silda saw him coming toward her she withdrew, frightened, into the doorway, precisely at the moment when Cleto was coming down the stairs. He was holding his trousers at the waist with both hands and mumbling some curses. Although he found Silda across his path, this time he did not kick her out of the way. When he saw that she was sewing he stopped and said:

"Willya lend me that needle a minute? I was goin' out ta buy one just now."

"What do you want it for?"

"Ta sew on this button. I got only this one pair of pants. Carpia, the big bum, stole my rope ta tie up her underskirt. So if I raise my hands, I lose my pants."

"Why don't they sew the button on for you at home?"

"'Cause nobody there knows nothin' about that."

"Well, who used to sew them on for you?"

"I did . . . when I had a needle . . . until I lost it."

"And who does your darnin' for you?"

"Nobody does no darnin' in my house; you know that. Whenever anything tears there they let it go till it ain't no good no more. It's everybody fer himself and the devil take the hindmost. Are ya goin' ta lend me that needle or ain't ya?"

"Do you want me to sew the button on for you?"

"Sure. So much the better. Here, take it. It's fixed with a little ring on it ta make it easier fer sewin'. I got a wooden one upstairs. If ya think it's better, I'll fetch it."

"This one's all right."

Silda took it in her hands. With her small white teeth she broke off the thread that she was using to mend Mechelín's vest and tied a knot at the end of it, using only the thumb and index finger of her left hand. (Sidora had practiced this operation with her a great deal because she always said that a woman who was awkward at tying a knot in her thread was a poor sewer.) With difficulty she pierced the heavy pants material with her needle, while Cleto held his hands on his belly to keep up his pants. Then she put the needle through the little ring on the button letting it slip down along the thread. Then she began to sew and to tighten her stitches, using all her skill for this job, the first she ever did for anyone outside her own house.

Cleto was not ugly. There was a certain sweetness and a great deal of sparkle in his black eyes. His features were regular, the lines of his body were straight and manly. But he was very dirty. An uncombed mop of hair covered half of his face, tanned by the weather. His face was splattered with spots of fuzz that some day would be a heavy beard. He nearly stopped breathing while Silda was using all the strength of her fat, round little hands to make the needle go through that tough cloth, which seemed almost like tarred paper. Mechelín surprised her in this task when he came up the street with his pipe in his mouth.

He stopped for a couple of minutes at the door, looking fixedly at this unexpected sight. Bubbling over with joy, he could not help exclaiming:

"Look at that, Cleto. Look at it well! Notice the way she draws out her hand with the needle. See how she pulls back the thread and how she tightens her stitches. In all justice, what more could anyone ask?"

Cleto looked at Mechelín, and then looked away without saying a word. Silda acted as if she had not heard those compliments and did not even smile.

The happy Mechelín continued hurling insults at Cleto and compliments at Silda.

After the task was finished Silda went into the house. Cleto devoted himself to looking at the button without opening his mouth. Mechelín did not close his mouth, talking to Cleto. The latter went away without saying good-by and the talkative Mechelín was still saying something to him, following him out to the street door. Then he leaned against the door frame. Tempted by his passion for talking, he began to look up and down the street, and the balconies and the windows across the street, at every passerby, saying with the richest and most picturesque variety of tones and volume:

"You should see that! I'm tellin' ya that ya hafta see it ta believe what those little hands are, comin' an' goin' as gentle as a feather in the air! And they never leave any mark. Ya tell her a thing once, and she has it. She works on socks and stockin's, an' does fine darnin', an' can sew on all kinds o' buttons, an' use a broom, or make a fire or cook a stew. In fact she can put her oar in for just about everythin' under the sun, an' with a grace an' excellence that makes your eyes pop out! If I have a pain on tha starboard side she warms up a brick, wraps it up in flannel an' brings it ta my bed. If Sidora gets sick, this little angel guesses her thoughts so that nothin' is lackin' from a cup o' good hot chocolate for food. . . . Food? You say food? Well, as far as food is concerned, she eats very little, but it all must agree with her 'cause she is gettin' fat. All the work she has ta do is light, an' she sleeps without a care in tha world. Ya never hear her say a word if it ain't ta answer what ya ask her, or ta ask what she really wants ta know. And dress? Why it's a pleasure ta see how any old rag is becomin' ta her. I can tell ya if I didn't know who her mother was, I'd take her fer some English princess, or at least the daughter of one of them businessmen downtown. An' ya should see the way she copies words outa the speller now, an' will learn ta read soon. An' what do ya say about the prayers she learned so quickly that even Pa'e 'Polinar is surprised at it? Why, I believe that if ya taught her music, she'd learn music, by damn!

"An' she's so neat an' trim in everything; the way she walks, an' the way she dresses, even with the few clothes that she owns. They even seem like silk in her hands, an' everthin's so clean. She's just that way by nature. Do ya know what I tell Sidora when she praises the excellence and the worth of this little angel? I says ta her: 'Sidora, she's not a woman, she's pure skill (*sotileza*); she's strong and fine spun like the leader (*sotileza*) of a fishin' line.' Sotileza . . . why . . . that's what we call her in the house. Sotileza here and Sotileza there . . . an' she answers quickly to the name. There ain't no offense to it. There's really lots o' truth in it; Sotileza, strong an' fine like a good fishline, by damn."

Consequently from that time on, the orphan girl Silda was called Sotileza, not only in Mechelín's home, but in all the other houses on High Street. Everywhere she was known for her beauty.

PART TWO

12   BUTTERFLIES

Among the sailor folk a clean person is almost as rare as a three-pound pearl. With the years, the instinct for cleanliness continued to grow in Sotileza. In my opinion, the contrast which her unusual beauty of form and dress made with the dirtiness of the persons and things of her surroundings must have caused the unusual fame which her beauty had in the Upper Town. The sailor folk there may have confused an attribute with the essence, or color with form. Here again the devil tempts me to compare her with a cat.

I remember well that the most striking characteristic of that beautiful twenty-year-old girl, at the height of her loveliness, was the extreme cleanliness of her dress, in which light colors always predominated, as if this were one more display of her beauty.

And her beauty was evident, not only when she was dressed up for parties or weddings in the neighborhood, or for mass and strolls on Sunday, which would prove little, but every day, at the door of her house, or in the street, or on the sidewalk weaving a fish net, or sweeping, or sitting in the doorway darning Mechelín's socks. She usually wore a short dress, with about two inches of a snow-white ruffle below, and a buff-colored short-sleeved cotton bodice with blue stripes. Also she wore a bright shawl of many colors with the corners crossing her chest and tied at her waist in the back, and a silk scarf, also light colored, neatly tied over the topknot of brown wavy hair that glistened like gold in the sun. The curiosity which brought out these attractive details moved the eyes of an observer to make further explorations. Then one noticed the fine lines of the bare feet and legs, which were visible below the white ruffle, and the well-shaped arms, the round, statuelike neck, and the well-formed shoulders, and finally the healthy face, like a breath of spring, and the gold earrings hanging from her small ears.

Such were the details that came to an observer on seeing Sotileza for the first time in her natural setting. Even with these details of her beauty, one might be rather far from appreciating how beautiful she was when her fame on High Street is considered.

Examining her still more closely, one discovers that the lines of her face were not exactly those of classic beauty: her forehead was rather narrow and her mouth, although small and beautiful, had a hard expression; the look of her large eyes was almost too blunt, and the general contour of her body was not entirely in harmony with classic Grecian lines. Taken separately each portion of her body was irreproachable; taken as a whole, her body was not a model for a statue in spite of its grace and ease of movement. In a word, Sotileza was not a beauty in the artistic sense of the word, but she had all the necessary attractions to be the admiration of all the boys on her street, and to excite the curiosity or even the frenzy of learned men who were more like slaves of evil passions than of esthetic sentiments.

Her natural aloofness did not change as she grew older but became more fixed. Although this quality never caused her to be coarse or provocative when envious women or bold men tried to make her talk, her sharp, biting surliness made her really feared and respected.

With the effect of her good disposition, and perhaps with the knowledge of her own beauty, she had acquired the courage that she had not had as a child. She even succeeded in dominating, with a mere look, the Mocejón women—a triumph that made her proud of herself—because it was one of the few in which she had used all her efforts since the time when she began to understand that a woman of her character needed only to insist in order to get certain things. Of course she knew that the women from the fifth floor were controlled more by force than by any change in attitude, and that they would take advantage of the first opportunity to hurt her. For the present these beasts were under control, although still growling, and she had, with the prestige she enjoyed on High Street, a weapon with which to torment their envious nature, and with her strong character she had the moral power necessary to command respect.

Cleto had seen her many times since that day when she sewed on a button for him. He had told her more than once: "Count on me for anything, even to givin' my mother and sister a beatin' if you want me to, 'cause they are very bad." And Sotileza had smiled, recognizing the quality of the motive that had made Cleto propose such an idle barbarity.

He was a frequent visitor at Mechelín's home. The poor fellow, by nature frank and kind, had developed a manner that was quite different from that of the other members of his family who were inclined to be dirty, ferocious, uncontrolled, quarrelsome, drunken and cruel. They could not understand how a young man like Cleto, who felt no necessity for being bad and found no pleasure in living as they did, could find anyplace else that something which he missed; that certain something—or inner spirit—which gnawed there deep inside him disconsolately. And this something appeared on the ground floor of the building where he lived. It was in Mechelín's joviality, in the simple kindness of Sidora and even in the cleanliness and orderliness of the whole house. There one could talk without cursing anyone. Meals were eaten at regular hours. They prayed prayers that he had never heard before. If he complained of some ache or pain Sidora herself recommended some cure and administered it herself. In short, he liked to be there, where he found so many things he had never heard about, things that gladdened his inner spirit which formerly had been so discouraged and sad, and made him catch a fondness for living. This taught him to distinguish dark days from sunny ones and harsh sounds from the pleasant ones; to talk and talk a great deal about everything they talked about, and to remember what he had been formerly in order to get more delight out of what he was becoming.

At the same time Sotileza had continued to develop. As she developed, Cleto noticed the changes in her lines and how she became more and more plump and the look in her eyes and the harmony of her voice, and how she was filling her home with light by her work and personality. Poor Cleto could have sworn that the light of the house came from her and not from the light of the sun. Afterwards, when he went back to his own home, where he found no supper ready for him and no bed in which to sleep, where he heard only curses and blasphemies, where those devilish women would have wanted to devour him merely because he was so attached to those "rascals" on the first floor. These daily quarrels at home made him remember Mechelín's home with more yearning. Whenever he had a free moment he returned there. More than once when he knew what was waiting for him upstairs, he was ready to get on his knees in front of Mechelín and say: "Let me stay here always. I don't need any bed or any food. I'll sleep on the brick floor in the kitchen and will eat a crust of bread in some café with what you pay me for working for you."

And it should be noted that Mechelín and Sidora did not disapprove of Cleto's apparent fondness for Sotileza. He was a good worker, honest, healthy, strong as an oak and would even be a good-looking fellow when he had someone to look after him or be concerned about his cleanliness.

Besides this he was destined to inherit a half interest in a fishing boat if Mocejón did not sell out before dying. What better arrangement for Sotileza than to accept him someday without repugnance! And why should the destitute orphan girl feel any repugnance toward him? Certainly in the eyes of her foster parents—if Sotileza's worth were considered—there could not be enough gold to equal it, nor was there any man, even a nobleman, who deserved her. But their love did not blind them to the fact that no nobleman laden with gold would ever come to their door. As they were sure that they could not count on such a bargain, was there anyone better than Cleto for her in the Upper Town? Of course they were not going to make him talk in order to get him to state what he felt, nor were they going to fill the girl's ears with praises of her suitor in order to gain her consent. But they would guard against barring the door against him or even closing it gradually.

If that reverent request that Cleto was forming in his mind so many times ever was spoken out loud, it would not be disregarded by Mechelín and probably not by Sidora. But there were other important considerations, one of which, denied by Sotileza, was her insinuated preference for Muergo when he was about sixteen. It was about this time that he became a member of the seamen's guild and also lost his mother, who fell while coming up the Long Ramp loaded with sardines—and alcohol. Sotileza then persevered in the same plans as when she was the little girl Silda. She felt that his nature was such that he should be helped to get away from the bad influences inherited from his mother, and the loneliness and abandonment in which he lived after his mother's death.

And the beastlike Muergo exploited these unexplainable weaknesses of the former victim of so many of his tricks at the boat dock and Maruca Beach. Now that he had no father or mother he visited his uncle Mechelín's home every day and tried to stay as long as possible in order to be there at mealtime, because on these occasions he always got a hunk of bread for his insatiable stomach. He was living with a family that gave him a straw mattress on which to sleep and his food for only a little less than what he was receiving as a member of the crew of a fishing boat belonging to a man from the Lower Town. It was the third on which he had worked since starting as a cabin boy on Reñales' boat.

On his visits to Mechelín's home on High Street, he frequently met Cleto. They hated each other implacably. They seemed like two big dogs with only one bone. For Muergo this bone was everything that was in the house, and he feared that the other might get some of it and there would not be enough left for him. For Cleto this bone seemed to be the crude monstrosity of Muergo, whom he hated even more in that setting. Certainly he was consoled a little by the apparent pleasure with which Mechelín and Sidora helped him to contradict the slightest attempt on the part of the ugly, grimacing Muergo to express an opinion. But this consolation was embittered by the persistent tenacity of Sotileza in helping Muergo either with or without reason. This was the real cause for Cleto's hatred for Muergo.

Oh, the monstrosity and crudeness of Muergo! You should have seen him when he was nineteen years old, at the time we see Sotileza again as she was presented at the beginning of this chapter! During the interval when we have not seen him, everything about him had grown at the same time: the thickness of his lips; the crossed eyes; the wideness of his pug nose; the tangled mass of hair; the big ears and the way they stuck out; the whiteness of his few teeth; the stooped shoulders; the fatness; the intensity of his copper color, which now shone almost like black leather; the savage harshness of his voice; his stupidity. . . . In short, everything physical and moral had become larger and more intensified in him. In order that nothing may be lacking in the harmony of this concentration of monstrosities, he was usually dressed in—or wrapped up in—a flowing, heavy, green flannel shirt, a pair of brown pants and a green stocking cap with a red border.

With this stiff, wooly outfit and his slow, waddling walk he looked like a polar bear, supposing, of course, that at the North Pole there are bears with the upper half green and the lower half brown. There was no other decent thing with which to compare him.

Sotileza had preached to him a great deal about saving some of his money in order to get a good suit for the holidays and Sundays. He already had part of it but did not want to use it without a coat and a Basque cap, which were lacking. He expected to buy them within a month and a half for the celebration of the Day of the Martyrs, the patron saints of the Lower Town. He would have been able to get them sooner if he had not gone so frequently to the Zanguina Bar, where he spent much of his money. One reason why all of his money did not end up there was that he did not collect all of his wages at one time. Muergo liked to drink, but the fear of losing the help of his uncle, Mechelín, of Sidora and of Sotileza made him control this vice to a certain extent.

He was able to carry a great deal of alcohol, but when he got drunk he was really wild. For that reason his companions pestered him with jokes and tricks when he was sober but kept out of his way when he was drunk. While in that condition he was capable of the greatest barbarities. Otherwise he was a contented, strong worker, quite pleasant and in rugged health.

And how far he was from mistreating Sotileza as he had the little girl Silda! What little sense he had, and something of a vile interest in Sotileza, and a great deal of the influence of nature itself, was working on his fat person during the period that the orphan girl was growing and becoming so beautiful, and who offered him with tireless persistence the only evidence of affection that he had ever enjoyed. She had gradually been taming him and humbling him until he was the slave of this lovely girl. He was like a ferocious beast that surrenders, almost hypnotized, to the caresses of a gentle woman animal trainer.

With this simile, and in no other way, can one explain the mutual affection of these two persons who differed so greatly. It was his egotistical self-interest and the irresistible force of a mysterious law; it was her vanity, satisfied by an achieved triumph, and the force of a reckless intention.

"See here, daughter," Sidora said to her one day. "This pamperin' you're givin' that brute will cost you dearly, 'cause blood will tell. If you play with wolves you'll get nothin' but bites and clawin's. I am not sayin' this because of the food he eats here, 'cause you want it that way and that's enough for me, but why don't you ask me to give it to someone who deserves it more?"

"Muergo does deserve it."

"That devilish, stupid, low-down fellow deserves it? Why?" exclaimed Sidora.

"Because he does," Sotileza replied dryly.

"I want a better reason than that. Though that reason may be worth any amount you wish, there are lots of better ones to be said against it, and even the blind can see them. Everybody, I suppose, is born with some sort of good luck, and that fellow has had it with you ever since the days when you should have hated him. Cursed be any injustice against the law of God! And see to it that you don't have your own way with Muergo so much that you forget to say hello to that good boy upstairs. He is as good as gold from head to foot. But nothin' seems too good for you to give to that pig of a nephew of ours."

"Cleto comes from a bad family."

"Then look at Muergo!"

"Everybody has his own tastes."

"And old people have had lots of experience, child, and they also have the obligation to advise young people when they wander from the straight and narrow way."

"And what harm am I doin' in lookin' with kindness at someone who is detested by all?"

"The harm comes in encouragin' someone who should not be encouraged."

"Just because he is ugly!"

"'Cause he is no good!"

"He doesn't rob or kill."

"Just because he ain't had the notion. If the notion ever does strike him, it won't be his good sense that keeps him from carryin' it out. And please understand that Muergo is not disliked because he is ugly but because he is a jackass with evil desires."

"Other men have 'em too, and they are accepted."

"That's because they also have some good qualities. Look here, daughter. Don't be offended and don't be angry with me. I could tell you more but I'm afraid that you will think that what you give this fellow to eat here is what bothers me and that that's why I'm talkin' like I do."

After these words Sotileza became silent. At Sidora's suggestion they sat down to finish sewing an old dress of hers because the next day was Sunday. They were doing this near Mechelín's and Sidora's bed by the light from a candle on a holder on the wall.

About this time Cleto came downstairs and met Muergo, who was coming in the door. Cleto had been listening to Sidora's advice to Sotileza. This inspired in him a sudden resolve. He said to Muergo very quietly, but very firmly, while holding the front of his heavy sweater with both hands:

"I don't want you comin' around here no more."

"The devil you say," replied Muergo in a whisper. "And who the hell are you to order me that way?"

"Are you, or ain't you goin' back where you come from?" insisted Cleto without letting go of Muergo.

"No, by God, I ain't."

"Then I'm goin' to give you a couple of punches in the nose. But don't holler even if you lose some teeth. And I won't holler either."

No sooner said than done. A couple of sharp blows were heard, and then a couple more just like them amidst the confused sounds of coarse interjections and heavy breathing. Then there was a heavier thud, like that of a head striking against the street door. About that time came an oath from Muergo, almost in falsetto, and then silence in the shadows of the entrance. Muergo spat out more blood than saliva and felt his teeth one by one to see if they were all in place. Cleto, in the meantime, after having relieved himself of some of his pent-up anger, started down street, fearful of what might happen to him if he entered Mechelín's home with Muergo, who might tell what had happened.

But Muergo was in no mood to tell anything. On a face like his a few more bruises made no difference. Consequently the women did not ask him anything about the three fresh ones near his mouth. He said good evening in a growl and asked where his uncle was.

"He went out to get some fishin' lines," replied Sidora.

"Ain't there no bait?"

"He got some just in case they were goin' out tomorrow."

"Well, have him get the boat ready early 'cause we are goin' fishin' for mullet after the first mass, before the tide begins to turn. If he can't go, tell him to stay in bed, 'cause Cole and me are goin' too. That's the message I'm bringin' from Andrés."

"Why didn't Andrés come himself?"

"He said that he was busy. Damn my hide, what a pile of silver coins he had on that table in his office! Bless my soul! There was enough to swim in, or even drown!"

Just then Mechelín came in. He walked more slowly and more dejectedly than formerly. On his face there was lacking that expression of joy which he knew years ago. Sidora repeated the message that Muergo had brought and added:

"If you don't feel like it, stay in bed. Muergo and Cole are going in any case."

"I'm all right," replied Mechelín looking at Sotileza, who seemed to encourage him with her eyes. "What I'm sorry about, and I'm sayin' it without meanin' no harm to nobody, is that Andrés, from the Lower Town, remembers more about these things than some people up here who work with me in the the same fishin' boat. Men feel that way all right, but these are Andrés' ideas of showin' his esteem for others, and they must be respected."

"Well, if we didn't have respect, Mechelín, where would we be?" replied his wife. "And speakin' of respect, who could help us any better on such occasions than good old Cleto?"

"Right!" replied Mechelín.

When he heard the name Cleto, Muergo turned around on the wooden stool like a bear struck with a thorn.

"What's the matter with you, you big jackass?" asked Mechelín.

"Nothin' that's any of your business."

Cole was a brave, skillful sailor, the same individual that the reader met at Padre Apolinar's house with the other wharf rats. Such cases are not rare among the sailors of Santander. We could mention several of the persons already known in this story, Guarín, Toletes and Surbia. They were three former wharf rats transformed during the years into fishermen with energy and dignity. Colo, from High Street, also turned out to be a good sailor after he stopped studying Latin and his mad uncle was put in the asylum.

By this time bits of a breakwater, big enough to stop the highest tides, could be seen. And the railroad track, starting at the dock itself, was making good progress. Locomotives were already puffing in that area. With their insides full of fire, they brought with them the start of a new life and swept away many of the old customs and habits that had lasted so many, many years. By this time the sailors of the Upper Town had only a small place to anchor their boats, and a small opening in the new railroad embankment to get their boats into the bay.

On High Street itself three or four old buildings had been replaced with new ones having white walls and iron balconies. These stood out like shiny false teeth in a set of dirty rotten ones. Many of these changes meant trouble for the sailors and fishermen, who faced all dangers bravely, not talking much with landlubbers and not frequenting the city except for a few favorite hangouts.

The new crazy ideas of Don Venancio Liencres were to blame for this and much more. He had been incredulous and astonished but got into business in Santander up to his neck. There was never a man more to be pitied!

13 ~ ANDRES' ORBIT

I call Don Venancio the most miserable of men because all others had to do was to tickle his vanity in order to have him be the first to organize preparatory groups, or the first to talk in these groups about the incalculable advantages of the daring, new undertaking. He was one of the first stockholders in the railroad company and one of the first to argue later whether the road should go to the right or left. He applauded the establishment of steamship lines between Santander and French Atlantic ports, and later he even swallowed the bait of the first credit associations which were organized in the province after the railroad came in. He lost his fondness for the old rocking chair in his office and gave himself enthusiastically to "modern" business with eloquent harangues and bright ideas expressed in the sidewalk cafés or on the governing board of the city's most fashionable social club.

His boy and Andrés had replaced him at the "old grind"—the name he gave to his old office. Tolín had turned out very well as manager of the department. The brokers and the correspondence section were in good order and there was discipline on all floors, in the office and the warehouse. He had a good nose, delicate taste and admirable subtlety of touch at the ends of his fingers in examining samples of flour, sugar and chocolate. Above all, he had a fondness for all this, which is the secret of successfully managing all these little details. Andrés helped him very little even though he was in charge of the cashier's office. He lacked any real talent for business. His feeling of duty and a very strong will at first and later mere habit made him adjust himself without too much displeasure to tasks unpleasant to one who did not enter into them with any real love. It was enough just to see these two friends to understand easily the differences in tastes and aptitudes in them. Tolín was a young man with a calm face, observant, and even meticulous in his gaze. He was somewhat choosy, or more precisely, methodical in his work, and very orderly in everything that he had to do with. His handwriting was plain, of the best Spanish quality. He used bits of paper, regardless of how small they were, to make his calculations, using figures that looked as if they had come out of a mold. He knew how to divide his attention conveniently, without getting mixed up, among several different matters at the same time. Although he was agile in his movements and not very prudish, there was not a spot or wrinkle on his clothing. In short, he was entirely at home in the office, like a statue on its pedestal.

Andrés was a confident young man, plump and rosy, with a fierce glance which was quick and changeable. He was well built and manly in all his movements. Seated on the stool in front of his desk, he made it creak with each stroke of his pen. While the shiny curls of his black hair were swinging in front of his eyes, his mouth did not cease to mumble some word or to whistle softly some currently popular tune. Any mistake made him break out in lamenting exclamations. For some insignificant blotch made on a paper he said the greatest atrocities to himself, forgetful that there were people listening to him. Even a fly buzzing around bothered him and the slightest noise in the street made him jump up and run to the window on the mezzanine floor. In the collections and payments of which he had charge as cashier, he would make an awful uproar while counting the money given him or when he paid out sacks of money on the counter, or when he made the silver coins bounce on the marble slab to test their genuineness. Furthermore, he was punctual for work and pleasant and helpful in everything and for everybody. But he couldn't contain himself and needed all this commotion and uproar in order not to smother while inside. As one can easily see, two more different dispositions could not be found than those of Andrés and Tolín. The only thing they had in common was the cordial affection each had for the other.

Within a few months after entering the office, Tolín became ill. His fever lasted for several days and his convalescence was long. Andrés knew how to paint pictures of boats with ink, indigo and a yellow vegetable dye. Tolín was pretty well spoiled by his illness and wanted his friend to entertain him day and night by painting pictures of boats and manikins alongside his bed. Andrés had the patience to stay there about two weeks painting and painting on a night table that was leaning on Tolín's bed and later at a table in the dining room. Luisa took in all these sessions of homemade art when she was not in school, and followed every stroke of the brush or pen without batting an eye. It seemed that Andrés' brushes and pens already knew how to paint without his moving them. They could make a stormy sea with a few shots of indigo, a set of sails for two or three masts with a swish of yellow and a hull and its gear with a couple of dozen lines made in just a jiffy.

"Now paint the captain," Tolín told him quite often. And Andrés would paint a form waving a cap on a yardarm.

"Now the mate," Luisa would say. And the mate was painted next to the captain. And then all the crew, the dog, the cage with the live chickens, the steering wheel and other things until Andrés would say: "There's no room now for anything else."

After several days, Tolín wanted to try his hand. As a boy he had had some experience at freehand drawing on walls and was by nature quite inclined to works of imitation which did not require any other virtue than patience and the dissolving of some dye in water. After spattering his fingers and lips he succeeded in painting as well as Andrés, who used to tell him so in a whisper. Occasionally he would tell the same thing to Luisa, at his side, whenever she pointed out, with astonishment in her eyes, what her brother was painting.

Tolín became so fond of this art that after he got back to the office he continued painting during his leisure. His father bought him a very good box of paints, a luxury in that day. He began to paint everything under the sun. He painted portraits of his father with a black coat, opera hat and cane; of his mother in a fringed mantilla, feathered hat and striped dress; of Luisa, in adequate finery; of the cook; of the maid; of the bookkeeper—

all in profile, facing to the left, because he didn't know how to arrange them to the right or front. Later he painted chairs and benches and tables, the cat, and figures from playing cards. When his father realized his interest in art, he tried to have him study drawing with a teacher who gave lessons in his studio in the theater building. But Tolín did not want to go back to the slow, tedious, preliminary school work after reaching the heights he had in art, and desired to continue cultivating it only with his persistent inspiration. He provided himself with drawing paper, which he had never had before, and started to do landscapes. Then he started to paint by sections and in detail, everything that he could see in all directions from his home. This work lasted years. At the same time he was working with enthusiasm and improvement in his father's office. Of course the panorama was enormous and his details were infinite. Botín's house alone, with pillars, one by one, and the green shutters, one by one, took nearly three months to do. Then came the dock, stone by stone, the Cathedral roof, tile by tile, and the ships and the mountains, and everything.

When we find him again filling his father's place in the office, this hobby was diminishing in importance. He painted only a few little things from time to time, but the fire of his love for art still smoldered inside him. For recreation he used to enter his room and look at his pictures that covered the four walls. They were all framed and bore his name and date of completion. He also enjoyed showing them to visitors. His parents and the servants showed them to everyone they could. They would go from picture to picture saying:

"This is the post office; this is Botín's house; this is Saint Phillip Castle, with the cathedral in the background; this is the ferryboat; the shipyards; and so on. Looks natural, doesn't it? Everything is right there! Of course he paints just for the fun of it. He never had a teacher and he never wanted one. Why should he when he does it this well?"

Andrés soon considered that Tolín did better than he did. It is true that any rivalry in art did not make him very excited.

When Luisa saw her brother paint boats so easily and decorate them so well, she said to Andrés one night:

"You better learn to do that too, boy! That is what you call painting boats!"

"I prefer to sail the real things, like I do," replied Andrés.

"Yes, and run around with low-down sailors and—and fishermen's detestable daughters," she answered with a great deal of meaning.

Andrés blushed, because it was true that he craved such companions and amusements.

But he was so much in the habit of being with Tolín during his convalescence that he was a constant caller at his home. Then later Tolín seemed to need him more because he rarely went out at night. Luisa and friends of the family frequently formed a part of the group. But many times there were only the three. Usually while Tolín was painting, Andrés would tell about his adventures sailing and fishing. Luisa would take in the paintings and the stories without missing a stroke or a word.

Sometimes she would butt into either operation and would say to her brother: "That green looks to me more like lettuce than the sea."

Or she would interrupt Andrés with these words: "That's not very becoming to a decent boy of good family like you. At best, you smell of boat grease—and maybe you say bad words, like the sailors, when we can't hear you."

Because he really liked Tolín, Andrés continued to go to his house in the evening. This pleased his mother very much and also Don Venancio Liencres, to whom Andrés was becoming more obligated every day. If someone who had authority to do so had told him: "Spend these two or three free hours wherever you wish," then he would not have gone so often to Tolín's home. That would have avoided the bother of changing his shirt so often, and the risk of meeting Mrs. Venancio, so serious and so stuck-up, and greeting her in a courteous manner when he was sure that all she would do would be to mumble something harsh. He was received more friendlily at Mechelín's, where he enjoyed himself much more. Or he would have enjoyed himself also at the dock or wherever there were sailors and fishermen. He knew most of them and talked with so many of them.

As he was growing up, his social obligations made him stay away from sailors some, but he was not losing any of his inclination for the sea. Rather, it was becoming stronger and growing as he grew. That is saying something, too, because he was broadening out and growing taller. At seventeen he was already more than six feet tall and could lift a hundred weight in each hand higher than his hips. In rowing, he could take the place of even the strongest sailor, and managed a boat or a launch with great skill. No strong winds or hurricanes bothered him. Against winds and tides he struggled triumphantly, not only fearlessly but gladly. I do not know what devilish attraction the sea had for that boy. He seemed like a water spaniel. As soon as he saw the water, he was there, looking for some reason to get into it. He already knew all the currents, the sand bars and all the mysteries of the bay as well as the best harbor pilot and had run all kinds of risks in it on account of storms, fogs, running aground and sudden squalls. Now he was beginning to learn something about the open sea and took advantage of every occasion to learn more. His first real opportunity came by chance.

The boats for the pilots do not have regular crews and they take the first ones that come. The pay is not much. Most of the money paid to bring a ship into the harbor goes to the harbor pilot and the owner of the boat. The rest is divided among the crew. Two pilots are on duty every day. They must be at the harbor entrance from dawn until dusk. If these two outfits are not enough, the chief pilot is told and another pilot and crew is organized.

This happened one holiday afternoon when Andrés was talking with some sailors at the entrance of the Zanguina Bar. Two more men were needed to make up a crew to bring in a ship. The matter was urgent and the pilot was impatient. Andrés thought: This is my chance, and offered to fill one of the places. Because he was respected there as the son of a sea captain, his offer was accepted. He was so glad that he ran to the docks ahead of the others and was the first one in the launch. He flung his coat under the seat, took his oar and braced his feet on the seat in front of him. . . . He was in his glory! Rowing and rowing, the launch left the bay. When it was tied up alongside the ship, Andrés went on board with the pilot. More glory for this spirited boy! To come into the harbor on the bridge of a ship under full sail and to witness all the maneuvers on board, to hear the commands and other sounds, to feel how the ship slipped along, controlled by the pilot, was as sweet as honey to him.

This experience pleased him so much that he repeated it many times after that whenever he had the opportunity. When he couldn't go as a member of the crew he sometimes went along as a curious onlooker.

In order to get to the Zanguina Bar even twice a week, he took time away from being with Tolín, either at the beginning or the end of the evening, according to the season of the year or the particular run of fish. Tolín knew this, but Luisa didn't. Both Tolín and Andrés could sidetrack her with some little lie, so that Don Venancio would not know either. Because this devilish girl, who was now becoming a young lady, had gotten the idea of meddling in Andrés' affairs as if they mattered greatly to her. She did this with objections, fuss and such urgent remarks that Andrés could understand where they came from because Luisa was like her mother and guarded the reputation of her home and the good appearance of those who frequented it.

Andrés used to go to the Zanguina Bar simply because the fishermen of the Lower Town spent more time there than at home. It was the center of most of their activities. They took a shot of liquor there before breakfast and at any hour of the evening, including the "night cap" before going home to sleep. There also they made their fishlines and bought sardines, made business deals, deposited their savings. When they came back from the sea loaded with raincoats and fishing gear, their wives would be waiting for them there. Some of the bad-acting women were there to insult and slap their husbands; some of the good ones, with food in a basket and the smallest child in their arms. These fishermen, although not as polished as those that appear in poems, liked to hold their children on their knee and give them something to eat while they were gobbling their food, even in a strange place, especially when they know that they might not be back home again for three or four days, as happens occasionally when fishing for sea bream. In this bar they would prepare their tackle for the following morning, and bait the countless hooks. Andrés used to gape at these fishermen, noticing how they put the baited hooks in the bottom of the basket, and the lines on the sides and edges. He had already observed this operation in High Street, but it was not the same to see one man do it as to see several doing it at the same time amid the noise of their conversations, their stories, the odors of the bar and the light of the reflecting lamps.

He knew so many people there and observed so many "characters"! He gradually learned the name, the purpose and use of each part of the tackle, the intentions or virtues of each fisherman, the amount of money he had saved or the amount of his debts, the affairs of each family, their joys, their thoughts. They surely seemed to live in glass houses! There he learned also about the service rendered by the lookouts who built fires on Big Cape to warn ships way out whenever a south wind was developing.

Andrés' parents knew that he was interested in all these things, but his father was far from condemning him. However, his mother had him in mind every hour of the day.

"Now you see," Pedro used to tell his wife, "that boy is taking after his father. He's a sea dog from head to foot. You can see that I was right when I wanted to teach him navigation!"

"Sure thing," replied Andrea. "At least for the present he is safe from storms and sharks, and that is so much to the good."

"Not even that much," replied Bitadura, "and one of these days he may become a sailor! And compare the glory of drowning in a washbowl when you could die in a hurricane at sea!

But you wanted it this way and that's the way it is, but it hurts me to see him the way he is now. He's strong, he's daring, he has courage—and such men aren't meant to wave their coattails and have their hands in gloves and their neck between two starched jibs in drawing rooms and parks. He has not failed in his duties and I hope he doesn't, but I repeat, I like the fiber he is showing! What I regret is that he may do some things badly or too quickly because he is doing them on the sly, and that is dangerous because he may be risking his neck. We'll have to talk about this, Andrea!"

"And about the other matter, too," she replied with zeal.

"And what other matter?"

"To get him away from that cursed place on High Street."

"You mean Mechelín's house? Why, that's the most honest and quietest place in the whole Upper Town! He's all right there, much better than in the Zanguina Bar, where I saw him one night when I went past the door."

"He's going to the Zanguina Bar! And at night! Doesn't he always go to Liencres' house?"

"Apparently the little dear is doing everything. When I tell you he is showing his fiber! But don't worry about the Zanguina Bar, I'll attend to that."

"But what will they say at Liencres' house?"

"They don't know anything about it. And if they did, what the devil difference would it make? Have I given them my son just to pay court to them every hour of the day? See here, between the two extremes I prefer to see him with the bad habits of the Zanguina Bar than infesting the city with ugly pictures painted blue and yellow like Tolín is doing."

"And I understand my point of view, Pedro."

"And I do too, Andrea, but we aren't together. What is God's will cannot be changed. And what isn't God's will, our boy shouldn't try and you shouldn't force him to try, because he doesn't need it, and it isn't good for him, if you want my opinion. And that's enough talk on the subject."

14 ✎ THE TEMPTER ON STAGE

It was soon after this conversation between Pedro and Andrea that Andrés resolved to tell his father about one of his desires—one of the strongest that he felt. That was to have a boat of his own, or in partnership with someone else, like many other young men of his own age. At that time there was quite a fleet of elegant private skiffs that anchored in front of the Swiss Café. I shall try to soften all the harshness that might come with this pretension when he told his father that he would use all his savings that he had made from his salary and bonuses received at the office. The captain smiled and offered to make him a present of a new skiff with the condition that he would not go to the Zanguina Bar any more than just in passing or in cases of necessity, because all the people of the Lower Town who had boats or were fond of water sports had some need to go to the Zanguina. Andrés accepted this condition willingly. Then Bitadura had a boatbuilder make a skiff under his own directions. It was an ordinary boat with sloop rigging—mast, mainsail and jib. It was so graceful and trim that it almost sailed by itself.

About that time Mechelín began to suffer from many illnesses which prevented his going to sea, or even getting out of bed. His small savings were used up and his family started to feel certain wants because Sidora and Sotileza did not earn enough in their work to meet all their needs. Andrés noticed this with grief, especially when he was convinced that most of Mechelín's illnesses were the usual effects of his trade, aggravated by the weight of his years. That is to say, they probably could not be cured and required great care during what was left of the sick man's life.

"I don't know," Sidora was saying one afternoon to Andrés, with sad-looking eyes, while her husband was groaning in bed, "I don't know how a man, lookin' at himself in a mirror, could be so beyond redemption as to choose this kind of work. Unhappy fellow! He's been fightin' these seas for fifty years, in cold, in the hot sun, in wind and rain and snow, with little rest, scarcely a whit of sleep and then back to the boat before daybreak. And we close our eyes in order not to see the vision of death, which gets away from port before any of the rest of 'em and is always waitin' out there for these poor fellows in order to finish 'em off when least expected, and where there's no help except in God's mercy! Just see here, Andrés, I don't know what is happenin' to me when they haggle with me penny by penny over the price of a pound of hake in the market; people who toss away a dollar for some piece of rag that they really don't need. If they only knew what it means to take fish from the sea! What dangers! What labor! And for what, good Lord? So that the first day the unfortunate fisherman has to stay in bed, his family goes without food, regardless of how honest or hard working he may be, just like poor Mechelín, who has no vices whatever. If he had only had enough savin's to buy even a small fishin' boat! You see, one hundred dollars in fifty and more long years of struggle isn't much to ask. If we only had that boat now, especially if he can't go to sea again, the boat itself would make a livin' for us by havin' someone else operate it. But we don't even have that, Andrés, not even that! And I don't work every day. My eyes ain't no good for sewing every day, and the small amount Sotileza here, who is my help and my consolation, gets for workin' for other people is small and irregular."

Sotileza, who was present, did not take her eyes from Sidora except to notice that Andrés was nearly crying.

As soon as he left, he went home and had a long heart-to-heart talk with his father, who knew Mechelín well and held his good qualities in esteem.

At the end of their talk, his father said:

"Don't let your mother know about this because she doesn't see things the same way we do, but we'll have to get Mechelín the boat he needs."

The Tempter on Stage

And Mechelín got it very soon, and from that day on joy bloomed again in his home in High Street, and the names of Andrés and his father were almost worshipped. About that time, Sidora told Sotileza:

"See here, daughter: from now on try to have a pleasant smile and a good word for Andrés, who is as good as gold, so that he won't think that we are ungrateful. I'm not saying this because you dislike him, but your face should never conceal your inner feelin's, not even when they are bad, and much less when they are good."

Although there was a certain degree of friendship between Andrés and Sotileza, it must be known that that was almost entirely due to his frank, communicative character. Sotileza was no more expressive with him than with others with whom she had any dealings, with the monstrous exception of Muergo. In regard to Andrés there was no dislike to be disguised on the part of this shy girl, who was by now reaching the limits of beauty which she reached a little later. She gladly gave herself to make the effort which was demanded of her by the more grateful than worldly-wise Sidora. The latter's surprise had no bounds when she noticed that Andrés' friendliness toward Sotileza decreased as her attentions toward him increased. The number of his visits to their home was even being reduced. What the devil was going on there? What was such a gentlemanly and good-hearted young man, that all doted on, resenting? Did he no longer consider them worthy of the good he had done them? Couldn't he see how they literally lived by the help he had given them, and how the poor, sick old fisherman gladly suffered all his ills because of it? Even though Mechelín had not lost his vision of ending his days in a charity hospital, he took advantage of any improvement in his illness to earn another share by working on the boat because it was his duty. Hadn't Sidora frequently gone from her humble home to the home of Captain Pedro Colindres with the very best fish caught that day, not as any payment for benefit received—because no price could be set on that and the giver would never have tried to collect any—but merely to show that they were not ungrateful? And if it wasn't this or something like it, what was it? Sidora worried and racked her brain in vain. In the meantime, the more she looked at Andrés, the more changed she found him.

She even consulted with her husband about the matter, and later with Sotileza. Mechelín said to the devil with it, and swore and reswore that he hadn't noticed any signs of such a change, and Sotileza, shrugging her shoulders, said the same as Mechelín. Then Sidora began to doubt herself and to think that she was seeing things. Although she did not forget it, she became accustomed to it, which was all she could do with the hurt she had inside. And the fact is that she had been right. What she didn't know, fortunately, was the cause of Andrés' shyness, which the reader is now going to learn.

The same day that Mechelín got possession of the fishing boat, Mocejón, now a sick old man, climbed the stairs to his home, vomiting from his big mouth the greatest curses and insults:

"Damn, double damn," he was saying as he bumped against the door and the walls of the corridor leading to the living room, where Sargüeta and Carpia were unraveling old pieces of rope and Cleto was smoking in gloomy silence near the wall. "What people have been sayin' is true! But, damn it, don't people have no shame no more? How can they do that? Is there a moral law of God or ain't there? That house! Is it a house or what is it? If they took that girl from my house because she was mistreated, how can they permit her to stay in that one? For some kind of monkey business? Because, by damn, the thing is clear—and as soon as someone who catches on to things quickly told me, I caught on right away. Double damn! What shameless wretches!"

They asked him for explanations and he began in his brutal way to link together the gift of the boat with Andrés' fondness for Mechelín's family and the budding womanhood of Sotileza. Mocejón began linking these things together, but then the two

The Tempter on Stage

women in his family took the matters of supposition to the most scandalous extremes. Cleto delayed a little in catching on, because he was a little slow. But as soon as he realized what it was he jumped like a tiger and exclaimed indignantly:

"By God, this is all a lie! All of you here are liars! And you more than anybody else, Carpia! I know this guy Andrés! And I know what each person downstairs is like, too, and I know what each one of you is, and I say that it is all a big lie, by God, and I'm sayin' that you are lyin', Pappy, because you're gettin' childish, and you, Mammy, because you never told the truth, and you, Sis, 'cause you're envious and nothin' but a loafer! Double damn!"

As Cleto was talking this way, his mother threw a wooden stool at his head and Carpia threw the tarred bits of rope at him and Mocejón, without strength to throw anything or even to slap him, swore at him till everything echoed.

While they were trying to hit him, his mother and sister kept up a constant stream of insults:

"Run along, you easy mark, you ungrateful son!"

"Take that, damn you, so that you can give it to her for a present!"

"They have sold her, by God!"

"She allowed herself to be sold!"

"And not for the price of the boat either, because she had already sold herself for less!"

"That's why she is able to dress so well!"

"And live at ease without doin' no work!"

"Go look for her now. Marry her now, you sucker!"

"But watch out where you bring her. If she comes in here, we'll burn the house down, by God!"

This, without relating what Mocejón said (because it is unprintable), is a short sample of what was yelled in the fifth floor in less than a minute, accompanied by ferocious and frightful gestures. Cleto started to froth at the mouth. Since he could not get revenge on his mother or father, he attacked Carpia and gave her the hardest wallop she ever got. Then he ran out of the house like a flash. His mother and sister did not continue to insult him from the balcony as they usually did. Although they were past masters at this art of insult, they realized that it might be a little dangerous to state these things from the balcony for all to hear. They also knew well that Sotileza did not have the patience of the frightened little girl Silda, nor were they ignorant of the esteem of the people in High Street and the support of the Council, which favored Sotileza more than themselves. What might happen in such a scandalous matter? Why did they need the evidence of the gift of the boat? Ever since Andrés and Sotileza were grown up wasn't each visit of his sufficient basis for such poisonous mouths as theirs to heap a mountain of infamies on him? The insulting sign would be put there on her door! That was all that was lacking! And it would be done without mercy, not only on the door of the house but also on the face of each person who lived there. But only when circumstances would present them the occasion, free from any responsibility for it, and when the echo of appearances would confirm the correctness of their denunciation. That's what they were waiting for with stubborn perseverance, with a watchful eye, working on the sly.

Cleto left the house horrified by those devilish abominations, but as soon as the fresh air of the street hit his flushed face and his poor wits had begun to get back in order and his heart was beating normally again, he noticed that there was something stabbing him inside like a thorn, and a horrible suspicion was buzzing around inside his head like a big fly in a bottle. If slander always leaves some trace, even in keenly intelligent minds and the strongest hearts, how could Cleto's rudimentary reasoning and irresolute heart be freed from the poison that his family's words produced there? Why shouldn't what he rejected as slander be true? Andrés was rich and handsome; Sotileza was a needy orphan who caught his eye; Mechelín and his wife two good individuals owing a debt of gratitude to Andrés. And if Andrés insisted, what might have happened?

The Tempter on Stage

And if he were not insisting, then why was he going there so often?

What unhappy days and nights poor Cleto passed struggling with these doubts! All he did was observe Andrés when he met him at Mechelín's, and watch the street in order to surprise him at unusual hours, and to look at Sotileza when Andrés was near her. This made him worse, because even the most innocent glances and the simplest words seemed to him irrefutable testimony of the cause of his distrust. Fortunately for everybody, he did not dare to say a word to Mechelín or Sidora, although he had it on the tip of his tongue to unburden himself, rather than to punish anyone.

But one night he stopped Andrés in the middle of the sidewalk and took him to the Big Wall, where the open space was empty at that time, and expressed to him, in a whisper and in his own way, all that annoyed him and took away his appetite and deprived him of rest.

Andrés was frightened because he did not know the real motives of Cleto's fears. Cleto had assured him that only the good name of that honorable family moved him to tell him what he did, and for a fellow as dull as Cleto to pay any attention to such trifles they must have gone beyond supposition. He investigated this point, and although Cleto assured him that he had heard only the members of his own family say anything about it, that was sufficient to spread it over the whole town. But he denied everything with solemn firmness, and shook hands with Cleto to swear that no such infamous thought attributed to him by the slander had ever crossed his mind.

Cleto, faced by such sincerity, began to see his way out of the difficulty. No trace remained in his heart of the terrible suspicion that had tormented him. Andrés understood that it was necessary for him to do something about these slanderous suppositions, and did not go to Mechelín's home that night.

But how fragile and miserable and lustful, as Padre Apolinar would say, is man. That Andrés, so scrupulous, so noble, so cautious, so wise and so generous, when he heard Cleto's evil confidences there on the Big Wall began to be something different without realizing it, when alone in his room, in the silence of the dark night, he had scruples about the reasons for conducting himself as he had with Mechelín's family. Even the strictest conscience suffers from a certain elasticity which, if not checked by an iron will and a good sound reason, reaches very dangerous extremes. This, of course, is a general statement. Then you can imagine, as happened in the case of Andrés, how the inexperience of youth conspires by means of an inborn weakness with the impetus of whims of a strong nature, ignorance, passion and enthusiasm.

Andrés had seen Sotileza grow up, and change gradually from a little half-sick vagabond girl into a beautiful, elegant young lady. But there had never passed through his head any idea that had the slightest connection with what the evil women of High Street accused him. Hence his sincere indignation when he found out, through the confidences of Cleto, and his own spontaneous decision to go less and less to this humble home, where his presence might compromise the honor of a girl. But, when the light of this flash disappeared and he examined things by the dim light of his reason, the first thing that presented itself before his mind's eye was the body of the supposed delinquent, but not in the scant clothing of the innocent companion of childhood games, or that of the good friend of early teen age, but with the incentives that a dreaming fantasy could accumulate on an abundance of womanly beauty like that of the lovely Highstreeter. Immediately, remembering again the slanderous suppositions of the Mocejón women, he said to himself: "Therefore, that was possible." And by a misinterpretation, quite usual and common in human speech, he again became indignant over the fact that he would be capable of committing a transgression, the hypothesis of which he had been enjoying just a moment ago.

Afterwards he came back to his plan to go less and less to Mechelín's and, without dismissing Sotileza the least bit from

The Tempter on Stage

his memory, he thought about how Mechelín and his wife would consider his conduct. To tell them the motive of his action would be like stabbing these good people in the heart. To conceal it from them would make him guilty of an error, at least as far as consequences were concerned, in regard to their affection and friendship. And all this, why? Simply because two shameless women on the fifth floor had had the idea of giving a wicked interpretation to a noble, generous act. And should the tranquillity of a clean conscience be at the mercy of the judgment of two uncontrollable women? And should he subordinate his legitimate pleasures, his honorable pleasures, to the opinion of two slanderers? Never! Consequently he would certainly take this warning into consideration. But he would not give the obscene family of Mocejón the pleasure of submitting to its desires. He would take certain decorous precautions in order to remove all pretext of gossip from their suspicions; he would go less than formerly to Mechelín's, but he certainly would go back. And let anyone dare to ask him why! Let some foul-mouthed person doubt his honesty, his loyalty or the nobility of his motives! He would stop any attempt against the honor and peace of an honest family. And if someone had then placed a crucifix in front of him and asked him to swear that all this was the truth, he would have sworn gladly and with enthusiasm. And he would have told the truth.

Nevertheless, if one could have entered the depths of his heart, how soon he would have found hidden there something that would have indicated the unconscious falseness of his oath! Because it is certain that ever since the first time that he went back to her home after having thought all of this out, still resolved to fight heroically against all evil thoughts that the tempter might suggest to him, and against the tempting easiness of some unexpected occasion, how differently he looked at Sotileza now from what he had before!

Which, provisionally, shows three things:

That Andrés, thinking and acting in this way, felt less honest and noble than on the Big Wall when he heard Cleto's secrets.

That, in the conflict in which these secrets had placed him, the most discreet and least dangerous thing for him and for the Mechelíns would have been to go less and less until he stopped completely.

And, finally, that Sidora was right when she affirmed that there had been a sudden change in Andrés.

If she had only known what efforts of will this change had meant to Andrés, especially when Sotileza started to shower him with attentions as she had never done before!

And thus more time was passing and Sotileza was reaching her full womanly development and Andrés was becoming a more elegant young man, skillful, valiant and strong on the sea, where he spent most of his free time, sailing his skiff *Zephyr*, helped by Cole or Muergo, who ordinarily took care of it; or fishing far and wide from Mechelín's boat, for the use of which he always paid scrupulously, to the great disgust of the sick fisherman whose conscience hurt to receive money from his hands. He enjoyed great prestige in both the Upper and Lower towns; in both his opinions were sought after and the captain of any launch would gladly have given him command of his boat in dangerous moments.

The best of the fish he caught went to Don Venancio Liencres' home, and, by intent, used to send them often by Sotileza, who also took some to Don Pedro Colindres' home. Because it should be noticed that, exactly as he proposed to take precautions about Mechelín's home on High Street, he got the idea that both his family and that of Don Venancio should recognize and admire the exceptional beauty of this elegant girl.

It so happened then that his mother told him one day that if such and such a girl set foot in her house again, she would do this and that to her. And the distinguished sister of Tolín told him one night more or less the same thing. Poor Andrés didn't know what to do, because he couldn't guess the reason for such excitement.

Andrés, in spite of these and other things from which he

The Tempter on Stage

was suffering, carried all the weight of his obligations in the office and that of friendship and courtesy for his pal Tolín. By this time Luisa was what was expected of her as a girl: a polite young lady, very bedecked and very scrupulous about etiquette. She was rather dull in talking, but not in the look of her big black eyes nor in the smile which showed her white teeth. She was quite fond of keeping distance between classes the same as her mother, but she made an exception with her father's clerk Andrés, whom she had known since childhood. She continued to be a busybody concerning the details of his life and doings, and whenever they were opposed to her likes and inclinations, she rarely missed a chance to scold him. He became peeved with such liberties. She used to become nervous with anger when she saw that he denied her the right to say what she was saying. Tolín used to arbitrate such quarrels and made peace; that is to say, he got them to talk about something else. He did not succeed in making what really could be called peace, because when the group broke up Luisa used to lock herself up in her room with a terrible temper, and Andrés went out cursing her as impertinent and meddlesome, and mumbling something that sounded like, "She finally will be the cause for me never returning here."

And these were the only unpleasant moments which the handsome young man had. Everything else was like a little golden bell that tinkled joys as soon as you shook it a little—and even if you didn't.

He had Cleto completely won over ever since that pledge and handshake. Cleto believed that anything in this world was possible, with the exception of the injurious suspicion of his family ever becoming true. Padre Apolinar was overwhelmed with joy watching and listening to Andrés. As Andrés was a wholehearted believer and had some money from what he earned in the office and knew how charitable the good priest was with any alms received, he used to have him sing masses to various saints. These were to request that Mechelín get better, or that his father return safely from a trip, or that he himself be free from bad weather on a fishing trip planned for the open ocean. Some of these masses were for five pesetas! And Pa'e 'Polinar, who was used to saying them for a peseta or even half a peseta, was very grateful and happy!

It was unbelievable to think that Andrés would spend his savings on society clothes or recreation, because these were unbearable to him. His friend Tolín could have all that! This was the one who enjoyed walking in the parks and main streets with an opera hat, kid gloves and a whalebone cane. Don Venancio liked it that way too because he thought that appearances in society were good business.

But Andrés and a half dozen other young men used to the smell of tar and the pleasures of the sea were the only survivors of that amphibious race of men who just a few years before filled the whole town with a spirit of youth!

Thus were the people, the things and the places of this story when Muergo and Cleto came to blows that night at Sotileza's doorway.

15   THE OLD STAND-BY

Cleto was walking up the street and then down the street, up the hill to the doorway and then back down again, saying to himself at the beginning of each climb: "This time I'm going in." He would arrive at the door but not enter. He was coming toward the Big Wall and always seemed to have a rusty nail inside his shoe which hurt every step he took. And that rusty nail was Muergo and the thought that he would have plenty to do if he tried to keep this stupid monster away from Sotileza by force. There was also the worry that because of this her door might be closed to him even if he did succeed in keeping Muergo away. That would be good pay for his trouble! If he only had some friends from whom to ask advice! If he could

The Old Stand-By

only talk with some good people who would believe him when he told them about this boiling force inside him when he was wide awake or dreaming, and which broke like a nor'wester against the walls of his heart as soon as he thought about Sotileza—and she was in his memory always. If he could only tell someone about that tickling sensation that came to him when he thought about what he might be if he lived with the Mechelíns, and what he feared might become of him if he didn't get away from his own family soon. If he didn't he might even jump out the window some night! Things were now in such a state that it would have to be one or the other—and soon. He remembered Andrés and thought of his influence with Mechelín and Sidora to get him out of his troubles. But now Andrés was giving employment to Muergo on his skiff and probably wouldn't help him in anything that might harm that brute. To go straight to the people concerned with his worries would be risking too much. That was because he had had little experience in dealing with people and did not trust his awkward speech and quick temper in picturing his inner feelings and the torments that bothered him. And thus thinking to himself, and walking and walking, he was going downhill on Rua Mayor. He reached the fish factory, deserted at this hour, and continued toward the Ribera (on the north side of the old dock). There he met Padre Apolinar. Immediately the idea came to him that there was nobody like this good man to listen to him kindly and to give him good advice!

He stopped him, greeted him with his cap in his hand and asked him to listen to something he had to tell him.

"If it's only a few words," the priest replied, while he was putting his hands like a visor over his weak eyes to see who the man was, "you've already told me them. If there are many, keep talking to me as we walk along, or tell them to me when we reach my home, because I'm in a hurry and can't waste more time in the street."

"Well then, I'll tell you at home what I got to say," answered Cleto, making a tack and coming alongside the priest.

Padre Apolinar at this time was living in one of the small houses on Alameda de Becedo. That meant that Cleto had to cross the city along Ribera Hill and San Francisco Street, the most important business streets of that day. There were waves of people of the better class and shop after shop well lighted and full of articles to port and starboard. Cleto didn't remember ever passing that way before. The noise and the wonders he was seeing surprised him so much that he nearly forgot about his feelings and sensations.

"You have to become accustomed to everything, Cleto, to everything," Padre Apolinar said to him when he noticed his amazement in looking at things in the stores and how he was bumping into passers-by. "But you fishermen are just like fish. As soon as you get on land and see rational, worldly people, you can't breathe easily. And the worst of it is that some of it sticks to you. You must know that if I had lived much longer on Ocean Street and seen so many fishermen, I'd be as much a fish as you all are because I am used to dealing with landlubbers. And now, dealing with those fishermen's kids that they send to me to scrape off some of their scales, I mean ignorance, you can see how I am even forgetting how to speak without using fishermen's terms. Some kids still come to my house. Some don't come because the distance is so great, and they may be frightened like you seem to be. At least they get a little airing along the way and don't smell so bad when they reach my house. I also get some children of the landlubbers, sons of God the same as anybody else, and in need, too, of some instruction and knowledge of the divine word. By darn! What rascals there are among them! But even at that I don't ever expect, as long as I live, to have a pupil as dirty and as ugly and as stupid as that Muergo."

This name made Cleto snap immediately from the bewilderment in which he was submerged. He shuddered all over, let out a good big curse and said with nervous vehemence, full of all the grief that annoyed him:

The Old Stand-By

"Let's row a little faster, Pa'e 'Polinar, so we get there sooner."

"What's the big hurry, darn you?"

"These worries that I got inside me, swimmin' in the hold."

A little later, with the poor light of a match which Pa'e 'Polinar struck, Cleto and the priest climbed the stairs of the latter's home and an old servant opened the door for them. They went into a room and closed the door. A tallow candle was burning on the table.

Being again with Padre Apolinar and examining him from head to foot, we might say that he didn't look a day older. He was wearing the same clothes we had seen before, and his face was the same. It didn't have a wrinkle or a scab more, nor was there a grease spot or patch less on his clothes. The same old Pa'e 'Polinar, with his red eyelids, his drooping head and his threadbare, transparent robe.

"See here, my boy. See whether you got any good eyes to see with," he exclaimed suddenly pointing to some big books and papers that were on the table, while removing his hat and cloak. "Look at them and tell me whether Pa'e 'Polinar, with this work at hand, has any time to spare to gad about the streets."

And as Cleto looked at him for a more understandable explanation, the priest added:

"This is like a fire that consumes my speech, my health and what little sight I have left. Because you must know now that this is a sermon which I have been selected to give for the holiday of the holy martyrs in Miranda Chapel the day of the feast day for the Lower Town. Which is saying something! Everybody will be there! Members of the Council, all the fishermen and half of Santander, with their mouths open, listening to Padre Apolinar! Do you think I can sleep with this coming up, or treat this subject in a happy-go-lucky way?"

Cleto had the idea of counting on his fingers the time until the 30th of August and saw that it was about a month and a half, and said so to the priest.

Pa'e 'Polinar then turned to the simple-minded boy, who was rubbing his cap with the sleeve of his jacket in order to clean it up a little before putting it on the table and said to him:

"Make it three months, because I already have been working at this table for as long a time as is still lacking, continuing dipping into the books and the inkwell—make it four months, it could easily be that long. And do you think that's time enough to write a sermon for such an occasion? It takes longer than it does to put a hook on a line! Here is where you can test a man, Cleto! This is where the best of them really sweat, by darn! And if some priest tells you anything different, he's not telling the truth, by gosh. He certainly would be a good-for-nothing preacher! All right, then. You'll see when you go to the chapel that day."

"Who, me? I'm not goin' there for that."

"That's true. You are from the Upper Town. But there will be some from the Lower Town who will hear me, and you will probably find out whether what I tell them can be learned in a couple of months. I don't think much of some of these young priests who seem to be educated at birth and the word of God already on their lips! And tell me now, what the devil's ailing you? What do you want of me? Why did you look me up? Why bother me?"

Cleto, who was in a hurry, didn't make him wait long for an answer, if you could call an answer that tide of guttural sounds, with short disconnected words, accompanied by hot oaths, rubbing of the feet together, swaying of the shoulders and head and creaking of the chair.

"All this is all right," said the priest, an expert in deciphering such a rare kind of puzzle. "But why the devil are you telling me?"

"So that you can give me some advice, and maybe help me a little."

"Oh, sure," replied the priest, wiggling inside his clothes. "That's what I was afraid of—as soon as you started to talk—

as soon as you sat in that chair—as soon as you stopped me on the street, by darn! Furthermore what is happening to you had to happen, because the hand of God reaches everywhere and you pay for what you do, and when you have something to pay for, I'm right here, as someone has said, handing over the money! Damn this lottery business. I got a bad bargain! And tell me, you darn blockhead, why did you put your snout in that house? What did you need there?"

"She sewed on a button for me one day."

"Yes, yes. You've already told me about that, and everything that has happened since. But later on, when you saw what was happening inside of you, why didn't you keep away? Because whenever I found you there, I always understood that it was just a question of talking a little and smoking a little with Mechelín in order to spend less time in your own home."

"That's what it was at first, but then! God! Haven't I told ya already how it seemed to gradually get into me?"

"Well, then, Cleto, then you should have beat a retreat, knowing as you do that between the fifth floor and the ground floor there could be no friendships or agreements. But let's see. Does she know anything about how you feel?"

"I ain't told her nothin'."

"Does Mechelín know anything?"

"Nothin'."

"Does his wife know?"

"Just as much as he does."

"How do they look on you?"

"The old folks, just so-so . . . and she, not so good, damn it. She accepts Muergo better, and that's what unrigs my capstan."

"And in view of what you tell me, what do you want me to do?"

"Give me some advice."

"For what?"

"To go later to tell her, like you know how to say it, that I wanta marry her."

"Holy heavens! If you've already made up your mind about that, why do you need any advice?"

"For nothin', I guess. The other is what you are goin' to do, and soon."

"May a northwest gale wash you overboard! Do you know what you are asking me?"

"All too well."

"Do you know what your mother is?"

"Better yet."

"Do you know what your sister is?"

"May lightning strike her!"

"Do you know what they did to me one day?"

"Sure I do."

"Do you know that any day is the day I do not dare to set foot on High Street if I see them leaning on the balcony? Twice, when I didn't see them, they gave me a complete rout all along the sidewalk."

"That's what I heard later."

"Do you know that before seeing you married to that girl they would be capable of setting fire to the house and the whole neighborhood?"

"It wouldn't be no lack of ill will that would keep them from doin' it."

"And knowing all these things, Cleto, why the devil are you getting me mixed up in it? Can't you see me martyred already? Can't you see me tortured, with spit on my face, bile on my lips and my hide in strips? Darn, either you don't like me or you are not in your right mind!"

"The devil I ain't, but if you refuse me flat, what am I goin' to do?"

"And why are you asking me? Did Padre Apolinar give you birth, by any chance? Does he owe you the bread he eats? The clothes he wears? Nothing, my boy. The same old story! All this merriment and candy for you alone, and as soon as there is any discomfort or any bump on the head, you all come to me to cure your hiccough or put a bandage on. That is as much as

The Old Stand-By

I'll ever get from you! Some people's luck, by darn; luck and nothing but luck! Of course it is true that it is my duty, if you look at it that way. But it is also true that duties must be performed with due reckoning and reason, and what you are asking me now is too much, and my answer is no, and no, and no! Do you want it any clearer than that, Cleto?"

Cleto shook his head, got up lazily from the chair, turned his cap a couple of times in his hands and mumbled a few incomprehensible words. Suddenly he straightened up angrily and said to Padre Apolinar, who was walking back and forth in the room:

"I don't know what I'll do all by myself as far as she is concerned. But for Muergo, Pa'e 'Polinar, if somebody don't knock him out by blows, he'll come to some other end or I'll get out of there."

"Man alive," replied the priest, standing in front of Cleto. "If that were not a mortal sin, I'd tell you that you might be doing an act of charity—Ave María! What nonsense one says in storms like this. Don't pay any attention to me, Cleto, don't pay any attention at all to what I say without thinking. But you are to blame, darn it! So, beat it! Don't worry so much about those things. Calm down! Get plenty of sleep—if you have a place to do so. Live peacefully! Don't bother that animal Muergo any more. He won't be doing what you are afraid he will. Forgive him. And who knows, man, who knows! It is always darkest before dawn. And . . . I'll drop around there a few times and start to prepare the ground as I see best—wisely, you understand, very wisely! I'll tell you when I have anything to say to you. And you, in the meantime, keep your mouth and hands quiet. Keep your eye on me. You can tell by the way I look and the way they receive you at Mechelín's, and I'll tell you something when it's time to tell it—and so, I've told you enough. Now run along and let me work a little, because I have lost enough time already for all we're getting out of it! Beat it!"

Cleto went out somewhat more encouraged, but not satisfied, and the priest leaned against his table. He sat down and unfolded a manuscript which he took from one of the books. All the while he was murmuring:

"With such entertainment and these preparations, do something substantial; get plenty of Latin expressions and polish up your speech so much that your listeners will be amazed."

Then he cleaned his quill pen on his jacket, tested the point on his left thumbnail and made a screen of the books placed on edge to protect his eyes from the direct light rays.

Then his housekeeper came in and said:

"Capuchin's wife is here, from the Prado de las Viñas."

"And what is bothering Capuchin's wife?"

"Her husband is much worse."

"Let her tell that to the doctor, darn it!"

"She has already told him. That's why she is here."

"She would do better to go to the drugstore."

"She would if she had any money, poor thing."

"So she came here for me to give her some?"

"She's asking for some alms."

"She surely came to the right place! Ramona, I would ask for some myself if I were not ashamed to do it, by darn!"

"The worst of it is that she doesn't even have a cup of soup for her sick husband at home. Not even a crust of bread, sir."

"Ave María! Ave María! He's got three children and a wife. He seems to be pretty good at that!"

While he was talking this way, the good priest slapped his pockets and put his hands in a drawer of the table.

"And what the devil would be there?" he murmured. "Because it doesn't have anything in it, there hasn't been any lock for many years. Nothing, Ramona, nothing. There's nothing. Tell that poor woman to forgive me for God's sake, because I cannot help her."

"What about that dollar you got this morning?"

"What dollar do you mean, woman?"

"The one from Andrés for a mass."

"Yes—put a greyhound on its trail. It went that fast."

"Since this morning?"

"Since this morning! What's the matter with you? How long did you think it would last me? Only till somebody asked me for it and they asked me for it this afternoon as soon as I left the house, and I do not have it any more. Darn it all! It seems that the matter could not be more natural or more common."

The servant was going out with this sad message for Capuchin's wife when the priest suddenly asked her:

"Listen, Ramona, before you go, and regardless of what it is, what do we have for dinner tonight?"

"For you, some meat and potatoes."

"What do you mean for me? What about you?"

"For me there are four sardines."

"And since when do we have different dishes to eat?"

"There is so little meat, and it is not enough for two of us."

"So there is just a little meat, eh? And how about the potatoes?"

"They are just about half cooked now, sir."

"Half done, half cooked—see here, by darn! See here! Bring me that meat now with the potatoes and everything."

"But, sir, if . . ."

"Bring it to me, darn it!"

The old servant went out and came back carrying the steaming food in a pot covered with a dirty pad.

Padre Apolinar held it close to his nose and enjoyed the succulent, fragrant odors. Then he put it away from him like one who flees from temptation and said to his servant:

"All right, all right. That stew is really all right! But since I have no appetite to speak of, give it to Capuchin's wife so that she can take it home to her sick husband."

After a few useless objections the servant went away to carry out her master's orders. In the meantime, he stuck his head out the door of his room and shouted to her:

"Be sure to tell her to return the napkin to us if she doesn't need it."

Then he went back to his chair and his papers, mumbling while he handled them:

"I have just read, I don't know where, that to keep one's health while doing such work as I have to do now there is nothing better than to go to bed hungry. That will be just right for me tonight, by darn! It surely will!"

16 A DAY'S FISHING

Andrés got up the next morning before sunup and went to the first mass that Padre Apolinar sang in San Francisco Church for fishermen of the Upper Town. Muergo, who had come to call him, was carrying the tackle and the basket of food for the day. They were the provisions Andrés' mother had prepared the night before as was her custom every time her son went fishing. And you should have heard her tell Andrés when she placed each object in the basket:

"Two, four, six, ten, an even dozen hard-boiled eggs I have put in for you. Will you have enough? In this piece of paper there are slices of fried fish—about two pounds and a half. Of course if you let those people get their big paws on that you won't have a chance to try any of it. If they would only swallow a dagger crosswise! Son, I do not know when you are going to lose this blamed fondness for such dangerous business! And all you get out of it is a bad case of sunburn or windburn, and smelling the whole house up with this messy dirt! And the worst of it is that some fine day you'll drown or get a sun stroke that will cause your death. Come, come, don't get peeved, because I am telling you this for your own good. Here is a ham and chicken meat pie. These are sausages—three dozen of them. Try to get those big hungry fellows to satisfy themselves with these so that there will be more of the other things for you. I have put in enough for five people. If there are more going—and you seem to pick up half the town—let them eat nails or else get along with what there is. I certainly would like to see your friend Muergo licking his big fingers and smacking his piggish lips! You certainly are getting good breeding and good manners from him! Boy, what wretched tastes you have! And how angry I get at you because I can't pull them out by the roots! But your father is to blame for all this. At least he gives you his consent, and probably applauds you for them. Yes! Yes! Andrés! I'm telling you how I feel, and you have to listen to me, because that is the least you are obliged to do. Here is a good-sized piece of guava jelly for you alone. There is also half of a Dutch cheese and two pounds of cookies, for everybody—six pounds of bread. How many bottles of wine shall I put in? Will you have enough with four? All right then I'll put in six, because those people have great capacity for eating and drinking. Here are my best napkins. Be sure not to let them wipe their big paws on them. They can use these big rags for that. This glass is for you. This other one is for all the others . . . knives and forks. It is a good thing that this basket is big otherwise there wouldn't be room for everything. Now you are supplied with all the necessary things. On your bed I'll put your fishing clothes and your raincoat in case a nor'wester comes up. And for the love of God, son, don't go very far out and come back early. If you only knew how I worry thinking about what might happen to you! What a mass I am going to have sung in San Francisco Church the day that this blamed fondness of yours for the sea comes to an end—and things go the way they ought to be going!"

Andrés, when he came out of the church, saw that Mechelín and Sotileza had also attended. That meant that both of them were going on the fishing trip. This had happened on several occasions because Sotileza liked to go, partly because she had few other diversions and partly because at home they catered to her whims. Whenever Andrés was consulted about this particular matter, he always did away with any pretension by saying how much it would please him. Sidora placed no other obstacles in the way of the beautiful girl than the condition that she should never go on such pleasure trips without Mechelín for appearances' sake. Since then, whenever Mechelín's health permitted him to go fishing in his boat with Andrés, Sotileza went along.

Cleto had suggested to the good-hearted Andrés that he give him a place in his boat, in which there were so many things that attracted him! First it was Sotileza whose will was his own, then it was Muergo, who did not deserve to be there and should not be so near Sotileza, and finally that abundant, tasty food that Andrés always took along to stuff everybody with at noon. And his suggestion probably would have been followed by Andrés, because he had mentioned the same thing to Sidora once. But she said that Andrés should not try to take Cleto on the boat because he was hated so by all other members of his family, who had enough to hate in addition to the boat. Cleto did not have courage enough to face the storms that waited for him at home if he rowed in his neighbor's boat. And Sidora and Mechelín wanted to have nothing more to do with those of the fifth floor.

For that reason Cleto did not accompany Andrés on Mechelín's boat. He was satisfied to watch the boat from a distance whenever Sotileza was along on one of these fishing trips.

"Fortunately, Andrés is with her," he would say to himself when he saw them leaving.

And that's what he did and said that Sunday from the Big Wall, while old Mechelín, Muergo, Cole, Andrés and Sotileza embarked just when the sun was casting its first rays on the beautiful panorama of the bay, and the light reflected like diamonds on the waves. There was an absolute calm, and the air was sultry. There were a few purple clouds on the horizon near the sun.

Although they put up the mainsail, it was useless just then because there was no wind. Muergo and Cole manned the oars. Mechelín, in the prow, took one also, so that they couldn't say that he was no longer good for anything. Trying to find the

A Day's Fishing

current, because the tide was beginning to change, they rowed toward the harbor entrance.

Andrés and Sotileza, seated in the stern, got the fishing tackle ready, laughing and talking all the while. Sotileza, who was so sparing with words and smiles on land, was very animated during these trips. And Andrés was no longer following his system of pretense to which he had spontaneously condemned himself because he gradually became persuaded that it was unnecessary, since no one remembered the motives that had caused it. Consequently he did not waste any opportunities to laugh heartily from time to time when she would say something sly or sharp that appealed to his playful and happy nature.

Sotileza, in all her Sunday array, was not as beautiful to him, although she believed the opposite, as when she was wearing shorter and fewer everyday clothes. Nevertheless she was quite lovely in the boat with her red silk shawl over her black, tight-fitting jacket, and her dark-blue skirt. She had on good shoes, and the topknot of her hair was covered by a good-looking scarf.

Muergo was seated two seats closer to the prow in front of her, and had his big, dirty, calloused feet braced on the seat in front of him. His powerful back was covered with a tight-fitting old white undershirt with blue stripes. These colors gave extraordinary luster to his bronzed, shiny skin. The same old stupid smile was on his huge lips, and his crosseyes shone through the heavy matted hair over his forehead.

Andrés was enjoying making a comparison of the buxom, fine features of the young lady with the details of the big head of the oarsman. He was mentally astonished by the contrast made by those two faces, when Sotileza whispered in his ear:

"I've never seen him as ugly as he is today."

"He surely is ugly," replied Andrés.

"It's fun just to look at him," added the girl, with a covetous expression, looking fixedly at the harshness of his face.

Muergo seemed to sense her gaze because he shuddered all

over and squealed like a wild colt. At the same time he made such a stroke with his oar that he caught Cole off balance and changed the course of the boat.

Then there shone on Sotileza's face something like satisfied vanity. At the same time she heard Mechelín's voice from the prow, back of the loose, flapping sail:

"What are you tryin' to do, you animal?"

"Nothin' that matters to you," replied Muergo, snorting again.

Just then Sotileza and Andrés tossed out their lines. By the time the boat was opposite the San Martín promontory they had already caught several pounds of fish—sea bream, haddock, mullet, sea bass. The fun of the trip really started then.

The useless sail was lowered. With the boat practically stopped, Andrés and Sotileza made their first casts opposite San Martín Hill, because some of the best fish were caught in a deep hole there near the rocks. Soon they passed beyond Tower Island, and then the beach in front, because the red mullet prefer a sandy bottom. And so on from place to place where they thought they could get different kinds of fish which they liked. The sea was like glass and they reached Mouro Island. Mechelín could not forget a daily custom of boat captains when they left the harbor. He took off his hat and said, "Praise be to God," and had everyone say the Apostles' Creed. Sotileza, who had never gone beyond the harbor entrance, began to feel the effects of the almost invisible but constant swell of the waters. Because of this unexpected misfortune, the boat went back inside the bay. Here again Mechelín observed another custom never broken by captains, exclaiming:

"Good Lord, bring us safe into port."

After sailing past the promontory they got ready their jiggers (four hooks at right angles) for catching squid. Carried along by the current, the fishing for squid got started. This can scarcely be called "fishing" because the squid are "taken" so easily. Sotileza, although she had an admirable skill for managing this collection of hooks in the water with the proper touch, lacked

A Day's Fishing

practice in how to remove the hooked squid without the spurt of black ink spattering on the person closest at hand. So it was that the first one she hooked made Andrés look as if he had taken a dive into an inkwell. She had to bite her lips in order not to laugh, and Andrés let out a rather strong interjection. Then she started to laugh like a crazy person. Then Muergo, who was looking fixedly at them, resting his elbows on the idle oar, exclaimed when she got another squid on her hooks:

"Damn! Now there's one for me, Sotileza! Throw the ink of all you catch on me, right in the middle of my face. Ha, ha, ha!"

Sotileza replied with a glance in which was written the intention of throwing on him all the ink she could. Muergo, abandoning his oar, sat down alongside her, ready to receive it. But the squid got away and loosed its ink right on Cole's chest. Of course he hadn't wanted it and hadn't any desire to get mixed up with the squids.

"How lucky you are, boy," roared Muergo, provoked.

He had no sooner said that when he received in his face all the dirty liquid from a squid that Andrés had just pulled in.

"That ain't the same, damn it," exclaimed Muergo, spitting ink and leaning over the gunwale to wash his face, on which one could scarcely make out the black spots.

And thus time passed until noon. The tide was going out, the weather was very warm. Puffs of warm air were coming from the south. These made small waves on the surface of the bay, the waters of which were taking on a deep blue color.

"Let's eat," said Andrés.

"Where?" asked Mechelín.

"The place where we usually eat, over at Ambojo's Grove."

"That's quite a distance from here," replied Mechelín. "Have you noticed that the wind is from the south and there are signs of a real blow?"

"So what?" observed Andrés. "Don't we have the guts to stand a little blow?"

"I'm saying that for your sake and for Sotileza's sake. You

may get your clothes soaked. As far as I am concerned, these trifling waves in the bay don't worry me! Hoist the sail, Cole!"

Cole, helped by Muergo, again hoisted the sail, which flapped in the breeze until Andrés hauled the sheet taut and took the tiller. Then the sail was smooth and motionless while the boat began to slip slowly along in the slight breeze, its prow pointed to the southeast.

A half hour later they reached the spot on the coast of the bay toward which they were headed. The wind had risen a little, and as the beach here is rather level, the backwash covered a good stretch between the open sand and the place where they had run the boat aground.

It was agreed that Cole would take care of the boat to see that it didn't get washed ashore completely, which might happen if too much time was used in unloading cargo and passengers. Andrés took from the basket a generous share of provisions for him. Mechelín, because of his infirmities, allowed Muergo to carry him ashore. Then, while Andrés was getting ready to carry Sotileza ashore, Muergo ran back from the beach, grabbed her by the waist and carried her ashore. She laughed heartily. Then Andrés jumped with one prodigious leap from the gunwhale to the dry part of the beach, where he sank into the sand up to his ankles.

Muergo, who was ahead of him, continued walking without putting down his burden. With Sotileza in his arms, he reached the edge of the paths which start from the sandy beach, and still showed no indication of putting her down. All the while she was laughing, insulting Muergo, slapping his face and pulling his hair.

"Put her down, you brute," shouted Andrés.

"Let her go, you big beast," said Mechelín.

They might as well have held their breath. Muergo ran and ran, and did not let her go till they reached the woods, where Andrés had planned to eat.

Finally he came out of the woods alone with his crosseyes

A Day's Fishing

shining and shaking his big head, making his long, heavy hair flop around it.

Mechelín talked harshly to Muergo because of what he had done with Sotileza, and Andrés also gave him a scolding. Muergo paid no attention whatever to what Mechelín said, but he did whisper in Andrés' ear, while rubbing his big hands together:

"By damn, that was really fun!"

Andrés replied to that by giving him such a kick in the stern end that it knocked him a couple of yards away. Muergo received this attention with a bestial shudder, a couple of jumps into the air and a loud snort.

Then he picked up the basket of food and a big empty jar that Mechelín was carrying. All of them walked toward the grove of trees, where Sotileza was waiting for them. In the meantime Cole had, with great effort, freed the boat from the bottom, had anchored it, and had lowered the sail. On board, he started to eat the food that had been left for him, and enjoyed the gentle slapping of the waves against the boat and its rocking motion.

The food eaten by the other four in the grove was very delicious and much talked about. The others had to restrain Muergo somewhat because he seemed to have no bottom to his stomach, especially in regard to drink. Andrés and Sotileza drank little more than cool water brought from a nearby spring. They also agreed between themselves to keep a good share of the food for Sidora, much to the disgust of Muergo, who would gladly have eaten all the leavings. Mechelín was grateful for this kind consideration for his wife, and because he felt so well, and under the influence of the pleasant surroundings, he became very talkative—something that only advanced age and illness had been able to lessen—and began a long series of praises of Sidora. One by one, he told of all her virtues and abilities. Then he went back in memory to the days of his youth and told of their love affair and marriage; then their happiness together and his adventures as a fisherman; and then his experiences as a grown man. Finally he hit upon the illnesses of his old age, without noticing that Muergo had gone to sleep in the middle of this long harangue, or that Andrés and Sotileza were listening more to what they were whispering to each other than to what he was saying. Then he was overcome by sleep, stretched out on the ground and started to snore.

Andrés and Sotileza looked at each other then without knowing exactly why. And perhaps without knowing the reason for it, they looked around and saw that everything was deserted and the only sounds were those produced by the wind in the trees.

Sotileza, because of the hot weather and big meal, had a flushed, red face, and as we have said, was more communicative than usual on these fishing trips. This excess of animation was revealed in the light of her eyes and the smile on her pretty mouth. With this and the flush on her cheeks Andrés saw her as he had never seen her before, against that lonely, lulling background. He recalled with indignation the slander of long ago, and in order to correct it he began to change the short expressions, used while Mechelín was talking about his adventures, into definite phrases. And those phrases were compliments. Sotileza, who had never heard him say these things before, did not respond as he had wished, either because of her surprise or some other effect which they produced in her. This inner struggle on her part caused a look to appear on her face that was hard to interpret. But Andrés, dazzled at that moment by the flash of his own internal storm, was able to interpret her look and changed everything into reality. Being thus deluded, he took one of her hands and put his left arm around her waist, while he was murmuring exaggerated, fiery expressions in her ear. Then the girl, as if caught in the coils of a serpent, shook herself loose from his gentle embrace. At the same time her eyes flashed angrily and the expression on her face changed in such a way that Andrés moved a good distance from her and felt that his enthusiasm was vanishing, as if someone had thrown a pitcher of cold water on him.

A Day's Fishing

"From that distance," the indignant young lady said fiercely, "you can say all you want to—provided you don't talk to me again like you just did. Not from you, who are from a much higher social class, and not even from my social equals should I hear anything that should not be said in front of Mechelín."

Andrés felt the force of this brusque lesson in the middle of his heart and said to Sotileza:

"You are more than right. I have done wrong, because . . . well, I don't know why. Please forgive me."

But, even though he expressed it thus, other wrong was still inside him. In such misfortunes good men's vanity suffers most, and Andrés' had been wounded badly. This was especially true because her rough scorn toward such a generous young man as he did not agree with her apparent approval of the monster Muergo when he had carried her in his arms not too long before. The allusion to the poor, honest fisherman sleeping near him also had touched his soul, not because it was undeserved, but because Mechelín must have had the same idea as Sotileza. Thus it would have avoided having a poor fisherman's daughter remind him of what was hurting his conscience most. In short: being put to shame in this episode, he thought and felt as any other man equally honorable, sane and reflective would have thought in an identical situation.

In the meantime, Sotileza, with no signs of her anger, started to pick up the tablecloths and to place the utensils and leftovers from the meal in the basket. In doing so she wakened the two sleepers: Mechelín by giving him a gentle shake, and Muergo by throwing water out of the jar on him. He sat up, letting out a roar. Mechelín stood up, yawning and rubbing his eyes. As the clouds were growing darker and the south wind rising, they all hurried to return to the beach about the middle of the afternoon.

No one had remembered Cole, who had stretched out to sleep on the sail, folded on the gunwale. The fish they had caught during the morning were in water in the bottom of the boat. The three people had to yell loud and often to waken

Cole, but finally he woke up. He hauled in the anchor and brought in the boat. The distance was shorter than during the morning because of the wind and rising tide. As it was not so easy to jump from the sand to the boat as it had been from the boat to the beach, Andrés allowed Muergo to carry him, and had to resign himself to seeing Sotileza again in Muergo's arms. She allowed him to do this without the slightest protest, but had been so harsh with Andrés for squeezing her much less.

When all were in the boat, Mechelín took control of it because he was the oldest and in view of the fact that there really might be a blow, because the wind was rising more and more. Andrés put himself under the command of this expert sailor. Mechelín sat down in the stern, took the tiller and adjusted the sheet to his own liking. The canvas snapped smooth and loud like the head of a tambourine. The boat started on its course, bouncing on the waves that were beating against the bow, like a fiery horse that finds a barrier on its road.

Andrés had thrown his waterproof over his shoulders, but Sotileza was unprotected because Mechelín had not wanted her to use his dirty old one. Muergo and Cole had no other protection than the clothes they had on. In order not to get her new dress wet, Sotileza had no other choice than to accept half of Andrés' raincoat, which he offered her insistently.

This handsome couple were seated close together under this waterproof covering, protected from the spray. Andrés, remembering the past, tried not to molest his companion, but it was impossible not to touch her somewhere due to the limited size of his coat.

Muergo and Cole were bailing out the water that was coming in. Mechelín kept his eyes on the course and the sails. Streams of water were running down Muergo's and Cole's faces and Muergo's matted hair was dripping like a thatched roof in a sleet storm.

Suddenly Andrés said to Sotileza in a whisper:

"This is about the place where my sailboat capsized one afternoon, with a wind about like this."

A Day's Fishing

"That's a lot of consolation for me," replied Sotileza in the same tone. "And how did you make out?"

"Another boat that was following me picked me up and then towed my boat in for me."

Then they both kept quiet for a while until the boat was closer in, near the first anchored boats. Andrés whispered then:

"About here a strong gust of wind upset my *Zephyr*."

"And you?"

"I had to hold onto the boat in the water until a rowboat from a ship came to rescue me. I didn't make out so well that day because I fell underneath the capsized boat, and the water was cold."

"Two duckings for you. That ought to be about enough for a fellow your age."

"Two, eh? That's what you think. I have already been upset seven times—and I hope today is number eight."

"What an idea, Andrés!"

"It isn't as bad as you think, Sotileza, because I would like to be in a situation where you would consider my arms as strong and useful, say, as those of Muergo."

"Listen to what a tune you are singin' now."

"Do these words of mine offend you?"

"Yes, they do, 'cause they have nothin' to do with the matter."

"Then that means that they are not wanted."

At that time, a big splash of water hit the boat when it entered a course between lines of anchored boats. Here the wind was stronger and the billows higher. Mechelín, in view of what he knew was coming, suggested to Andrés that they proceed to the leeward of the breakwater instead of going to the High Street docking space. That is what Mechelín did very skillfully, much to the pleasure of all.

Andrés picked out the fish he wanted sent to his home and to Don Venancio Liencres, leaving the rest for Mechelín to do with as he chose. He said good-by to everybody good-naturedly. He took leave of Sotileza half affectionately and half resentfully, and started to his house, while the others took everything movable and edible from the boat. After leaving it well tied up, they started up High Street carrying the equipment. They were followed at a distance by the silent Cleto, who had witnessed, without being seen, the disembarking, saying to himself:

"While Andrés is along to protect her, I don't mind."

17 ✒ THE NIGHT OF THAT SAME DAY

Andrés slept badly that night. The foolish step that he had taken in the grove was a failing in his obligations. The old couple on the ground floor, Sotileza herself and the shy Cleto liked him, even loved him, precisely because he was honorable, because he was meek and generous and because they believed him capable of sharing with them his last crust of bread, and would fight it out with anybody in the street to defend the life or good name of any or all of them! What would Sidora or Mechelín say if they had seen him in that moment of madness, or if they had read his thoughts on many other occasions? How would the trusting Cleto judge him if he suspected? Cleto, who had found him so indignant and so noble when he told him of the slander with which the women of his house persecuted him! But especially, what would Sotileza think of him?

He could not live tranquilly in the situation which resulted from his action that afternoon, as he examined it there that night with his head on his pillow. Consequently he would try to see Sotileza face to face as soon as an opportunity was presented. He would talk with her about what happened, calmly, coolly and slowly. He would blame his slip on the temptations presented by the place, the murmuring of the wind, the salt air— on anything at all. Perhaps he would give as his motive a sudden desire to test her virtue—that all could be decided in due time. The important thing was to be as he should be, and in his place. If by talking his prestige should grow in her eyes, and she should carry this admiration to the extreme . . . Then, and then only would be the occasion of changing roles and letting Sotileza get the lesson that she deserved! That is what he planned to do unless the very strength of the desire and the obviousness of the wish should oblige him to yield! But in this light, it was a different matter, and not being to blame, he would also be free of all responsibility.

Regardless of how important all this was, it was not his only reason for sleeping badly, for often disturbed thoughts have the habit of linking themselves with others!

As soon as he reached home from the fishing trip, he went straight to his room without replying a single word to the many said to him by his mother, half lovingly and half angrily, about the risks he ran, his appearance, the girl he was making love to and other things. There he shaved, washed and changed into clean Sunday clothes which he found all ready for him within reach. These had been prepared ahead of time by his mother who doted on that boy who was so noble, so gallant, so handsome but still such a ragged fellow! Why that very night, if she had not examined his dress carefully, he would have gone out with a cane, an opera hat, but no necktie.

"It is too bad that with the face and build you have the good Lord did not give you the art of being a decent person to the same degree that the devil gave you to out-do the most slovenly, poorly dressed fisherman!"

That is what she said to him while tying his necktie. Then, while straightening out the folds of his tight-fitting Prince Albert coat, she arranged the pleats of his shirt front, brushed his shoulders with a clothes brush, adjusted the hang of his trouser legs over his patent leather shoes, the tops of which were red moroccan leather.

"If you were another kind of person, there would be no need for your mother to cause you this unpleasantness every time you dress like a gentleman. But since you are as you are, son, how angry you make me sometimes! I wish that your father would hurry up and get back from his trip and start to keep his promise not to sail again! When he can look after you we'll see whether he can do with you what I have not been able to do. It is all right if you go to sea once in a while, but not so much as if it were your work! What do you think? Look at those hands! They even have callouses on the palms! Putting kid gloves on hands like that! At least for the sake of repaying the attentions that the Liencres show you, you ought to be a little more thoughtful about certain things. To whom would it occur, except to you, to go fishing all day when you knew that you were invited to go to the theater tonight with such a distinguished family? Well, we'll see how you behave! Be careful not to leave in the middle of the show. Wait until it is ended, and accompany them home. Give your arm to Mrs. Liencres or her daughter when you leave their home to go to the theater, and the same thing when you come down the stairs from the boxes. Because now you are going straight to look for Tolín, who is waiting for you in his room. That's what he told me this morning when we came out of eleven o'clock mass at the Church of the Jesuits. Now, you are properly attired, and you are tall and handsome, by gosh! Why shouldn't I say so if it is the truth?"

These incessant naggings bothered Andrés a great deal. If they were to the point in regard to his tastes, they were scarcely deserved in regard to all the rest. She wanted him to be elegant and distinguished by dint of adornments, glances, wit and kindnesses. That is to say, by making him a slave to his dress, to his speech and the stupid rules and regulations imposed on drawing rooms and public parks by a few dudes who weren't worth anything. Andrés, with his natural gracefulness, his manly bearing and his ingenuousness, was one of the few individuals who fit in well everywhere.

He went, then, "in full regalia" to Tolín's home. When he was crossing the vestibule, going to Tolín's room, he met Luisa, already arrayed in all her finery for the theater. This impetuous young man thought it very becoming to her and that's what he blurted out to her for a greeting, because he had enough confidence to do so:

"You really are lovely, Luisa."

"And what difference does that make to you?" she replied, passing along without stopping.

Andrés took this literally, and for that reason was quite surprised by her gruffness. In fact, he was so surprised and so resentful that he complained about it to Tolín as soon as he reached his room.

"I'm telling you, pal, that some of these days I am going to give her a piece of my mind. She seems to have taken a dislike to me."

"As if that were a dislike," replied Tolín while waxing the drooping ends of his thin mustache.

"Well if it isn't a dislike, what is it?"

"Just a whim to have fun with you. There are so many confidences between you two!"

"Well, I don't like that kind of fun!"

"Sure, man, yes. It is nothing more than that—or perhaps some resentment she might have."

"About what?"

"How do I know? In any case, the whole incident is not worth a damn."

"To you, maybe, but it is to me."

"And why to you?"

"It seems to me, Tolín, that when one comes into a house every day and is received this way . . . Because this has been happening to me for several days."

"Man, if you look at it a certain way, that indicates affection and esteem. If she tried to kick you out of the house once and for all . . . because that girl has a way of getting things done quickly."

"I'm beginning to see!"

"What do you mean, you're beginning to see? What you should see is what she does with the fellows who really annoy her. I surely felt sorry for that poor Calandrias."

"Calandrias—who is Calandrias?"

"Don't you remember the kid we used to call Pachín (Francisco)? Well this fashion plate is sighing for her all the time and walks up and down in front of our house nearly the whole day—and she gives him only harsh rebuffs, and slams the door in his face—and makes faces at him from the balcony. At the dance we had at a picnic on St. John's Day she refused to dance with him—but in such a way! I'm telling you, I don't know how that man has the courage or the dignity to continue walking up and down in front of our house for my sister's sake. Well, there are several fellows like him, but she is the daughter of Don Venancio Liencres. Now you see! She treats them all the same way—harshly and coldly. And the worst of it all is that their families are all intimate friends of ours and visit us often— since they are of the best families! Mother is beside herself with these fits of temper of Luisa's. And she is right. What more could she want, man, at her age, than to have so many and such good suitors from whom to choose the one she likes best. Well, nothing—she is like a stone—just like a stone. So, now you are complaining. Of course all these things I am telling you are so that you can make up your own mind and in the confidence of our friendship. You understand?"

At this moment two loud knocks were heard at the door and Luisa's voice, which said:

"We are going!"

Andrés opened the door immediately. As his friend had finished dressing and primping, both of them went into the corridor, where Andrés had to greet Mrs. Liencres, who, although somewhat old and dried up, was as elegantly dressed as her daughter. Don Venancio was holding forth just then at the Recreation Club and would come to the theater at the last minute, if other more interesting matters did not prevent him from doing so. Tolín stepped up to give his arm to his mother to go down the stairs, and Andrés offered his to Luisa with the expectation of receiving a rebuff. But he didn't get any, fortunately. However, he did get rather a frigid look and she said these words, which left the poor young man confused and perspiring:

The Night of That Same Day

"But don't step on my dress and tear it like you did the last time!"

On the way they stopped at the door of Don Silverio Trigueras, a wheat dealer with plenty of money. The elegant Angustias, daughter of the family, came down putting on her gloves, with plenty of shining ornaments on her head. She was the famous beauty of Santander for whom Tolín Liencres was sighing in his pensive moments and for whom he was waxing the ends of his mustache. He outdid himself greeting her. She accepted the customary greetings of the other two women, and from Andrés the best the poor fellow knew how to make, and all continued together toward the theater.

Once in the box, Tolín sat down back of the young lady of his dreams. Andrés sat very near Luisa in order to leave more space for her mother. Having got up before the sun, and having worked a great deal all day, he spent most of the time sleeping during each act, and in the intermissions he went out to the corridor to smoke. All that he could remember about the whole affair was that Don Venancio Liencres asked him whether the performance was in verse or in prose.

"I think that it's in verse," Andrés had replied. "I mean, no, maybe it is in prose."

"It's all the same," Don Venancio had replied.

Then came the departure from the theater. Again Andrés offered his arm to Luisa, because Don Venancio gave his to his wife, and Tolín could not be kept away from the lady for whom he sighed.

In the street, one could see the well-known row of hand lanterns held by servants who were waiting for their respective families. Even in those days, in spite of the fact that gas lights had been installed for over a year, there was quite a remnant of that old class vanity, expressed by a big lantern with four glass sides, with three or four candles, so that the rich people could go around the streets in the late hours.

Andrés noticed that the wind, which had gone down some when he had left home, had grown much worse. As he knew that the wind would be blowing harder at the street intersections near the docks than any place in town, he dared to advise Luisa to continue holding his arm until they reached her home. This time he was not snubbed. The others thought this a wise observation and they obeyed it to the letter. Andrés and Luisa were ahead of all the rest, except of course the servant with the lantern.

When they came to the Street of the Martyrs they could hear the wind whistling in the rigging and cordage of the boats at the dock, and its loud roar at the nearby intersections. Some passing gusts made Luisa's silk dress rustle. She became so frightened that she violently seized Andrés' arm, as strong and firm as an oak branch.

"Hold on hard and don't be afraid," Andrés said to her. "This wind won't take me away regardless of how hard it blows."

Luisa held on with both hands so hard that he could almost feel her heartbeats on his right arm, especially while they were near the dock taking Angustias Trigueras to her home.

As soon as Andrés was again in the relative calm of a back street, he said to Luisa in order to calm her, and especially to say something:

"If you should ask me, I would say that it was blowing harder this afternoon."

To which Luisa replied at once, and without the slightest tinge of humor:

"Well, if I had made the wind blow this afternoon, you would have taken a nice dive, I assure you."

Andrés felt that his blushing made his face burn. He remembered that he had said something very similar to Sotileza while they were sheltered from the waves by the same raincoat. He knew that Luisa could not have heard him say that—but she might have seen him.

"What a disposition, woman," he replied confusedly to the remarks of his friend.

"One doesn't need a bad disposition to say those things.

They are just necessary caution, or even works of charity, if you ask me!"

"Caution—works of charity!" exclaimed Andrés now more in control of himself, because Luisa was leading him into the field of insolence, which annoyed him. "Well, what did I do wrong this afternoon?"

"Man alive," replied Luisa very resolutely. "To be exact I do not know, because the sail kept me from seeing half of the boat, and in the other part I could see only three wet forms that turned my stomach."

"I was holding the tiller," said Andrés, resigned to passing as one of the forms that turned her stomach whenever Luisa was convinced that he was not occupying the part of the boat she could not see, where Sotileza was.

Luisa, not deceived by these words, added, without paying much attention to him:

"Well, if you didn't do anything this afternoon, you certainly did enough during the morning."

"During the morning!"

"Yes, sir, during the morning! Do you think that you weren't seen out there going back and forth, hour after hour, with those clumsy sailors and that vulgar woman?"

"That vulgar woman!"

"That's right. That vulgar woman! The hussy! Do you think that is all right? What will people who saw you say?"

"And what could they say?"

"They could criticize, and plenty."

"Well then, why did they look if it was so bad?"

"Well, why do you have to be doing these things where people are looking? Because one does look when it is right in front of the house and one has a good pair of binoculars to look with."

"Yes and a desire to butt into other people's business."

"Other people's business," exclaimed Luisa with a shudder which Andrés could not appreciate, either because of his anger or because of the force of the wind against him.

"Yes, in other people's business, in something that doesn't matter to you," replied Andrés calmly. "Because I have not offended anybody and furthermore was doing my duty."

"Well, it is my business," confirmed Luisa with a voice somewhat changed and nervous. "And it does matter to me a great deal, because you are a friend of the family and a companion of my brother and I don't like to have people say that Tolín has friends who are out at all hours with toughies from the Zanguina Bar and shameless, dirty women. For that reason, and only for that reason, does it matter to me. And if you force me just a little, I'll tell my father so that he can tell your father when he comes back, and get you out of this evil life. And now, I do not need your arm any more and I don't even want you to speak to me."

So saying she let go of his arm. It was true that she did this after having been in tow at the last intersection, and when she was protected from the wind in the vestibule of her home, while the maid who had gone ahead was knocking on the inner door.

The fresh memory of these events was the second theme of the worries which kept Andrés from sleeping in the early hours of that night.

Tolín's sister had never been so meddlesome, so impertinent or so unbearable. For the first time he had heard from her lips the threat to go to her father with the story so that he could tell it later to his father. This pampered, spoiled girl was capable of doing what she said. The matter was certainly not a trifle, but there would be no telling what she would say or what details she would add, in her desire to win her point. Don Venancio was a very formal man and concerned about the good repute of people with whom he had dealings. The airs of his wife could be seen here, as well as the thinking of Andrés' mother. No longer was his father the same light-hearted, impressionable Bitadura whose indulgence could be relied upon by his son who had known how to get at the weakness of his eternal boyishness. Now he was more than fifty years old, and was rich and fat. All of which had changed his disposition. Andrés himself did not have the strength to submit in silence to certain whimsical impositions. He did not know to what extremes a conspiracy plotted by a busybody girl against his honest procedures, might drag him. With such elements, what sauce might not be prepared by the devil for a few days in the body of the tenacious daughter of Don Venancio?

But, after all, this was just a mere supposition. It remained to be seen what time would bring. It could be seen coming, and he could fight against it from a distance. But the other, the other matter, was more urgent and more dangerous for him! And thus he battled with his thoughts until, hours later, he turned over on the other side and went to sleep.

18 GETTING FLEECED

For the first time in his life Andrés, with a perseverance that was somewhat unusual in him, was looking for an occasion to see Sotileza alone. Also for the first time in his life he deceived Tolín with some pretext to be away from the office for a couple of hours.

This happened in the middle of the morning, on a day when Mechelín was out fishing in his boat and Sidora was in the Plaza. Sotileza was working at home, in her usual house dress, which was clean, short and quite scant, as has been described elsewhere. Dressed thus one could admire her sculpturelike beauty better than in her Sunday finery. Andrés had observed that well. He was very glad to find her that way, even though he had hoped he would.

"I have to talk with you," he said as a beginning, not quite sure of his voice.

She noticed his confusion and asked him, startled:

"And why do you come at this time of day, and under these circumstances?"

"'Cause . . . because what I have to tell you should be heard only by you. Sit down and listen."

Andrés sat down in a chair and moved another one close to her, but Sotileza did not want to sit in it. She remained standing, leaning her bare right arm, round and white, on a chest of drawers, while her heavy breathing showed the internal struggle she was having, and replied in a firm voice and a stern look:

"Remember what I told you that Sunday in the woods."

"It's that very thing that I came to talk about."

"I thought that that matter was settled there."

"Not entirely, and for what wasn't entirely settled I have come now."

"Well, since then, we have seen each other a couple of times. Why have you kept still until today?"

"I have already told you. Because it is something for us alone."

"And I have already told you that I do not want to hear you say anything that can't be said in front of decent people."

"It is precisely because you have told me that that I have come to see you. Sit down here, Silda. Sit down, please, and I promise not to take any liberties in word or deed. I want only to take from you the grief that others caused you, and take from myself a burden that tires me very much."

Sotileza, gasping and pale, mechanically placed her beautiful body on the chair which Andrés indicated.

As soon as she was sitting beside him so close that he could hear her breathing, he exclaimed:

"And you may be sure that I need all my will power to keep that promise when I see you so beautiful—and we are alone like this!"

Silda got up quickly and went back to lean against the chest of drawers.

"Don't think that I'm afraid," she said, "to be with you,

'cause I have strength enough to handle anybody who fails to show respect for me."

"Then why did you go so far away from me?" asked the amazed boy.

"Just because I don't want to hear you say things when I am near you that show you to be somethin' I don't like to see in you."

"Well, then, so that you can see me with no displeasure, and only for that reason, have I waited for this occasion. Please believe me, Silda. I swear by these crosses," he explained as he crossed his thumbs and index fingers.

"You're sure takin' a good road to begin!"

"That was just a saying. I swear that I will not keep any of my thoughts from you so that you can see me with my heart in the palm of my hand. But if this frankness offends you, you will never hear the like again from my lips. I swear it, Silda. Please sit down here again, and tie my hands if you think I will offend you with them. Then, after you hear me, if you think that my words hurt you, tear my tongue out for saying them—but, please, sit down here and listen to me."

Sotileza sat down again, but mechanically and very pale, half haughty and half affected. Andrés, who had always considered her cold and distant, in complete control of her unfathomable emotions, was surprised by that sudden, unexpected disturbance and show of strength. He saw that the girl had emotions also! And thus his own increased! Vile human frailty! But he had just sworn that his procedure would be honorable. Arming himself with sufficient will power to carry it out, he began to talk as follows:

"Silda, that afternoon I said some words and I went too far in some things that brought a scolding from you which was very harsh! Thus, because of the misdeed which I committed, I confess that I deserved the punishment. During all the years we have known each other, I have not given you any occasion to suspect my intentions by any bad word or any indication of any evil thoughts. In this house everybody, and you first of all, would have been willing to have me guard your honor. Would you be willing to do that after that Sunday afternoon? Tell me frankly, Silda."

"No," she replied without hesitating.

"Well, that is the pain that I have here inside my heart, Sotileza. That grieves me here inside and keeps me from sleeping at night and makes me restless during the day. I do not want anyone in this house to mistrust me, where I am accustomed to have all doors open for me, like the sun, when I arrive. I want to get back to those times, Silda, back in your esteem and the confidence of everybody."

"You ain't lost my esteem or the confidence of anyone, Andrés. Everyone here knows what he owes you, and I, too, know what I owe you. There ain't no ungrateful people here."

"I don't want to be liked merely for the favors that I do, but because of my own worth, and I know that I am not now as worthy in your eyes as I was a short time ago."

Then Silda exclaimed with a warmth of tone unknown in her:

"And if you was calculatin' on that, why didn't you spring it at the proper time, in order not to do what you did?"

"In the reply to that question is exactly the apology for that act and for those words. It is the only reason that I can offer you to get back in your esteem and your confidence. Now you see why this reason couldn't be given in front of witnesses without disclosing the cause for it. That remedy would be worse than the illness itself."

"I do not know," said Sotileza with a tone and an expression of crudest sincerity, "that there can be any apology for those things in men of such a high social class as you with women of such low social class as I am."

Andrés felt the force of this argument.

"Well then," he replied, seeking in the false effects of his voice and his attitude a determination which he did not find in his arguments, "are you one of those women who believe that there are any differences in class that matter when it is a ques-

Getting Fleeced

tion of those things? Your beauty, covered by those few ragged clothes you have on, clean as silver, is it not as lovely as that adorned by silk and diamonds? What a rude, coarse young man feels toward you, cannot that same emotion be felt, perhaps even more keenly, by a man of my social conditions? That which the amenities of the country and the influence of nature, in all its splendor, may make him feel toward a woman like you, cannot they make me feel that too? And while we are talking about this matter, what would be so strange about it, with the occasion so propitious and the place so pleasing, if I should try to take advantage of these opportunities to test your virtue, as is often done in plays?"

Silda replied to this confidential interview with a cold, jesting smile.

"That is to say, you don't believe me?" asked Andrés, very provoked.

"No," she replied calmly.

"Why not?"

" 'Cause a lie can be seen from a long ways off, even in the way it comes. And don't tire yourself with useless words about that. It is the pure truth. For that reason I would have believed you more today in the grief which you say you feel by weeping over it here wholeheartedly than by tryin' to use a trick."

Andrés remained for a moment without knowing what to reply to these cruel, conclusive words. Later he replied, just to have something to say:

"It is not enough, Silda, just to make a statement; you have to give reasons."

"I would gladly give one, just one that is worth many more," replied the girl, restraining the impulses of her character.

"And why don't you give it to me then?" asked Andrés, not as valiant as he seemed.

" 'Cause I'm afraid that you'll resent it."

"I promise not to. Why was that the truth?"

" 'Cause I recognized the evil thoughts that made you do it."

"You recognized them? How?"

"'Cause I read 'em many times in your eyes."
"When?"
"For quite a while."
"Silda!"
"That's what I said, Andrés. You wanted my reasons, didn't you? Well, now you know 'em."

Andrés was disarmed and wounded in the deepest part of his conscience. Sotileza knew that and hastened to say to him:

"You promised me not to be offended with the reason I would give you. Keep your word."

"I'll keep it," replied Andrés, more with his lips than with his heart. "I'll not even insist on the way your eyes deceived you when you read that in mine. But tell me, Sotileza, when you discovered these evil thoughts in my eyes, why didn't you tell me?"

"'Cause, if my eyes did not deceive me, you should have left those thoughts outside this house. It wasn't up to me to toss them out of it."

This was another thrust in the heart. Andrés by now did not know which side of this struggle to get on, as it was a struggle without a single advantage for him. He appealed to the suggestions of his pride, which was what was bothering him most, and then said to his tenacious adversary:

"Then those thoughts of mine didn't frighten you?"

"I was afraid they might be noticed by people who would have cried over them as a real misfortune."

"But for yourself you were not afraid?"

"Why should I? I was sorry to see 'em in you, but nothin' more."

"And why were you sorry?"

"'Cause the time might come . . . the time that's here now."

"You mean the time for giving me a lesson like the one you are giving me now?"

"I don't know enough to do that, Andrés, and I'll do only

enough to defend myself by replyin' to the matter, as is the law of God."

"But you have already told me that, once you discovered my bad thoughts, it was not up to you to toss them out of this house."

"Yes, that is what I said."

"Then I should toss them out. That is to say, go away from here forever, since I will be carrying my thoughts with me."

"Or come without 'em. That would be the same."

"And what am I to do so that you will believe that I do not bring them?"

"Just don't bring 'em. That's enough."

Andrés, out of self-respect, did not wish to lie by insisting that Sotileza was mistaken in what she said about his evil intentions. From what he was hearing, he knew that his intentions were showing through. To insist on denying them was to be more and more unworthy in the eyes of that virtuous girl who liked him more as a repentant sinner than as a man of false virtue. But, at the same time he considered that those evil ideas, so hated in him by Sotileza, in another brain might not frighten her so much. He even remembered the pleasure with which the scrupulous girl allowed herself to be squeezed by the arms of the stupid Muergo on the Ambojo Beach. It was that same Muergo in whose eyes he himself had read lewdness of such a degree that Sotileza surely must have noticed it. Then what was not a misdemeanor for the ugly, dirty Muergo was a crime for him, a cultured, genteel youth. It was so great a crime that it would close the door of her home to him. Was he less in the eyes of Sotileza than that monster? This was incredible, and it would be a real folly even to manifest doubts about it. But the fact of her preference for Muergo existed. This showed that Sotileza did have more scruples about the persons who were motivated by such thoughts than about thoughts of that kind. This fact did not lessen the virtue of Silda in Andrés' eyes since he knew how much influence is exerted in the meaning of certain acts by the condition of the person who performs them or consents to their being done. But being in the faulty position he was, that fact offered him a way out. Perhaps he could take advantage of it to get out of the position which Sotileza presented to him with her tremendous reasons. To get out of it in that manner, that is to say by adjusting himself to Silda's conditions, was to oblige him never to return to her home. Because any man who had sworn to what he had should sacrifice everything for the good reputation of the woman who complained about his evil intentions. To not return to her home was an undertaking too great for his strength of character, particularly since he had given cause for not returning and since he had just become convinced that the moral confusion which had so surprised him in Silda when he began to talk to her was not the realization of his fond hopes that the roles which each of them had enacted in the scene in Ambojo Grove should come to be reversed. Nevertheless, let anyone ask him at that moment how he was faring in the way of high and honorable thoughts. No one else's could equal them! Such was the power of pride!

All this which has taken so long to tell here—and I hope that it has not been of little worth to the reader—became jumbled in Andrés' brain during the few moments of silence which followed the last words of Sotileza. Taking, then, the point of view of suspicion by reason of his mental reasonings, Andrés began to recall, in a complaining tone, the happy years of their childhood and early youth, when he spent so much time in the company of this innocent orphan girl and her kind protectors. In recalling these pleasant incidents he talked about affection, abnegation, serenity, peace and noble confidence. Suddenly a slight spot appears in the smiling background of that picture. There is a breath of suspicion. The spot becomes a cloud, the cloud spreads out—then good-by light and confidence and gladness! The old friend, the old stand-by, is now the bad man from whom it is necessary to keep virtuous girls, the playmate of his childhood . . .

"I can't submit to that, Sotileza," exclaimed Andrés at the

end of his lamentations. "I cannot leave this house because of that suspicion, after having entered it as I have."

"Well, who's throwin' you out, Andrés?" asked Sotileza, astonished after having heard, without emotion, his declarations.

"You are, because you tell me . . ."

"I never said that," replied Sotileza calmly. "I did tell you that you shouldn't come back with those thoughts which have come out here 'cause you have wanted them to. Is that throwin' you out of the house? And who am I to do that?"

"You always come back to those blessed thoughts," exclaimed the impetuous young man, irritated when he thought of the zeal with which they were placed in front of him so that he might crash against them. Then allowing himself to be carried away by the impulses of his injured pride, he added vehemently: "And if by chance you were right, Silda; if those evil thoughts had taken possession of me, what would have been so unusual about it? Haven't you ever seen yourself in a looking glass? Don't you know that you are beautiful? And am I made of stone, by any chance?"

While Andrés was talking thus, Sotileza had changed expression again. Moving her chair at least two feet from him she said in a tone and with an expression impossible to describe:

"Andrés! When you try to make things better, you only make 'em worse!"

"I don't know how they are getting," exclaimed Andrés, beside himself. "What I know is that I have to tell you what I told you, because it burns me up inside when I try to keep it quiet."

"Holy Virgin! And with all that you are darin' to deny . . ."

"I am not denying or affirming, Silda. I am doing both. You do the same!"

"'Cause I am on the side where I belong. You are killin' me with grief, Andrés!"

And Andrés saw then in the eyes of Sotileza an expression, and something like a veil of dew, that he had never noticed in them.

"You say that I am killing you with grief? Why?"

" 'Cause that ain't the way I want you to be in order to like you, but the way you were before."

"And why can't you like me the way I am now?" asked Andrés blinded by despair and vehemence.

"Because, just because," said Silda. She did not take her eyes from Andrés and got up quickly from the chair. Then she backed up a couple of steps holding onto the chair and continued thus in an attitude produced by the peculiar mixture of haughtiness and supplication in her. Then she said: "By the Holy Virgin, Andrés, don't ask me any more about that—and listen to what you have obliged me to tell you! You know as well as I that ever since you picked me up in the street the people of this house have given me, out of charity, much more than I deserve. I was alone and destitute, and here I have parents and a home. I could die, like any other young girl. But they are already old and in the course of events I may be alone again the world. In order to be of some worth in it, I have no other wealth than my honor! Please, Andrés! You know how much that is worth to me. You helped me when I was an innocent little girl. Now guard my honor more than anyone else!"

"Do you think that I would steal that from you?" exclaimed Andrés, sincerely surprised at her suspicion.

"Not steal it from me," replied Sotileza at once with brave spirit. "Not you nor no one else can do that. But appearances are all that are necessary, and you know well what scandalous tongues are like."

By now Andrés was reckless. His impetuous rashness took him from injury to injury. But his nature was noble and his heart always responded to the calls from its depths. Furthermore, the insistence of imposing himself by force of despair on such an indomitable firmness as Sotileza's, which he had never recognized until now, was entirely useless.

"You are right in everything, Sotileza," he said with an attitude that well suited the sweet tone and meaning of his words. "And you are telling me such things with such reason

Getting Fleeced

that I realize that even with the best of desires, I have, in my persistence, at times gone along roads that honorable men do not use. Please remember what I swore to you when I came in here not long ago. That is true, and that is why I came. All the rest came out because—because the devil mixed up my ideas and then used my words to his liking for the ruination of souls. Forget about them, Silda. Forget about all that and forgive me!"

Then, surely, Andrés was talking with his heart. He was such an impressionable young man!

As Sotileza knew him well, she came closer to him and said:

"That's really talkin'. That is puttin' yourself in your true light, Andrés! Now that you are in control of yourself, now that God has removed the bandage from your eyes, don't wait for the devil to get back. Go away and let me alone as I was. Only with that, will I pardon you with all my heart for all these things."

Andrés got up from his chair ready to leave. The stinging sensations of his hurt pride, irritated again by the last words of Sotileza, did not prevent him from recognizing the power of the reason for her wanting him to leave.

"I'll do what you ask," he said to her. "But, is it your intention to close the door on me forever, when I go out now? I will not submit to that, Silda, and much less now than ever because I know this about you."

"Don't get angry again, Andrés, for heaven's sake! I do not wish to close these doors on you forever, and I couldn't even if I wished to because I do not have the authority to do it. What I wish, you already know too well. The evil is not just enterin', but in the occasion which you sought to enter, because there are eyes and tongues that live only to hurt others. And if I, for what I am, do not seem to be worthy for you to consider in this matter a little, do it at least for these poor old people, who would die of shame the day that I lose my good reputation."

"Silda!" exclaimed Andrés, then in the midst of one of those bursts of enthusiasm which he occasionally had, "I am not worth as much as you deserve!"

Without daring to look at her, because she was really a temptress at that moment, he left the house quickly.

And he had gone in there believing that the roles played by each of them in the little scene in Ambojo Grove would be changed!

But how the devil had that shy, silent girl had such sensibility and strength to give him the lesson she did? How was it possible for a woman of such balanced judgment and such high thoughts to become a mountain bramble with him and the people who loved her most and be a soft ball of combed cotton with a beast like the horrible Muergo? What unusual inclinations did such noticeable preferences indicate? Of what material was that woman made, who did not have a girl friend of any intimacy in the whole street, and who did not miss the company of anyone, who seemed not to be moved by anything, yet who was sensitive and intelligent and virtuous and grateful and courageous and at the same time had given voluntarily the sweetness of her heart to a stinking, abominable person?

This Andrés was thinking as he stepped outside. He was so distracted by what he was thinking that he failed to see the fish seller, Carpia, who passed him some ten steps down the street. He noticed neither the look she gave him when she stopped a moment, nor did he hear the words which that terrible woman said, with the idea that everyone in the street should hear them:

"The devil! He's going so fast that he's burnin' up the road! I should say so! Mechelín's at sea, and Sidora's in the Plaza, and the young girl's all alone at home. And there goes decency out with the sweepin's! Wow! That for her, the little pig! Ah, the devil take me! If I had only been at home! There'll be another time, 'cause he'll be back to get the same bait! I want to catch both of you in such a situation as this, in broad daylight, so that your face will show what little shame you have! Indecent girl!"

19   HOW ABOUT THE MOAT IN YOUR OWN EYE?

During all this time poor Cleto was not getting over his love for Sotileza. Pa'e 'Polinar had tried on three occasions to carry out his promise to sound out the wishes of Sidora and Mechelín. But he was never free from a certain fear. Those devilish Mocejón women were always on the balcony, or on the sidewalk or shouting in the middle of the street. It was fortunate that they did not discover his intentions when he went up or down the street at full speed as if his duties called him far from there. Cleto was calling at his door every day at nightfall. Inside of his house the good priest was really sweating over the task of writing his sermon. Cleto would say to him:
"Ain't there nothin' new?"
Padre Apolinar would tell him what had happened, encouraging him with hope for better luck another day. Then Cleto, sad and crestfallen, would go to spend a few moments in Mechelín's home. He usually found Sotileza rather cool, and the old folks as affectionate as ever. From all appearances they had not found out anything about the blows that he and Muergo had exchanged at the entrance to their house. Since that time these two fellows had met only once and that was inside this same house in front of the people there. Then they growled and bristled at each other but this did not attract any attention because it was nothing new for them to act that way.
The last time he had seen Pa'e 'Polinar Cleto was told:
"Darn you, Cleto, I wish you would take these things with less enthusiasm because your sighs do not coincide conveniently with my work which right now is real swell . . . really swell, by darn! So, either cool down your forge a little or keep bearing the delay good-naturedly because that is what you need most. See here, Cleto, either I am greatly mistaken or that morsel is not for you. By darn, you certainly aimed high. And

with Sotileza and her dislike for your whole family . . . I'm telling you, Cleto, that even the devil himself could not have piled up so many obstacles in front of this longing that you say is consuming you. Let me get back to my books and my papers. Time is flying and the sermon has to be a good one that will be worthy of notice. I can tell you now that it will be a regular three-masted one!"

All these reflections were fuel for the fire in which Cleto was being consumed. He left Pa'e 'Polinar resolved to do for himself as much as his strength and his power of speech would allow.

Walking toward High Street he met Colo about the time he reached the intersection. Cleto liked Colo because he was a fellow with a good disposition and good conduct. They were good friends, and because they were, Colo had told him several times about his love for Pachuca (Francisca), the youngest of three daughters of his neighbor Chumbao (sinker), the owner of the fishing boat on which he worked. If the next draft for compulsory naval service did not get him, they would be married as soon as the drawing was made. Everything was all arranged for that. Cleto had heard all this many times and it made his mouth water. Who better than that good friend, so expert in these matters, to listen to him with affection and to help him with his advice?

He approached him rather cheerfully. In order to make his problem seem big, he made such a point of beginning way back that Colo, thinking that he was talking to him about things that he already knew well, stopped him in his story to ask him with lively interest:

"Do you know what is goin' on, Cleto?"

"What?" asked Cleto with great curiosity, fearful that what was happening might have some relation to what he was telling his friend.

"Well, it so happens that the people from the Lower Town are goin' to challenge those of the Upper Town to a boat race on the Day of the Martyrs."

"Let them challenge, by God!" exclaimed Cleto, kicking the ground angrily. "I thought that it was something else. We can talk about that later, man! Let me finish my story first."

Colo was not inclined to do that because he was in a hurry. He told Cleto:

"I just came from the Zanguina Bar where they were talkin' about the race. As far as the men there are concerned, it is all set if we do not back out. The prize will be $16 in gold. It seems that there will also be a big prize for climbin' the greased pole. It's all goin' to be a big fiesta to help amuse the summer visitors as well as the folks in Santander. The way I see it is the fellas from the Lower Town wanta try to make up fer their loss to us two years ago on St. Peter's Day. Just as if they could get even! Now I'm goin' to run along to tell Sobano what's up. See whether they can count on you this time like they did before. So watch out, Cleto. I ain't got nothin' more ta say."

The excited Colo spoke no more and hurried off up the street, leaving Cleto with the bitterness of his grief unexpressed. Right away he thought of Andrés and decided to confide his heart's secret to him. The scruples that had prevented him from doing this before were of no value. But Andrés did not go to Mechelín's home that night.

The next day Cleto waited in the vestibule of Andrés' office to see him.

Since his conversation face to face with Sotileza, Andrés seemed like a different person. He was less boisterous in his movements and much more absent-minded and less gay in his speech. At times he expelled the air from his lungs like a southern squall, making sounds with a trembling effect and a variety of tones, as if he were thus trying to get rid of the thoughts that caused his chest to swell.

Cleto, who had plenty to do with his own inner longings without noticing anything new in the appearance of his well-to-do friend, explained to him in a few words what he wanted to tell him. A kick in the shins would not have produced in Andrés as deep and sudden an impression as Cleto's declarations.

His first reaction was to insult him and strike him. That such an individual would dare to set his ambitions on an object of such value! And furthermore that he should ask him to help carry out his plans. And after what he himself had just gone through, and what was happening to him now! Didn't that all seem like a joke that cruel fate was playing?

But he controlled himself to such a degree that Cleto noticed only a few flashes of the inner storm which appeared in his eyes. The poor afflicted Cleto thought that these flashes were a sign of how great the idea seemed to his good, rich friend. Andrés confirmed Cleto's suspicions at once by showing him all the obstacles in his way and answering him with a few harsh words. In short, he was trying to show him how impossible his love was, and to confuse him with threats. As a result, Padre Apolinar's opinion seemed rosy in comparison.

He left Andrés without saying good-by to him. There seemed to be such a heavy fog around his plans that he drifted through the streets in order to find a way out of his grief, wondering all the while where he could anchor in a safe harbor.

And he was correct in all this thinking, because at this same time Muergo and Sotileza were alone in the front room of her home. Sidora had not yet returned from the fish factory and Mechelín, just back from the tobacco store, was smoking his pipe on the sidewalk.

Muergo had appeared there earlier than usual because the news about the race was entirely correct. He wished to tell his uncle about it as soon as he heard it.

When he reached the house he asked Sotileza where Mechelín was.

"He left to buy some tobacco."

"Gee, I am glad about that. And where is my aunt?"

"She is still in the Plaza. She'll be here in a few minutes."

"Well, I'm sure glad about that too."

"Why, you animal?"

"Well 'cause you're alone, which is just what I like, ho ho! Do you know that there's goin' to be a boat race?"

"When?"

"On the Day of the Martyrs if you Highstreeters don't get scared and back out, by damn. You will really see what pulling an oar is. And you'll lose the gold prize money. A whole ounce of it, Sotileza. Damn, if that was only mine! I sure know what I'd buy ya with it! Man, what a day that's goin' ta be. All that and a sermon by Pa'e 'Polinar. And I'm goin' ta wear my new suit for the first time, new from head ta foot, even with brand-new shoes an' everythin'. Damn."

"Do you already have the cap and the jacket, Muergo?" Sotileza asked with as much interest as that of a mother who watches over the selection of clothes for her son.

"Didn't I tell ya? Since ya insisted so much about it, I saved and saved and saved . . ."

"And just because of that, Muergo? Did you save just because I insisted?"

"And for what other reason?"

"Was it just 'cause I asked you to?"

"Damn. For what other reason do I do anything?" exclaimed the big brute, shuddering from head to foot. "Why don't I go on a drunk every day? And why do I stand workin' for such a guy as Mordaguero? Damn! Just ta please ya, Sotileza. Just because ya wanted me to I got the good suit. For that alone! Tonight I can't eat here, but will ya gimme some bread? I'm hungry!"

What a peculiar girl Sotileza was! In the very same room where she had tamed the impassioned impulses of Andrés with her disillusioning words and her scornful countenance, she was listening to the crudities of Muergo with a smile on her lips and joy showing on her face.

"Listen," she said to the beastly Muergo, on whose hair and clothes still shone the scales of the sardines that he had taken out of the net on the fishing launch, "as soon as you put on that suit, come a runnin' so that I can help arrange it on you before the others notice it. 'Cause you do not know all the details of elegance. Boy, you will be worth seein'!"

"Damn," exclaimed Muergo when he saw the look of joy on her face. "I'll be as pretty as the religious procession, but I won't look as good as you, Sotileza, by damn, 'cause you'll look better than all Christendom dressed up. When ya gimme that bread could ya find a couple of slices of bacon too?"

While Muergo was saying this, with his big bare feet firmly anchored to the floor, with his arms at his side and his cap on the back of his head and his long hair over his eyes, it began to grow dark in the room. With this motive, if not pretext, Sotileza left Muergo standing there and went to the kitchen to light a candle.

When she came back she looked toward the front door, saw Mechelín, and called him to tell him that his nephew was looking for him. Muergo's displeasure at the arrival of Mechelín could be seen clearly on his face and by a certain shudder of his stooped shoulders.

In other times goodhearted old Mechelín would have been excited by the news that his nephew gave him. Now that he did not have the strength to personally take part in the rivalries of the two towns—and his aches and pains robbed him of much of his enthusiasm, or even curiosity—he gave little importance to the events announced by Muergo. However, he did tell him not to take part in the rowing contest if he had any idea about his own worth as an oarsman because it was evident that the Highstreeters would win. Muergo held his ground, arguing in favor of the Lower Town. It made no difference to him how much his brutal assertions hurt his old uncle. Sotileza intervened with a couple of sharp reproaches that made Muergo as soft as a tanned sheepskin. He then agreed with his uncle that the fishermen from the Lower Town were nothing but lazy loafers. After that he began to gnaw on the crust of bread that Sotileza had given him and went out the door, headed for the Zanguina Bar to find out how the plans for the big fiesta were coming along.

Later Sidora came in and repeated what she had heard about the big plans while in the Plaza. She suggested that Mechelín go to the Seville Bar, where people from High Street would be discussing the whole affair.

Cleto arrived soon after Mechelín left. He had not met Muergo on the street because he had come up another way. However, Muergo did meet Andrés. If he had to meet one or the other, it is not known whether he gained or lost by meeting Andrés.

As soon as Cleto had left him earlier Andrés had felt the need for more space in which to ride out and to control the storm loosened in his heart and in his head. To him it seemed that what Cleto called his inner storm was really muffled and would not be driving him onto dangerous ground. But Andrés felt that his own inner storm was a furious hurricane that beat around him and carried him hither and yon, beating him with its foamy blows, bitter as bile. Fleeing desperately, he walked around for an hour without knowing where he had been or recognizing anyone that he knew.

And for what reason? Simply because he fell into the notion that Cleto was a good match for Sotileza, and that she or her foster parents would quickly recognize this when Cleto, or someone speaking for him, made known his intentions and desires. And, in conclusion, Cleto and Sotileza—Sotileza, so lovely, so beautiful, so elegant—had caused him to fail in his obligations as a friend and as an honorable man. With hardened scorn, he was mulling these thoughts over in the depths of his brain. He felt certain that it was villainy to oppose Cleto's plans merely because of the motives that were buzzing in his own brain, or to work so that Sotileza might again be alone and helpless in the world. But, by examining his thoughts more closely, was he sure that the reasons were not just the result of his own rejected love? Continuing this examination of his innermost anxieties, he even considered the possibility of marrying her himself. And to think that with an excess of generosity in his heart he himself had been capable of giving Sotileza to the first decent man that deserved her!

But would Sotileza deserve this sacrifice? Would she deserve what he had imposed on himself by swearing to her what he had in her home when he was alone with her?

Cleto had told him that not a single word nor the slightest sign of any understanding had been exchanged with Sotileza concerning his amorous intentions. But Muergo—that stupid, hideous Muergo in whose arms she had allowed herself to be carried on Ambojo Beach! Here he was again on the same subject that he had examined so frequently since promising Sotileza not to return to her home with any evil thoughts in his mind! There was no malice perhaps in her moments of carelessness, but they were not becoming to such a decent girl who had put him out of her house for much less important misdemeanors. He would have to talk with her at least once about this alone, and soon, and to Muergo too!

And on such an occasion it was that Muergo met him at one of the street corners near the Zanguina Bar.

"Where did you come from?" Andrés asked him.

"From up there," replied Muergo.

"From High Street?"

"Yeah."

"From your uncle's house?"

"Yeah. I went to tell him about plans for the boat race in case he didn't know about it."

"And who was there?"

"Damn," exclaimed Muergo, scratching his ugly head with both hands. "When I got there, just imagine how glorious it was ta find her all alone."

"Who?"

"Sotileza, by damn!"

"So . . . Sotileza alone . . ." said Andrés, scarcely able to hide the grief which bothered him. "Well . . . what did you tell her? And what did she say?"

"Just imagine that she didn't say nothin'," replied Muergo, shuddering. "'Cause at the best part of it she went to the kitchen ta light a candle and then my uncle came in."

How About the Moat in Your Own Eye? 205

"So . . . at the best part of it," Andrés stressed with a tone that nearly threw sparks. "That is to say that something good had already happened. Isn't that right, Muergo? Come, man, tell me frankly."

Muergo scratched his head again and, after laughing in his own way, said to the impatient Andrés:

"To say that it was good . . . well it wasn't as good as it coulda been . . . but it was good just the same . . . by damn, that little time we was together. I was tellin' her some things and more things. I didn't tell her half of what I woulda if I'd knew how to say it!"

"And she?" prompted Andrés, almost in a bellow.

"Well, she . . ." replied Muergo rubbing his big hands together while bending so low that he almost formed a ball with his body. "Well, Andrés she . . . ho ho! . . she's just like glory . . . she's pure honey for me!"

"That's a lie, you ass," roared Andrés. "Any sweetness from a woman like that is not meant for a beast like you. I forbid you to tell this to anyone or even to believe it yourself . . . !"

"Damn!" exclaimed Muergo rudely. "And why shouldn't I believe it if it's the truth? And who is there to tell me not to try that honey again if I like it so much?"

"Well, I do!" replied Andrés, fearing that he had showed his hand too much. "Because I have the obligation to watch out for Sotileza's good reputation, which would be spoiled by boasts of such suppositions as yours. Do you understand me, you barbarian? That's why I forbid you to brag about her in front of anyone as you have boasted in front of me, because what you said is a damned lie."

"By God, it's the pure truth!"

"I tell you it's a lie, you pig! If what I say isn't enough to cure you of such slander, I'll also tell you that someone with more authority than I have will close the door of that house to you forever."

As Andrés was thus giving rein to his anger in a fierce, unrestrained voice, a sort of tickling sensation was rising in Muergo's chest. His hair was starting to stand on end and his crosseyes were rolling around in their sockets.

"Ah, by God," he said quickly, clenching his fists and roaring loudly, "what bites you is not that I'm tellin' a lie, but that I'm tellin' the truth."

Andrés was dumfounded with shame when he realized that a beast like Muergo had been able to discover the mystery of his imprudent rage.

Then Muergo added: "Yeah, by God! What's happenin' to me here and other people have been tellin' me I thought was just ill will, but I seen somethin'. By God, it's all clear now!"

"That's another slander, you animal."

"No, no, by God! Otherwise what's stirrin' inside me now never woulda started to stir, by damn. How it stings! Andrés, for you I'd jump headfirst into the sea for anything else; but in this, no by God! Don't cross in front of my bow in this business . . . 'cause I'll give your tub such a ramming that you'll sink ta the bottom!"

The only reply that Andrés could think of quickly for Muergo's unexpected and even eloquent speech was a blow with his fist. But the street was not deserted, and because it wasn't, such a blow might have repercussions that would not be to his advantage.

The monstrous Muergo noticed something about it because he considered that he had been given an answer. Andrés, fearful that the reply of this insubordinate animal would oblige Muergo to fulfill his threat to "sink" him, went away quickly.

Each step that he took in that unfortunate adventure was another stupidity that would cost him more misfortune. The poor fellow was burning up the road toward Blanca Street, while his monstrous rival was entering the Zanguina Bar.

20   CLETO'S LOVE AFFAIR

The next day the *Montañesa* came into port on the return trip from Havana. When the captain went ashore this time he was resolved to give up his seagoing life forever.

"Now is the time, Pedro, now is the time," his wife said to him, holding him in her arms, after hearing him swear that he would not break those good intentions. "What a pity it is that you didn't do it many years ago. We have so few years left to spend together without more of the worries that have turned my hair gray."

"Come on, don't complain, you dear ungrateful thing," replied the captain, looking at her from head to foot after freeing himself from her arms. "I have more gray hairs than you have and I am still slick and smooth of skin as a well kept horse. I also have more dents in my hull. Now somebody else can work while I rest. Let's see how my first mate Sama grows fat on the job that he inherited from me. He knows all the ropes. The worst of the whole deal is the ship, which can't take many more storms, just like its captain. Fortunately, after so much hard work he has saved enough to buy food and to give himself the last overhauling in a safe port."

By this time Don Pedro Colindres was a heavy, well-tanned man with nearly white sideburns and hair. His wife was a lovely matron, with gray hair and a majestic bearing. She continued the conversation with her husband, who was looking at her enraptured:

"It's a good thing you are doing that, Pedro."

"Well, what's the matter with Andrés now?"

"I don't know. But for a couple of weeks he is not the same as he was before, and the last week I scarcely know him. It worries me a lot. He doesn't even try to eat, his sleep is restless and I believe that he doesn't know where he's going. Last night he came home very early, like a stunned pigeon. I tried to get him to talk but couldn't get a single word out of him. Consider how cheerful he used to be and what he is like now."

"Just apprehensions of yours, Andrea, just apprehensions, because you women have such a way of loving."

"I tell you that they are not just apprehensions, Pedro!"

"He seemed pretty calm to me this morning when I saw him, and I'll be darned if I noticed any change in him."

"That's because he puts on an act in front of you. See here, Pedro, I'll bet you my hat that they have turned his head up there in that cursed house where you can't get him out dead or alive."

"From what house?"

"The one on High Street."

"Bah!"

"But I'm telling you it's true."

The captain didn't want to talk about this matter any more. Whether she believed him or not, he assured his wife that there was nothing to worry about there.

At the same time that this was happening in Andrés' home, Pachuca, Colo's sweetheart, was urging Sotileza to finish the new dress which she was sewing that same day, which was Saturday. But Sotileza, regardless of how much Pachuca pressed her about the sewing, doubted that the job could be done.

Pachuca was seated near Sotileza looking at her and trying to help her with certain involuntary movements of her hands. As a result of her impatience she talked and talked without once closing her mouth. And talking and talking she talked about Colo, praising him to the skies as was to be expected.

"When are you goin' to get married?" Sotileza asked her.

"I can't tell you that, girl," replied Pachuca, sighing. "As far as wanting to get married is concerned, we would have been married long ago, because he wants to and I do too, but you know that there is going to be another draft for navy service—and I don't want to get married today just to be a widow tomorrow."

Cleto's Love Affair 209

"Right you are, Pachuca. It is better to wait till they come back."

"If they do get back, poor devils."

"What else can they do but get back?"

"Some of them may never get back, poor fellows! Out on the big wide ocean! Maybe God will want him to be called this time, but it would be a miracle if he ain't called regardless of how small the quota for the draft is. I have already offered a mass for one peseta to St. Peter if he ain't called."

"Well, see here, Pachuca," replied Sotileza in that dominating tone that was characteristic of her, "if it's a question of his bein' called now or later, I would offer that mass to have him called this time."

"But why?"

"Because they come back from there very different men. They even learn to walk erect and wash their faces every day. You'll get all those advantages if you marry him after he returns from the service."

"And you, Sotileza, when are you going to be married?" asked Pachuca impertinently.

"Me?" she replied looking astonishedly at her friend. "Who to?"

"To anybody you choose," said Pachuca without hesitating. "Isn't this whole street yours from top to bottom? Is there any girl on it more sought after than you?"

"I'd rather stay single than marry any of the suitors I got."

"Greedy! What do you want? A rich merchant from downtown?"

"Who said that?" exclaimed Sotileza at once, in a harsh voice and with a deep frown.

"I was just sayin' that to say somethin', woman," replied Pachuca, fearful that her friend had taken her joke the wrong way.

"The fact is, Pachuca, that some words are more to be feared than slaps," replied Sotileza with poorly concealed anger, "because there are tongues which scatter these words like the plague, and you know well that there are some on this street that are worse than the mange, and they are lyin' in wait for a chance to ruin someone's reputation."

Poor Pachuca, who hadn't thought about such rumors when she said what she had to Sotileza, continued to swear it to her in order that she wouldn't be offended.

"If I am not offended at you, Pachuca," she replied making an effort to give her face and her voice all the mildness she could, "it's because I know well that you do not dislike me. But there are others who can't see me and are out to get me, and from these blows, which hurt me, come other complaints which I can't help. Some other woman, in my case, might not tell you, but I am tellin' you this way 'cause as far as gettin' a rich merchant is concerned, even the devil could not have had such an evil idea."

While Sotileza was talking thus, old Ramona, the housekeeper for Pa'e 'Polinar, came in asking for Mechelín.

"He's out after sea bass and won't be back till later," replied Sotileza.

"And Sidora?" asked the old servant.

"She's in the Plaza."

"Well, I was looking for them to tell them that Pa'e 'Polinar wants them to come to his house to see him tonight without fail. They already know why he can't come here himself. So you will tell them when you see them, beautiful?"

"Yes, I'll tell them," Sotileza replied without ceasing to sew.

"God bless you," said Ramona while leaving. "How plump and good-looking God made you. You should be thankful to Him."

Then she left, dragging her sandals, while Pachuca, looking at Sotileza, laughed at these exclamations of the priest's housekeeper.

As soon as Pachuca left, Sotileza no longer had any obligation to talk and used all her mental powers in trying to guess the reason back of the message brought by the servant. Padre

Apolinar had never done anything like this before. But, for some time now, peculiar things had been happening.

The hours rolled on and Mechelín and Sidora, dressed in their good clothes and nearly devoured by curiosity, went to keep the date with Padre Apolinar.

Cleto, in the dim twilight, saw them leave. He was seated in the Seville Bar, with his hands in his pockets and his shoulders squeezed between the end of the counter and the wall. His face was half hidden in his sweater. The poor fellow had not closed his eyes all night and had come back from a day at sea without remembering anything that had happened. Pa'e 'Polinar was doing nothing for him, and Andrés was doing all he could to stop him. There was nothing else to do now except to make use of his own efforts. He was ready to do as God and his love would show him how. When he saw the two old folks leave, he was thinking about this.

He suddenly got up from his bench and waited for them to go around the corner of Hospital Hill. Then he looked at the balcony of his own home and up and down the street. When he saw that all was clear, he reached the doorway in a couple of jumps.

Sotileza continued sewing Pachuca's dress by the light of a candle that she had just hung on the wall. When Cleto was standing in front of her, he realized the difficulty of his undertaking in spite of the firmness of his resolve. The word, that blamed word, always failed him when he wanted to say it!

"I came along," he stammered shyly, "I came by, from across the street . . . and I said to myself: 'I guess I'll go in.' That's why I came in. Gee! That's a nice dress you're sewin'. Is it for you, Sotileza?"

Sotileza told him it wasn't, and out of courtesy asked him to sit down.

He sat down quite a distance from her and looked at her in silence for a long time, as if he were trying to become intoxicated through the eyes in order to thus break the bonds of his tongue. He succeeded in saying:

"Sotileza, once you sewed a button for me, outside there, remember?"

"Yes, but a lot of water has gone under the bridge since then."

"Time has gone slowly for me," he said, more encouraged. "It seems like only yesterday."

"All right, but what of that?"

"Well," Cleto continued, "after that button, which I still got on this pair of pants . . . See it? Well, after that button, I kept comin' to this house 'cause I didn't like to stay in my own. Sotileza, you know that well, by gee. That isn't a home up there, and my mother and sister and my father ain't much good. Well, I didn't know nothin' better than that house, and 'cause I didn't, that's why I gave you that kick that day. You remember? Damn me! If you only knowed how much that kick has hurt me since that day."

Sotileza was surprised by what she heard because Cleto had never said anything like that before. She looked at him. This seemed to not only cut off his speech, but even his breathing. Then she said to him:

"But why are you tellin' me all these things?"

"'Cause I gotta tell them to ya," Cleto dared to reply. "That's why, and 'cause nobody ain't wanted to come to tell them to ya for me. Damn! It seems that I am not offendin' nobody with it. 'Cause you'll see, Sotileza, you'll see what's happenin' to me. At first I didn't realize it, and allowed myself to be carried along by the big ground swells I got comin' in here inside me and you kept growin' and growin'. Gee, what trim riggin' you was developin', Sotileza! I wasn't offendin' nobody lookin' at you, it seems ta me, and not by tryin' to gladden my insides by the companionship of the people in this house once in a while. Upstairs there wasn't none of that, nothin' but blackness, and people's reputations tossed out the balcony like garbage, no devotion for nobody. God, that makes for a bad disposition, even though you gotta good one. That's why I gave ya that kick that day, Sotileza. If it wasn't, I'da not did it, I know, 'cause if someone here hada told me: 'Cleto, jump off the Big Wall head first,' I'da did it, if you woulda been pleased by it, tho' I wouldn't jump for no other reason. All right! I never had those feelin's before, Sotileza. I learnt them here, without askin' for them and without hurtin' nobody. Now ya see it wasn't my fault. I liked such feelin's, by damn, I liked 'em a lot, they tasted like pure honey, since I had been in such a sad situation before. Those feelin's were enough for me 'n I tried to stuff myself with 'em, until they got possession of my chest. Then tossed this way 'n that by those tides inside me, I couldn't sleep 'n there was a knot in my gullet. See here, Sotileza, I used to think that there wasn't no troubles like those of my house. But I used to sleep better with them than with those feelin's that I got down here now. See that, by damn! It seems ta me that I ain't offendin' nobody with that, am I, Sotileza? 'Cause at the same time that this was happenin' ta me I was likin' you more 'n more every day, 'n I was lookin' atcha with more 'n more respect. I wanted more 'n more to see your wishes in your eyes so that I could serve ya without ya askin' me to. 'N so months and months passed, and one year 'n another, with that feelin' in my heart without knowin' how ta come to get outa the jam. You see, Sotileza, it's one thing for a man to feel somethin', an' it's somethin' else ta tell about it without words, like me. Then what you are, 'n what I am—nothin' but trash compared ta you. But I couldn't stand it no more. I went to men who understand such things to have them speak for me, but since it didn't hurt them like it did me, dammit, they slammed the door in my face. That was lack of charity! 'Cause there wasn't no harm in that for nobody and nobody was not offended. You are gettin' what I'm sayin' about this? 'Cause nobody wanted to do it for me, I came to tell it to you myself, by damn."

For Sotileza this amorous feeling of Cleto's was no news because she had seen it before in his eyes. She was not surprised at this disconnected account. But surely she was surprised by the unexpected boldness on the part of the one who was telling it. She looked at him calmly, and said:

"It is true that there is no harm in all that you tell me, Cleto. But what's the big idea of tellin' me now?"

"Damn," replied Cleto, very surprised. "What's the idea that such things are always told? So people will know them!"

"Well, I already know them, Cleto; I already knew them."

"You knew them! You might just as well not have known them. But that's not enough, Sotileza."

"And what else do you want?"

"What else do I want? Damn! I want to be a man like so many others I know. I want to look for a different kind of life from what I got now, with that light that you have lit inside of me here. I want to live like you folks live in this house. I wanta work for you, and be clean and neat, and be able to talk correct, like you do. I want to sweep the floor for ya wherever ya go. Whenever you ask me, I'll even bring in mermaids, that nobody ain't never seen, from the ocean. Does that seem a little to you, Sotileza?"

Cleto was really transformed at this moment, and Sotileza was surprised at it.

"I never saw you so spirited as you are now, or using so many words."

"That's because the wave broke, Sotileza," he answered more excitedly than ever, "and I believe that I ain't the same as I was before. I used to think that I was a fool, by damn! Now I swear that I ain't no fool with this feelin' I have here in my heart that makes me talk in spite of myself. If this is a miracle you have made without tryin', what miracles could you do with me when you really tried? Look, Sotileza, I ain't got no vices. I'm a good worker. I don't know how to dislike nobody. I don't need much. I never knowed more than sadness and grief in the best of my life. Seein' somethin' different here made me like it, and who is to blame for that? In this house they need a man—you get me, Sotileza?"

Sotileza understood all too well. For that reason, she told him with a certain gruffness:

"Yes, but what good does it do you to have me know?"

Cleto's Love Affair

"There you go again! Or do you want to turn me down that way courteously?" he asked exasperatedly.

"See here, Cleto," Sotileza replied coldly, "I have no obligation to answer such questions. That's why I stay at home without tryin' to make anybody talk. I do not dislike you, and I know very well how good you are. But I have here in my heart my own feelings and I want to keep them there for the present."

"That's all right, Sotileza," exclaimed Cleto discouragedly. "That's the hole in my hull that'll send me to the bottom."

"It's not that bad," said Sotileza. "But Cleto, if I said 'yes' as you want me to for example, instead of the 'no' that you fear I'll say, what good would that do you? If you have to hide from your own family to come to this house just as a pastime, what would it be like if what you want would happen?"

"That's exactly the same thing the others told me! Damn it, that's not right. I didn't pick out the family I got."

"But who told you exactly what I told you, Cleto?" asked Sotileza, without noticing the poor fellow's exclamations.

"Pa'e 'Polinar, first."

"Pa'e 'Polinar, and who else?"

"Andrés."

"You went to him with that story, stupid? And what did he tell you?"

"A thousand indignities, Sotileza. It nearly killed me."

"Don't you see? When was that?"

"Yesterday afternoon."

"You deserve what you got. Why did you sing these tales of woe to anybody?"

"Damn it, I already told ya. This feelin' was chokin' me. I lacked courage to talk to ya about it—and was lookin' for somebody to do that for me. Today after I have been able to talk, I wouldn't need them, damn it all. But that ain't the point, Sotileza."

"What is it, then?"

"Just 'cause they are bad upstairs, do I get the punishment?"

"I'm not givin' you any, Cleto."

"You're givin' me plenty if you shut the door in my face just because of my family upstairs."

"No, I haven't even gone that far, Cleto. You were carryin' it too far. I just informed you. Do you understand now?"

"I'm afraid I do. Damn my luck. But tell me straight, 'cause that's why I come here—and don't let fear make you hesitate, Sotileza."

"Don't make me talk any more."

"What ya ain't sayin' is worse. What am I here for? Come on, Sotileza. Does that seem a small matter to ya? Tell me what you'd like me to be, and I'll be that way regardless of what it takes. Is there someone else better than me, maybe? I'll be more than he is, if ya insist."

"That is really being stubborn, man."

"It's worth more than life to me, Sotileza. Why would I risk it otherwise, damn it? Look, it's all a matter of havin' a little tenderness in your heart, and the rest takes care of itself. Ya can say ta me: 'This is what you gotta do,' an' I'll do it gladly. I'll not be no bother to you. Some little corner is all I need—even worse than the one I got now at home. I'll eat what is left over from what I earn so that you can live easily in comfort. Right now I'm living on practically nothin', Sotileza. Just as sure as God is in heaven, what I thrive on is a little devotion, a bit of kindness and some joy around me. God, what pleasure that would be! So you see what I'm askin'. I don't want to offend nobody, you understand? 'Cause I'm not askin' nothin' impossible."

Sotileza finally smiled, listening to the poor fellow. He insisted in vain on getting a definite answer from her. His stubbornness annoyed her more. Finally Cleto, worried and sullen, said:

"Well, at least tell me that what I've been sayin' wouldn't sound no better to ya from no other man."

"And what difference does that make to you, stupid?" she answered in a bold, angry tone that froze Cleto's blood in his veins. "Who are you to demand such things from me?"

"I'm nobody, Sotileza, nobody at all. Just trash—and not even that much," he shouted, realizing the indiscretion he had committed. "Grief blinded me, and I spoke without thinkin'. That's all it was, I swear."

"Let me alone now."

"But don't hold no grudge against me."

"Get out of my sight. I've stood it long enough."

"Damn my bad luck! You won't forgive me?"

"Not if you don't get out."

"I'm goin' then."

Cleto left her home, gloomy and sorrowful, when he thought that he had been within a finger length of coming out triumphant and rewarded.

21   VARIOUS MATTERS; AND MUERGO ALL DRESSED UP

It would offend the reader's judgment, regardless of how dull it might be—and I am not supposing any such thing—to repeat as important news that Pa'e 'Polinar called Mechelín and Sidora to his home in order to talk to them about what Cleto had requested. The poor priest, with the work and worry about the sermon for the fiesta, and the fear that the Mocejón women instilled in him, took this way out in order to lose less time and not be in a fix that he feared worse than fire.

He fulfilled his promise with little enthusiasm, and even with the warning that he had nothing to do with it and under the condition that, if the matter took shape, not even the flies in the air should know that he had had even a little to do with serving the confused young man.

"Cleto is a good boy," he said finally. "From one point of view, it would be a good thing to have him as a helper in your household. He would cause no trouble in it. But others would, if for no other reason than because he had a peaceful harbor there. You know about whom I am speaking. You remember, Mechelín? You remember, Sidora? Gosh, what people! On the other hand, the girl is really beautiful and really decent, and consequently deserves a nobleman. But marquises probably aren't looking for daughters of fishermen, Sidora. Sooner or later she will have to put up with some High Street sailor. And this Highstreeter, with more or less matted hair and more or less ability to read and write, will be about on a level in looks and literacy with Mocejón's son when he is cleaned up and shaved. You understand what I am saying? Well, knowing the wish of the young lady concerned, talk over in the family the pros and cons of the matter so that I do not get mixed up in it, by gosh, and may God help me out of the whole darn business!"

Sidora and her husband saw the same pros and cons in the matter as Pa'e 'Polinar. The only difference was that she found a solution, and Mechelín, at best, thought it all wrong to compare Sotileza's burnished gold with the dirty copper of her suitor. It is true, of course, that for Mechelín no man had yet been born who really deserved her.

Sotileza had understood from all that Cleto told her and the errand on the part of Pa'e 'Polinar's old servant that the same subject had been discussed at the priest's home as had been aired between her and Cleto. Sidora and Mechelín had agreed that it was their duty to find out from Sotileza as soon as possible what her wishes in the matter were. From some remark of Sidora's, Sotileza started to tell them about her recent interview with Cleto.

"So much the better for us, then," said Sidora. "It saves us the bother of telling you."

"Right," confirmed Mechelín, hitting the floor with one foot.

Silda remained silent and continued sewing. After a moment's silence, Sidora added:

"So, what do you say, dear daughter?"

"What do you want me to say?"

"Just what your opinion in the matter is."
"You know that without me sayin' it."
"That ain't sayin' very much."
"Half that much would be enough."
"I would like for you, daughter, to be informed about it all. Right now you need nothin', thank God, but tomorrow and the day after, you see . . . we are only mortals, and we are old, and besides, not in good health . . . you might be left alone . . . and it could be soon. It is true that this family is bad, very bad. It couldn't be worse. But he is a fortunate fellow, good as gold. With a little cleanin' up and some good clothes, he'd stand out 'cause he's a good-lookin' fellow. I am not praisin' him to the point of tryin' to force him on you, but this is a matter where everything has to be made clear, so that you will not be deceived in makin' up your mind."

"Right," said Mechelín, hitting the floor again with his foot.

As Sotileza gave no response, Sidora, somewhat annoyed by it, added at once: "But daughter, tell us somethin', for the love of God, so that we will know your feelin's. If you are afraid of makin' a mistake, do you want us to ask advice, for instance, from Andrés?"

"Please do not even mention it to him," she burst forth immediately. "His advice is not needed, nor from nobody else. I know very well what suits me."

"Well, that's what we want to know, daughter; what suits you at the present time."

"Right."

"I want you to leave me in peace about these things, and don't talk to me no more about them. Because I do not need any more, 'cause everybody knows what he wants and I have more than enough words to express my opinion when it is needed. That is what pleases me now—God alone can say about tomorrow. Do you understand me now?"

And that is how that matter remained then.

Another different matter had been discussed with much more enthusiasm in all the gatherings and kitchens of the street, ever since the night before. This matter was about the boat race proposed by the Council of the Lower Town and accepted by acclamation by the whole body of the Council of the Upper Town at a meeting in the Seville Bar. In those days, most of the Santander sailors had not even thought about any more adventures than those furnished by their own work, and a project of such a nature caused great enthusiasm among the young folks of the whole city. It also warmed the blood in the benumbed bodies of the older ones. It was not a question of a race between two rival boats, but an affair which took on all the solemnity of the great conflicts between two bordering or neighboring nations. Nor was it just a group of a few fishermen from the Lower Town who challenged others from the Upper Town. Neither was it a matter of winning, in open competition, a prize offered by an individual or city government, nor episodes in which there was room for skills in order to divide the booty among the competitors, where there is scarcely any pride. This was a whole guild challenging another, just to celebrate the day of the patron saint of the challengers—a solemn holiday in Santander. The race would start at the afternoon high tide, about half past three, with the docks crowded with people. The prize would be an ounce of gold taken from the very heart of the contending guilds. The fishermen from the Lower Town were conceited because they were many compared with the smaller number in the Upper Town. In short, particularly for those of the Upper Town, the event came to be almost an international question. Consequently it is not to be wondered that even the cats and dogs on High Street were interested in it.

With this motive, the home of Mechelín had more visitors than usual at night. As he did not like to go to the bar where the big race was discussed, his real pals—and there were many of them—came from time to time to rejuvenate his spirits with what they heard in the bar, or to ask his authoritative opinion whenever it was needed.

All this displeased Andrés greatly, because it kept him away

Various Matters; and Muergo All Dressed Up

from Mechelín's home just at the time when he felt most need to visit it for a chance to be alone a few minutes with Silda—who was so jealous of her honor—in order to tell her how dangerous her honor was in the mouth of the savage Muergo. In doing this he was not failing in his pledged word, because when he made the vow he wasn't counting on what he heard later from that beast. And even though Sotileza thought that he had failed in his word, what of it? If he were deceiving her, he would be a fool to keep from her such undeserved considerations. If Muergo was lying, it was even his duty to warn her about it. But there was all this coming and going of strangers—also the attitude of his father, so different from other times. How the captain warned him and watched him; and Luisa could carry out her threats when least expected. Baffled by all these obstacles, at the same time spurred on by the impulse of his impatient, fiery character, he rambled on in his mind about the most absurd things. At times he came up with projects for distant and dangerous places. The worst of it all was he was not frightened by it. It all seemed right to him to do in exchange for the chance to have his own way. The reader already knows the difficult thoughts in Andrés' brain and his wild resolutions.

On the other hand, Cleto was glad in his own way about more visitors to Mechelín's home. He could enter now without being noticed so much, going in like so many others. Sotileza had no pretext to blame him for being obstinate. He could observe without anybody noticing him, or see without being seen. He was able to do this now, and that suited him since Pa'e 'Polinar had told him that the old folks were on his side. How sweet that bit of news was to him. With what he had told Sotileza and what they had told her later, his wishes might be fulfilled when least expected. In the meantime he would keep his eyes open and try to be prudent at all times. And that is the way he was behaving, with his heart full of hope.

Muergo went back to Mechelín's home that night after his argument with Andrés. With the sorrow which this encounter left inside him, the tension over the approaching boat race and being half drunk, he caused such a disturbance in the house that his uncle told him not to dare come back till the race was over, because tempers were touchy everywhere in the city.

The guild from the Upper Town asked the challengers from the Lower Town about the time and distance of the race. Everything was ironed out. The race was to be to Rat Rock from the steps at the dock and back—the course usually used.

That same day preparations were started by both guilds. The bilges and gunwales of their boats were scraped and scraped until they were as smooth as silk. Benches and oarlocks were cleaned and tightened. A thin coat of tar was put on the sides and then painted. Finally, soap was applied to the bilges and sides to make them slip smoothly through the water. Soap was used instead of tallow because the latter might not be slippery enough.

The boat to be used by the guild from the Upper Town was painted white with a red stripe. The one from the Lower Town was blue with a white stripe. Cleto and Colo formed part of the crew selected by the Upper guild. Cole and Guarín were in the one from the Lower guild. Muergo did not get a chance to row because he could not be trusted in such a delicate undertaking; not from lack of strength, but because of his brutish unreliability. In his own way he felt this snub, but he consoled himself by thinking that he would wear his new suit for the first time that day, with shoes and all, and also with his plan to make a try at the greased pole after the race.

And so the 30th of August arrived, to the great joy of all. On the part of Pa'e 'Polinar there was some sweating. He had scarcely closed his eyes during the last week, as he was engaged in trying to memorize everything that he had scribbled down for three months.

By dawn of that day Muergo was down by the water's edge at the Long Ramp scrubbing his big head and feet in the water. Then, letting them dry by themselves, he went back to his

Various Matters; and Muergo All Dressed Up

room to put on his new suit. He dried his face with his cap and combed his hair with his fingers.

An hour later, gladly fulfilling the desires of Sotileza, he went up High Street, nearly bursting his new suit and slipping on the sidewalk with each step in his new shoes because of the stiff, smooth soles.

The prominence which his ugliness acquired in such good clothes and clean shirt seemed incredible to those who saw him. How his skin shined! How his hair came out back of his wide cap! What an arching of his arms! What a smile of pleasure, and what a gait!

Sotileza crossed herself three times as soon as she saw him. Then she put her hands together and opened her eyes wide, as if she were surprised that the whims of nature could reach two such extremes.

"Hold that position a minute, Muergo," she said enthusiastically. "Let me look at you a bit from a distance. Bless my soul!"

"Do you like me this way?" he asked, standing with his legs wide apart in the middle of the room. Do I look all right with these trimmin's? Where's my uncle?"

"Both of them are at mass. Don't go away until they come back—I want them to see you this way."

"We don't miss them now, by damn. 'Cause they'll probably throw me out again. I come on accounta you, Sotileza—'cause I promised to come—and besides, I have ta tellya sompin' that's botherin' me here inside, by damn!"

"Well, see here," she replied with a resolute gesture, "if you came to tell me about some things that I haven't asked for I'll put you out in the middle of the street and you won't ever get back in here. Do you understand?"

"Damn it! You too? But if I've got a thought, what's wrong in bringin' it outside?"

"It can come out when it should."

"Well, by damn, it's comin' out now."

"I tell you no. Don't be stupid. Holy heavens, what a way to dress! Come here, you animal."

Muergo advanced a couple of steps toward Sotileza and after looking him over from head to toe again, she untied the poorly tied black silk necktie, tied it as it should be done and pulled out the pleats of his shirt. Muergo let her do all this without daring even to breathe. He liked that gentle handling and was trembling from head to foot.

"What a mess of hair!" she exclaimed after finishing his tie. "Why haven't you had some of this sheared off, you scatter-brained, slovenly fellow? Ain't there no combs in the whole Lower Town?"

Saying this, she pulled his cap from his head, and began to straighten out his hair with her fingers.

"Holy heavens! This is like a wood full of trees. Wait for me to arrange it a little before I start to comb it." Then she sank her hands into this shock of hair. Muergo let out muffled roars from his throat. Sotileza, far from being frightened by them, pulled here, untangled something there. The more he roared, the more she sank her hands into this heavy nest. Suddenly Muergo let out a real howl.

"Does that hurt?" asked Sotileza, without letting up any.

"No, damn it!" he replied, lowering his head more. "Haul her in more—and more—I like it a lot! Stronger, Sotileza . . . Damn . . . that's the way, pull ahead . . . more! More yet! Ouch!"

Sotileza jumped back a couple of steps, because she felt his big paws around her waist.

"Not that!" she shouted to him at the same time.

"Yes, by damn!" roared the monster. "What did ya think?"

And he advanced toward her trembling and bristling, indomitable, frightful.

In one corner of the room was a club which Sidora had used to beat the lumps of wool in a mattress a few days before. Sotileza pounced on it, and before Muergo succeeded in even touching her clothes, he already had received two heavy blows

Various Matters; and Muergo All Dressed Up

on the head, which brought forth curses from him. Muergo stopped then, roaring and yearning. Sotileza gave him a couple more wallops with the club.

"Back up! Farther!" she shouted at him fiercely and resolutely.

Muergo backed up three steps.

"Still more," she insisted, wielding the club. "Back there against the wall."

And only when Muergo put his shoulders against it did she stop her threatening attitude. Muergo was puffing and Sotileza even more. Then she spoke to him, as if she wished to nail him to the wall with her words:

"That is your place, and this is mine. You understand? Well, the day that you make that mistake again will be the last time I ever look at you. Do you agree?"

"Yes, damn it," replied Muergo, like a wild beast would roar squatting in a corner of his cage.

"Here, take your cap," Sotileza then said solemnly after picking it up from the floor.

Muergo stretched out his hand to get it.

"First straighten up your hair a bit," she said to him while shaking the dust from his cap.

Muergo obeyed without saying a word.

"Put your head down."

Muergo obeyed. Then Sotileza put his cap on him as it should be worn.

"Don't touch it," she said after he had straightened up.

In his chest could be heard noises like distant breaking waves.

"Are you glad, now?" she asked him.

"Look at me like ya used ta," replied Muergo. "That's the way! Like that! Oh, what satisfaction!"

Sotileza began to laugh and said:

"Tell me now, what were you going to tell me?"

With these words Muergo woke from the stupor in which the recent scene had put him. He started to tell Sotileza about his meeting with Andrés near the Zanguina Bar. Just then Mechelín and his wife returned from mass and the story remained untold.

"Praised be the name of the Lord!" exclaimed Sidora, looking at her nephew. "When the devil was here on earth he must have looked like you do today."

"Sure, you look like a dressed-up piece of plaster," added Mechelín, crossing himself.

With this, and what had happened previously, Muergo's patience came to an end. After a couple of curses and a harsh interjection as his only good-by, he left, resolved not to stop till he reached the Miranda Hermitage, where the flag of the Lower Town Guild had been flying since dawn. The bell was ringing loudly. The flag and the bell amused the eyes and the ears of the devout fishermen who were approaching.

22 ≈ THE UPPER TOWN AND THE LOWER TOWN

The great Sardinero Beach was nearly deserted in those days, because only a few people came to enjoy the sea bathing. There was only one building on the whole beach. A beloved citizen, Brigadier Buenago, had drowned one day when there was a heavy undertow. That event had made sea bathing less popular. Later a few more people came with tents in the summer; there were picnics and country dances. A trip to Madrid was a three-day affair. The people of Santander who had seen Paris could be counted on one's fingers. For young people there were fewer organizations and opportunities for amusement than today.

Even in those days the landlubbers in the city were little interested in the boat race. It was primarily a fiesta for seafaring folk. However, there were some, of course, who favored one guild or the other. There were even some visitors from the interior of the province.

Although the sun was warm and there was a big picnic in the Miranda Meadows, by two o'clock in the afternoon the edge of the dock was crowded with people. Soon others came, forming a second, third, or fourth line of onlookers. It seemed a miracle that with all the shoving and jostling no one fell into the water.

The ladies in the houses near the dock began to group on the balconies. Guests, of course, were given the preferred seats. Men's bearded faces could be seen in the background. Bright-colored parasols gave each balcony the appearance of a big flowerpot full of large flowers.

Soon the band from the orphan asylum began playing in the distance, then closer and closer until it came to a street near the docks. Then it went down the steps. Going individually from boat to boat, the musicians reached a two-masted coastal lugger, on whose bowsprit was the greased pole sponsored by the City Council. There the boys started to play again. Firecrackers were popping everywhere to add to the noise and gaiety.

The launches and boats that surrounded this lugger extended in a wide line north and south, all full of people, forming a wide channel. At the end of this open space, near the stairway leading from the dock, two boats were anchored in line, parallel to the dock. These were for the officials of the race. Opposite them was another, with the colors of the Port of Santander at its prow, flapping from a short pine stick. That flag would be the sign of triumph, and would be taken by the first boat that came back from Rat Rock, a distance of about three miles.

A slight breeze was blowing from the northeast. Taking advantage of it, the luxurious skiffs, with their sails and pennants flying, tossed about in the background of this lively, picturesque picture. The *Zephyr* was there, manipulated skillfully by Andrés, who had some of his friends with him. Tolín was not there, because he preferred to be on the balcony of his home, standing near Silverio Trigueras' daughter. Not too far from the launch with the flag and the lugger with the greased pole, right in the front row, was Mechelín's boat, with Sidora, Sotileza and several friends and neighbors. Some were there because of their friendship for old Mechelín, others to help him with the rowing. Pachuca was there with her new dress. She and Sotileza, a really beautiful young lady, occupied a preferred place in the center of the side that faced the open channel. By a cruel whim of fate, the Mocejón family, filthy, quarreling and alone, was in its dirty boat just the second one from Mechelín's.

Suddenly a murmur is raised among the people in the boats and on shore, This drowns out the tooting of the musicians. From the south, almost like a lightning flash, in a whirl of foam, there comes a white boat with a red stripe. There are eight oarsmen on each side of it. They are bareheaded, and are wearing tight white shirts with horizontal stripes. Almost at the same time, from the opposite side, another boat appears. It is blue with a white stripe, and is moving swiftly with the same number in its crew. The captain, standing in the stern, guides each boat with an oar instead of a rudder.

These two boats cross in front of the stairway like two flashes, amidst the gay shouting of the crew. They slip and move in arcs and curves, leaving white, foaming waves behind them. Either of these boats could write the name of the guild in the water with its keel. Later the rowing is slower. They are moved only by the blade of the oars. Then they slip away again and come in with the oars raised above the water, rocking on the white, churning water. In all these movements they seem like fiery steeds controlled by their riders to check their impatience before entering the arena for a tournament. There is something of this in the bubbling rocking of the boats before the race, because the oarsmen do it to get warmed up. Get warmed up that way! With half of that, a strong errand boy would have more than enough energy to last him four days!

Finally the tide is at its height. The music is heard again.

The Upper Town and the Lower Town

The officials move down the stairway to the two boats anchored there. The boats enter the channel. Each pulls alongside one of the official boats. The landlubber judges stop them there while members of the crew get set for the contest. The signal is given—and away they go!

The Upper Guild—the white boat—is at the right. By the second stroke of the oars it is opposite Mechelín's boat. Then, amid the creaking of the oars and the thongs on the oarlock pins, the shouting of the crowd and the oarsmen, the voice of Cleto stands out. He is rowing in the bow and hollers these resounding words:

"I'm dedicatin' this to you, Sotileza!"

And Sotileza saw him bend his robust body back, and with all the strength of his arms curve the heavy oar as if it were of Toledo steel.

The magnificent Highstreeter did not reply. The emotion she felt in such a situation deprived her of speech. She would gladly have said something, not just for Cleto alone, although she did not fail to esteem his courtesy, but for the bit of local honor which was being put to a test in this contest. On the other hand, old Mechelín, warmed in his enthusiasm by the fire of such things, waved his Sunday cap in the air and shouted as loud as he ever did in his life:

"Hurrah for you, strong boy—and for all the other Highstreeters!"

The two launches go by as if some mysterious hurricane impels them. In about three seconds they are beyond the boat with the flag of honor, which seems to greet them by flapping loudly. The wakes of the two boats become one. The tips of the oars rise and fall in unison as if only one arm moves them all. The backs of the oarsmen bend forward and back in changeless rhythm. To the dazzled eyes of the spectators, men, oars and boats make one single unit moved by a single will.

And thus they move away. Even the best pair of eyes cannot notice the slightest advantage of one over the other. On such occasions the result of the struggle often is decided by strategy, something like a timely trick, or by courageously coming alongside the other boat by surprise when it cannot change its course—all within the rules, naturally. In this case they play clean and open.

At half the distance they are a little farther apart, because the dropping of the tide will start soon. They must take into consideration the drift which will separate them from the shortest course if they should line up the Rat Rock with the prow. Two minutes later, without binoculars one could not notice any appreciable difference between the colors. A little farther on they become two blurred forms, almost shapeless, and the movement of the oars can be distinguished by the reflection of the sun on the water that runs off the blades while in the air.

Finally one of the launches disappears behind a small island and immediately the other one does too. They then reappear to the east of this rock, with the first one maintaining the slight lead it had before disappearing.

But which one is ahead? Many spectators are in doubt. Some who have binoculars say that it is the High Street boat, and according to their statements the advantage is such that it has won the race, even though the other crew redoubles its efforts.

Little by little the two forms take shape and get larger. Movements can be seen and the colors distinguished. Now even ordinary eyes can measure the distance which separates the two boats. The Highstreet boat is a couple of lengths ahead.

However, no one lets up rowing. Everybody is rowing with the same spirit as at first. Since only one can win, the merits of the loser will have to be judged by the experts.

The High Street boat comes over the finish line like a flash and reaches the mouth of the wide channel. From there, with oars abandoned and trailing in the water, the captain controls the craft very skillfully. It pulls up alongside the launch with the flag. Cleto pulls it in with one grab amidst the shouts and applause of the people. Without losing any of its momentum

The Upper Town and the Lower Town

the boat reaches Mechelín's launch. There Cleto, standing up glowingly, says with a loud voice, trembling with enthusiasm:

"Take it, Sotileza. Fasten it on our boat with your own hands!"

Amidst the applause of everybody, companions and bystanders, he gives her the flag, which in that moment is the honor of the Upper Guild. The beautiful girl places it, as Cleto asked her, on the prow of the triumphant launch. Firecrackers are exploding everywhere. The musicians on the patache play very loudly.

While Sidora and Mechelín, mad with joy, embrace Cleto and Colo, who come alongside to receive the applause of the enthusiastic Pachuca, a chorus of curses is raised in Mocejón's boat because of the shameles thing done by their son. The blue launch of the Lower Guild has come in. The High Street boat has covered the distance of six miles in twenty-five minutes.

When this first part of the celebration was finished, the contenders for the greased pole climbing were on the deck of the lugger, dressed only in breechclouts.

Muergo was one of them. He was in very bad humor because he had just witnessed what Cleto had done. The defeat of the Lower Guild added to his gloom and ill humor. He intended to get revenge on Cleto by offering to Sotileza the flag from the top of the greased pole.

When the people saw him take hold of the pole, an exclamation of astonishment spread over the crowd on the dock and on the boats surrounding the patache. He looked like an Australian bushman, or a savage from Polynesia.

After climbing a couple of yards on the pole, he lost his hold and his balance and fell into the water, making splashes and kicking the water. There he looked like a chimpanzee felled by a bullet from the top of a tree in the wilds of Africa. He was blowing in the greenish water, diving and reappearing on the surface, as if he were in his natural element, like a baby whale. In fact he looked like anything but a man. Taking the laughter and exclamations as applause favoring his gracefulness, he made more and more nonsense at each attempt to climb the pole.

After his first tries, Sotileza was ready to leave. Sidora and Mechelín were of the same opinion because he did not greatly amuse them. They and their friends rowed to the dock, made the boat fast, took the oars and walked slowly to High Street.

23 THE FEMALES OF THE MOCEJON FAMILY

That night the Zanguina Bar was full of customers and many were standing and sitting at tables on the sidewalk underneath the arched portico. The prize money for climbing the greased pole was divided among all the contestants. This was agreed to by the referee because no one had been able to reach the top without falling into the water. Muergo could not find his shoes when he left. He had tried more or less unsuccessfully to remove the grease from his body. However, it had not come off in spite of all his duckings. With his share of the prize money he decided to give his own stomach some pleasure and to buy a white handkerchief to give to Sotileza. Of course he was raving mad because of the loss of his shoes, but later consoled himself with the thought that they weren't much good to him because he had not really learned to walk in them. After this he forgot about them. While everybody else around him was excited and talking loudly about the events of the afternoon, he was silent and unconcerned. He was stuffing himself with fried foods, fresh bread and plenty of red wine, especially when he remembered about the victory flag after the race or the blows with the club that he had received that very morning, when he had dreamed about something quite different. He also thought of his meeting a few nights ago with Andrés and the fact that he had not been able

The Females of the Mocejón Family

to tell Sotileza about it. Andrés! He had seen him that very afternoon in his skiff near Mechelín's boat in the bay. And what eyes the rascal had for Sotileza! In order to kill such troublesome thoughts, he took a double drink, and thus he was able to weather the storm.

In one of the groups that were talking outside the Zanguina Bar was Pa'e 'Polinar, who was quite annoyed. Picking up a word here and there he had reached the conclusion that his oration about the holy martyrs of Calahorra had not pleased the councils to any great extent, and that in the opinion of some people the sermon was not worth much.

This indignity left the priest quite perturbed.

"Cuss my luck!" he exclaimed. "What the devil are they used to hearing, anyway?"

"As for that, Pa'e 'Polinar," a boat captain replied to him, "and without any offense to anyone, there has been only one good sermon about the martyrs since the year '49, when we built that chapel with our own hands because they had torn the old one at the Point down to put up those big buildings that are there now. Only then were first-rate things said about the holy martyrs, by men of fluent speech and great wisdom. The truth comes first, Pa'e 'Polinar, without offense to anyone."

"First-class things! First-rate things, the devil! What things they were! A couple of more periods here, and some commas less there, always the same old stuff. The heads of the martyrs were cut off in Calahorra, and then the executioners tossed them into the river, and a lot of 'ohs' and many 'ahs,' and the rest just trifles, and finally nonsense, by gosh! Drivel, nothing but drivel! Had you ever heard the legend about the stone boat, for instance?"

"Who would not have known about it here, Pa'e 'Polinar?"

"Sure, man, sure. But like I told it? How did the boat come? What route was it taking? What kind of weather was it? What kind of seas combatted it? How did it get into this port? Why didn't it go into some other port first? Had anybody else told you all these golden bits before, with such grace and art? Did those other fellows know it the way I know it? Did even the Council itself know anything about the Rock of the Martyrs, that most people call the Horadada?"

"We knew something about that, Pa'e 'Polinar."

"Something, yes, something. To know something is the same as knowing nothing in such important matters, by gosh! Now you know it with all the details. Now you know that lovely arch in the rock was made by this miraculous boat when it bumped against it and cut it in two. And from whom did you learn it? Did you get it from the mouths of those other silk and satin preachers? No, you knew it because you heard me tell you this morning: me, this humble priest, who, by telling you so much in one sermon, took three tiring months to prepare it, and used more than fifteen of the best Latin texts, but didn't succeed in pleasing you. Pearls before swine, man, that's what it was, pearls before swine! But some day you will be in another situation like this, and that will be the best punishment you could get, by gosh. A lot of jabber from those blusterers. I'm not saying any more, by darn, because you still feel the sting of your defeat in the boat race this afternoon. I don't mean that I'm glad you got beat, but consider it a punishment from God and, by darn, it could have come from Him, without any vanity on my part. Wow! Tongues, tongues, corrupt tongues, miserable flesh, corrupt flesh! And good-by, boys, I've got things to do. Of course, your failure to appreciate my efforts in the sermon does not free me from the obligation of serving you. The door of Padre Apolinar's home is never closed to anyone. But be careful never to call there about more special sermons from me, because I'll not open it for you even if you knock it down. Even if you knock it down on me, by darn!"

Pa'e 'Polinar went away, much less angry than what he himself believed.

In the meantime, celebrating did not stop on High Street. There was singing in the bars, conversations in all the balconies and windows, merriment on the sidewalks and dancing in the street. The whole neighborhood was crazy with joy—everybody,

The Females of the Mocejón Family

that is, except the members of the Mocejón family. They remained inside their cavern, doing nothing but cursing poor Cleto for the insult he had given them by what he had done with that devilish girl after the race. . . . To add to the displeasure of the two furies, the matter was talked about all along the street with no indication of shame. It was on everybody's tongue that no girl was more deserving of what had been done by Cleto's gallant gesture than Sotileza. Some people even discussed whether or not they were a good match, and whether or not there were any mutual, serious intentions between them, and if there weren't, there should be. The people on the fifth floor had heard much of this. Later they closed the windows of the balcony in order not to hear any more. The Mocejón females preferred this recourse to giving loose rein to their poisonous anger on an occasion so compromising for them. They had more than enough will power, strength of tongue and skill to stir up the whole street in fifteen minutes. They had done it so many times already. But the proper occasion and the right excuse were lacking. Just a little motive, or the appearance of one even, was all they needed, and when they had it—and they would have it, because it seemed to be close by all the time—then, then that so and so on the ground floor would pay for it all at once and would find out what the bad son, the infamous brother, the indecent, the animal, the shameless wretch, the little pig Cleto didn't know!

And they kept on talking while Mocejón buzzed like a horse-fly in the corner. In the Seville Bar, indifferent to all the excitement around him, the accursed young man was smacking his lips over the sweet memories of his latest adventure.

By the time Andrés reached Mechelín's home there were almost more people than there was room for. He believed that he had to drop in for a few minutes in order to congratulate the old fisherman on the victory of the Upper Town, and to chat a while with the family on such a special occasion. Sidora was nearly bursting out of her skin with joy. Her husband seemed to have thrown off twenty years from each shoulder. Sotileza, after the excitement of the afternoon, was now down to her usual calm level.

The rejuvenated Mechelín said to Andrés as a fitting close to all his comments about the race:

"Well, man, that was surely a good idea that Cleto had. You musta seen it, 'cause you wasn't very far away. I'm referrin' to the flag which he gave to Sotileza for her to put on the boat. I'm tellin' ya that I didn't think he had it in 'im. I liked that action; why should I say I didn't? And you, Sidora, you was almost cryin' from pure joy. And this little angel who turned so pale and her little hands trembled so much—all the people of the street are talkin' about this!"

"Would you believe it, Andrés," added Sidora, "the poor fellow is wandering about now as if he had committed a mortal sin against us? Isn't he a poor devil, though? Don't you see? Other fellows, in his case, would be braggin' about it all the time."

"Right," confirmed Mechelín.

To ask Andrés if he had heard about the matter, when he hadn't lost a single insignificant detail of it! To extol what Cleto did, and the merits of Cleto and even the gratitude of Sotileza, when he had had it all together in one lump in his throat for a long time now! But how was this honorable couple to suspect—even if they knew about what happened in the Ambojo Grove, and what went on right here in this house—that a young man in such apparent conditions could possibly have the mania of not enduring patiently even to have flies become entangled in the curls of Sotileza's hair without his permission? Sotileza knew this somewhat better, and because she did, she read with one quick glance at Andrés' face the bad effect the praises for the gallantry of Cleto were causing in him. For that reason she tried to change the conversation, but she did not succeed. Mechelín, aided by his wife and the friends present—among whom were Pachuca and Colo—insisted on his favorite theme. And since everything looked rosy to him then, and he wanted everybody around him to be happy and gay, he finished his praises and congratulations by saying:

"Tomorrow's goin' to be Sunday for you too, Sotileza! Since ya like fishin' and sailin' so much, you're goin' to come along with me in the boat in the middle of the mornin'. By the middle of the afternoon, we'll be back."

"There's lots of sewin' to be done," replied Sotileza.

"It can't be tomorrow mornin'," said Sidora, "because I have to be in the Plaza all day. You'll go with him some other day, won't you, darlin'?"

"For the love of God!" exclaimed Mechelín. "Maybe some other day I won't be in the mood I'll be in tomorrow. But I'll try to be, won't I, daughter?"

When Andrés left their house shortly after this conversation, and while he was going down toward the Cathedral, he could have sworn that he had a hornet in each ear buzzing those same words. A little farther on, these words, which sounded in his ears, were the beginnings of thoughts going through his head. And as he kept walking and walking, those thoughts brought about plans. Those plans filled his mind with memories. Those memories produced violent struggles and serious reasoning; the reasonings gave way to dazzling fallacies, and they in turn to more plans. These plans produced disturbances and surgings in his heart.

Thus he arrived home, and thus he spent the night, and thus he woke up the next morning, and thus he went to the office. For the second time in his life, with some poorly concocted excuse he deceived Tolín during the middle of the morning to get out of his obligations at the office.

A quarter of an hour later he entered High Street from Hospital Hill, not without first having passed by the fish factory to make sure that Sidora was there on the Plaza under her canvas-covered stall. At the same time Carpia, who was leaving the house, backed up quickly into the doorway and ran upstairs. On the first landing she waited in hiding. From there, trying not to be seen, she saw Andrés enter the apartment on the ground floor. Right away she went to the fifth floor as fast as she could to speak a few words with her mother and came back down the stairs to the entrance of the building without making much noise. Then on tiptoe, and even holding her breath like a fox about to attack a chicken house, she approached the door of Mechelín's home. By stretching her neck slightly but being very careful not to have her head appear in the open doorway, she knew from the sounds reaching her ears that the brazen couple were not in the front of the corridor but at the other end of the room. She listened more, and heard occasional words which sounded like recriminations of Sotileza and excuses and impassioned laments on the part of Andrés. Regardless of how sharp her hearing was she couldn't catch an entire phrase which would inform her about what was happening there.

"And what does the truth about what can be happenin' between them matter to me?" she said to herself, realizing the futility of her curiosity. "What does matter to me is that everybody will believe the worst, and that is what they're goin' to believe right now." Then she put her disheveled head in the doorway and looked at the lock of the door. She saw that the key, as she had presumed, was on the outside, which greatly simplified her work. She advanced a couple of steps quietly, extended her arm and pulled the door toward her, with great care so that the hinges would not squeak much. She began to close it ever so slowly while the murmur of the conversation increased on the inside. When she closed the door and turned the key, she removed it from the keyhole and put it in the pocket of her skirt. Then she went out to the sidewalk and called her mother. As soon as her mother answered from the balcony, she told her calmly, as if it were an everyday matter:

"Now!"

Then there were a few moments of silence. There were only a few people on the street, a few women mending clothes on the balconies or leaning out some window or other of a lower floor, or talking in a doorway. Carpia was in front of her building, leaning against the wall with her arms crossed. Dirty kids were playing here and there. Suddenly the voice of Sargüeta was heard:

"Carpia!"

"Yes, madam."

"What are you doin'?"

"Somethin' you could never guess."

"Come right up here as fast as you can."

"I don't wanta."

"I've told you many times never to stand where you are now. You know very well why. You have a good home of your own to enjoy without botherin' no one. Come on up. I'll not be tellin' you again."

"I'll be darned if I wanta. You hear that?"

"Come up, I tell you, Carpia. And don't make me lose my patience. You don't have nothin' to do where you are."

"Yes I do have somethin' to do, mother; a lot. More than you could ever imagine. I'm guardin' the honor of the stairway in this buildin'; indeed I am! In fact the houses of the whole neighborhood! From now on everybody has to know how each and every other person is—why my face is tanned because of the bad weather, and why some others have such white, clean faces. By God, I can't stand it no longer. Right in front of your eyes, and in broad daylight! Is that shame, mother? 'Cause I am here right now to throw it in her face. So that we can have this over with once and for all and people of honor can stay in their homes and the dirt goes out on the trash heap. That's why I'm here—the indecent hussy!"

"But, daughter, what is it? What's happenin', Carpia?"

"Well, that ink-slingin' clerk and the nice young lady are all alone, poor little angels, in the house and the door is closed. And this buildin', from the main entrance up is not meant for that kind of actin', by God!"

By this time the kids started to gather around her, a few passers-by stopped, closed balconies were opened and women who had been seated inside were now leaning over the railings.

From the balcony, Sargüeta then answered her daughter, who started to swagger on the sidewalk in front of the doorway:

"And that astounds you? Why are you gettin' excited about that, darlin'? But with all that, watch out for any embarrassment, because some of your listeners may ask you to prove what you're sayin'. Because there wouldn't be any people with evil lives if there weren't shameless women who *conceal* much evil. And right in the face of God, she is such a scoundrel that she sold herself for some mere rags which she praises so much. There are lots of women like her who conceal crime, by God, and they are the ones that entice nice boys and get them started on the road to perdition; and show disrespect for good people. There . . . these . . . And the way they hold on for all they're worth. That's why I'm without a son right now. That's the way the rascals took him away from me. He wasn't even thinkin' of her. He was livin' in peace here at home." Suddenly Sargüeta noticed a neighbor across the street who was looking at her. "What are you lookin' for that you lost, you big bum? Does somethin' I said annoy ya? Is your conscience botherin' ya?"

"Keep quiet, you slanderer, you foul-mouthed thing," replied the woman spoken to, who didn't even remember how to start a fight, but who did not refuse one when it was so close at hand. "You ask what I have lost here? What else could it be but my health just lookin' at you and your house?"

From below, Carpia butted in:

"Don't pay no attention to her, Mother dear. Even garbage would get dirty if ya threw it in her face."

"Me let her alone?" exclaimed Sargüeta untying the knot in her scarf only to redo it with her hands trembling with anger. "Me let her alone? I'd leave her with no hair on the top of her head, by God, if she was only a little closer."

"You'd do that to me?" replied the woman, who was beginning to get excited. "You boot-licker . . . you egg-sucker . . . you low-down devil."

"Yes, to you, you gossip, you concealer of criminals . . . and also that other sucker that is provokin' you against me."

Then the other woman from her balcony:

"Shoot brimstone from that devil's mouth, you snake, you scandalmonger, you drunkard."

The Females of the Mocejón Family

Carpia spoke thus from the street without the women upstairs keeping quiet:

"Scandalmonger! Ask her, Mother, why her husband gave her a cleanin' the other night. And if she don't dare to tell ya, let her rascally neighbor tell ya, 'cause she runs some secret errands for her and gets a share of the liquor she buys for her, by God."

Then this woman cut in while all the others were still yelling:

"Me? Me anybody's errand boy? Shameless wench! Loafer! Envious rascal! Did she tell ya that by any chance?"

"The person told me who saw it with her own eyes, and she ain't told me no lies yet, 'cause she ain't so far away that she can't hear you. Lean out the window further if you want to see her. Damn it, don't act hypocritical, 'cause everybody knows what I'm sayin' about cha."

The woman in the window chimed in amidst all the other shouting:

"For me to tell you those things I would need to go downstairs to exchange words with you and remind myself of that indecent scarecrow, like that other wench. And you, you long-tongued bitch, why are you makin' anybody else talk, when you are a whole sack full of evil yourself, just like your filthy mother? Both of you are uncontrollable and have to sleep off your drunks in the balcony 'cause you don't have no beds—just like big old sows!"

Carpia shouted, "What more do you want, you impudent, shirtless thing, that I would allow you to ever mention my name?"

The woman in the window said as she let out a mouthful of spit: "Well! There goes your name right now. Come down to pick it up in the trash in the street, because it's contaminatin' the garbage."

I am going to cut off here this sample of the cloth of the process by means of which the Mocejón females go in involving other fighters in the contest, and at the same time subdividing it into many others, each from a different motive. So that in less than fifteen minutes the whole street is quarreling. Everybody yells, but nobody understands anyone else. They shout at the top of their voices and vomit forth words whose crudeness cannot even be expressed here by symbols, because there are none which show their filthy character—drunken, dirty, foul-smelling, all at the same time. All the women taking part in the quarrel shout at once. No one tries to reply to any nauseating insult with one that is more filthy, but simply to expel from her mouth, with all the strength of her lungs, as many abuses, as much lewdness, as many filthy words as keep occurring to each of the violent women involved. For the success of such fights, the human voice alone is not enough, regardless of how loud it may be. In the midst of this infernal uproar gymnastics are also used as a help, because even simple vulgar mimicry doesn't quite suffice either. For that reason one woman with arms akimbo will stamp her feet, another bends till she almost rolls over, at the same time she is tying and untying ten times in succession the scarf around her head. Another nearly squats and rises, wtih her eyes flashing and the veins on her throat almost bursting. Another hits herself impudently on the hips with her closed fists, or strikes her butt with the palm of her hand. Someone else leans way over the balustrade of the balcony, with her hair hanging over her eyes and her jacket unbuttoned, and waves her arms wildly. Others, like the Mocejón females, do all of this in a moment, and much more still, without giving any rest to their throats or cursing tongues.

This spectacle was not new on High Street, and because it wasn't, passers-by gave it little importance when they saw it. But when they asked the motive of the first spectator leaning against the wall, or standing in the middle of the sidewalk with legs spread wide apart, they heard about the supposed seduction in Mechelín's house. That was why Carpia was there, more attentive in spreading these rumors through the street than to stand her ground in any quarrel, especially since it had already reached the desired pitch. The passers-by and onlookers of all kinds were crowding up, one by one, little by little, until they formed a dense group in front of the door. The questions continued. Names were given, curiosity was stirred up and the usual comments made.

The Females of the Mocejón Family

From time to time the locked door vibrated, shaken from within. Then there was some savage obscenity on the part of Carpia for the culprits on the inside who were thus trying to show that they were locked in against their will.

The honorable reader, without any effort, will understand the situation of the unfortunate Sotileza and Andrés. Because of the emotion of deep disgust which the sudden arrival of Andrés produced in her, and attentive only to reproach him with harsh words for his reckless action, Sotileza did not hear the slight noise that the door made when Carpia closed and locked it. Or if she did hear the sound, she attributed it to something else. Andrés was out of breath, confused and stammering—a sign of the wildness of his decisions to come. As far as he was concerned, not even a cannon shot would have distracted him from the state of bewilderment in which her resolute attitude put him. Neither did the first confused words that Carpia spoke to her mother attract Sotileza's attention because she was more than used to hearing them shout from the street to the balcony. When she finished her harsh scolding of Andrés—who had no good answer —she left him in order to observe from the living room what was going on outside. As soon as she noticed that the door at the other end of the passageway was closed, she ran toward it. When she found that there was no key and the door was locked from the outside, she exclaimed in fear, putting her nervous, convulsive, clenched hands near her mouth:

"Holy heavens! What they have done to me!"

Then she looked through the keyhole and saw Carpia near the street door, and around her some onlookers who were questioning her and looking toward Mechelín's home. She felt a mortal coldness in her heart and lacked breath even to call Andrés, who, bewildered and motionless, was looking at her from the small living room. Finally she made a sign with her hand to have him come to where she was. She was as white as a dead person. Her beautiful eyes were distorted and she was trembling from head to foot.

"Do you hear that shoutin'?" she said to him. "Well, look through here and see what it is."

Andrés looked through the keyhole for a moment and then didn't say a word. He didn't even dare to look at Sotileza while she asked him, half in anger and half in anguish:

"Do you know what this is? Do you know why that door is locked?"

Andrés did not know what to say. She continued:

"Well, all this has been done to put an end to my honor. Look how they are trampin' on it in the street. Holy Virgin! And you are to blame for all of this, Andrés. You, you are to blame. Don't you see how what I feared most has happened? Are you content now?"

"But where is the key?" asked Andrés in a rage, his dismay suddenly changed to despair.

"Where is the key? Can't you guess? In the hands or in the pocket of this wench who has locked us in—'cause she's been lookin' for a chance for a long time to ruin my reputation. She saw you come in here, and so that you and I will be seen by everybody when we get out that door together, she and her mother probably started that fight—'cause that's part of their trade. Are you gradually understandin', Andrés? Do you realize all the harm that you have done to me today?"

For a reply to these deep-felt exclamations of the unfortunate girl, Andrés rushed to the door. In vain he added to the strength of his arms all that his desperation gave him in order to spring the lock and open the door. Then he hit the blackened boards with his hard fists. He made no progress whatever.

"Give me a pole, Silda, a club, anything. I need to open this door right now, because I want to choke somebody with my own hands."

"Don't get excited," Sotileza told him with a tone of bitter resignation. "It will be opened in due time. That's why they closed it."

The Females of the Mocejón Family

Andrés left the door and ran to the living room, remembering a window that was there. But the window had a heavy iron grill. He couldn't even think of moving it. He saw the club that Sotileza had used to shake the dust from Muergo. He tried to remove the lock by prying one end of the club against the door, but the lock was held by heavy clinched nails. He put the club underneath the door and pulled up on it, and the club broke right away. Then he got on his knees and tried to raise it with his fingers, pulling with all his might—but nothing happened. Not even a splinter broke from those tough oak boards.

In the meantime the uproar outside was increasing and the group of onlookers in front of the door was getting bigger. Sotileza, feverish and worried, frequently looked through the keyhole and knew everything that was going on. She could see the anxiety, caused by this scandal, in all the faces turned toward the door and could hear the defaming words against her honor which Carpia was vomiting from her hellish mouth. In each instant that passed without being able to get out of that ignominious jail, she felt in her face the pain of some new thorn that this scourge of shame was driving in there. What would the honorable and affectionate Sidora say when she came back from the Plaza and found the street crowded that way and found out what was happening before she could tell her the truth? And poor old Mechelín! Holy heavens! What a blow it would be for this unfortunate old man when he came back in the late afternoon so cheerful and gay.

These considerations were what worried the unhappy girl most. In the vehemence of her desire to get out as soon as she could in order to bring the dispute concerning her honor to the whole community, she also began to beat the door, making threats and to unburden her desperation by shouting through all the cracks around the door.

As soon as Andrés was convinced that there was no way to get out of there by force, he again fell into profound bewilderment, which intimidated him so much that he covered his ears in order not to hear the tumult from the outside, and asked

Sotileza not to annoy him any more with the weight of her very just remonstrances. Then he saw with perfect clarity how senseless and criminal this matter was and the frightful extent to which his unpardonable foolishness was going to reach.

In one of these moments when he was sitting down with his elbows on his knees and his head in his hands, and Sotileza was in the middle of the living room with her fists on her hips and her gaze lost in a cloud of thoughts, her mouth half open, her face pale and her chest panting, Andrés said suddenly, raising his head:

"Silda, everyone pays for what he does, and if this is the law in matters of little importance, in questions of honor it surely should be even more so. I am ruining your good reputation . . ."

"What are you tryin' to tell me?" Sotileza asked peevishly, coming out of her distressing thoughts.

"That any blotches that fall on your honor because of me I shall wash clean, like decent men should do."

Sotileza bit her lips and said to him instantly:

"You wash the blotches from my honor! You will have all you can do down there washin' away those that are already fallin' on yours!"

"That is not a just answer, Sotileza."

"But it's tellin' you the truth about the way I feel. Oh, Andrés, if you had that idea to restore so little by doin' me this great harm, it is too bad that you did not warn me about it before."

"Why, Silda?"

"Because you could have excused me from telling you that I would never accept the solution that you're offerin'."

"You mean that you never would accept it?"

"Never."

"And why?"

"Because . . . 'cause I wouldn't."

"Well, what more can you ask of me, Sotileza? What is it that you want?"

"From you I want nothin', Andrés—nor from nobody. What I want now," said Sotileza, turning impatiently and convulsively toward the door, "is that that door open—so that I can get out of here as soon as possible to the street in order to look at the people there face to face. That's what I need, Andrés; that is what I want; because each moment that passes in this jail with no exit, something burns me up inside."

"And what do you intend to do when we do get out?" asked Andrés, disheartened again on thinking about this critical moment of trial.

"You are asking that of a woman like me?" said Sotileza, who was getting braver by the moment. "But where can I get out, for God's sake? And I want to get out. I'm choking in this place. Holy heavens, what troubles!"

Andrés, upset by the situation of the desperate girl, ran from the living room resolved to make another try on the door. When he approached it his feet kicked some object that made a metallic sound when it slipped along the boards of the floor. He picked it up. It was a key. Who could have put it there? And what difference did it make?

Andrés was so afraid of going out into this uproar that continued in the street that he doubted whether he should show his find to Sotileza.

"What are you doin', Andrés?" she asked him from the living room.

Andrés ran toward her and showed her the key, telling her where he found it. She let out a yell of delight.

"Oh, the wretch! She threw it under the door. Right! So that we could open it up from the inside and that people will believe what she wants them to. Well, we will see if such a trick is any good, you big rascal!"

While she was saying all this, Sotileza was trembling with emotion. She grabbed the key and took one angry look at it.

Andrés, having forgotten for a moment the extremely compromising situation in which he was, looked with astonishment at the transformation which was taking place in that girl whom he couldn't understand. She was no longer a woman of cold aspect, of calm reasoning and harmonious speech. She was not the discreet young lady who extinguished fiery, clever arguments with an icy, solid stare. Nor was she the provocative beauty who caused storms in hardened hearts with only one glance. Nor had she the elegant loveliness of a distinguished lady. In the opinion of the confused Andrés, all she needed to do to be a great lady was to change clothing and living quarters. Finally she was not the shy young lady who had been crying just a few moments before on account of the risks which her good reputation was running. She was now a ferocious woman. By this time she was showing traces of the former vagabond of the docks, and of the beaches at low tide. Now in her eyes there were bloodshot lines, and in her usually harmonious and pleasing voice there were tones of the fish seller, like so many of those who were right now in the street.

Andrés saw her go away from him like a flash, reach the door, open it with a trembling hand, go into the vestibule and hurl herself into the middle of the group on the sidewalk. In the meantime, he scarcely had strength in his legs to stand up straight. But he considered that such an attitude was the best testimony against his supposed crime. He came to suddenly and changed. He came out behind Sotileza resolved to do anything, but with no other plan than helping her.

When she appeared in the doorway, Sotileza saw the hated Carpia in the middle of the group. She did not hesitate one moment. With all the courage of a pursued beast, she walked between the people who made no effort to stop her. Putting both hands on Carpia's shoulders, she said to her, looking at her with a fierce glance:

"Lift up your rotten head and look me in the eye! Do you see me, you wench? Do you see me, you vile thing? Do you have me where you want me now?"

Carpia, being what she was, did not dare to protest against the shaking Sotileza was giving her. The fierce glance and resolute attitude of that young woman, who acted like a wounded

The Females of the Mocejón Family

lioness, held her bewitched. It is possible too that the weight of her sin influenced her unusual timidity.

Sotileza, becoming more and more excited as Carpia became more intimidated, did not let go of her.

"And have you thought that it was enough for a ragamuffin like you to want to dishonor a decent woman like me, just to have your own way? When did you dream that up, you dirty wench? You watched my door like a treacherous fox, and when you saw a respectable man enter my house, a man who enters it every day in plain sight, you locked us in there, thinkin' that when we got out by usin' the key you returned under the door, you was goin' to insult me here in front of the whole neighborhood, which you and your rascally mother had assembled by means of one of the scandalous fights that you know so well how to put on whenever you wish. Well, here I am! Now you have me in the street! And what are you goin' to do now? Do you think that there is anyone here, regardless of how low he may be, who would dare to think of me what you want them to think?"

As Sotileza continued shouting, the other quarrels calmed down as if by magic. Everybody was looking at her and all minds were hanging onto her words and gestures.

Sargüeta withdrew quickly from the balcony, like a reptile hides in its hole when it hears sounds nearby. Carpia thought that the world was falling in on her when she saw herself in the midst of that silent multitude, yet alone with her implacable enemy, and so burdened with sin.

"Do all of you see it?" continued Sotileza without taking her hands from Carpia's shoulders and looking violently at the groups in the streets and on the balconies nearby. "She don't even dare to deny the evil that I'm throwin' in her face. The infamous wretch must be pretty well abandoned by God. Look here, you envious, soulless rascal. I got out of the jail you made for me with a desire to drag you along the ground pullin' your hair, I was so blind with rage. But now I see that for your punishment, in addition to what your own conscience is givin' you, this is more than enough!" And with that she spat in her face. At the same time she gave her a hard shove and left her.

There was scarcely anyone in the street who did not have some score to settle with the insulting tongue of Carpia. For that reason, when in a fit of anger she tried to attack the dauntless Sotileza after being insulted in that manner, a whole chorus of abuses frightened her. A wave of people shoved her up the street. Then a girl approached the triumphant Sotileza and told her:

"I saw it all from over there in front. I saw her close and lock the door of your house."

"And I saw her throw the key under the door when she thought that my back was turned," added an old man with a running nose. "I'll say it now, because I am a truthful man. You have to be careful of vicious dogs when they ain't chained."

"I couldn't have been mistaken, because it couldn't have been nothin' else!" exclaimed Sotileza rejoicing over these two unexpected testimonies. "But it is a good thing that somebody saw her—and I hope to God that you will dare to say it out loud some other place, if anyone who has authority to punish these infamies asks you about it."

Poor Sotileza could not take any more. A sob checked her voice in her throat. She put her hands over her eyes and ran to hide her grief in the farthest corner of her home. There she shed seas of tears surrounded by the loving compassion of Pachuca and other girls from the neighborhood who let her cry because only by crying could she alleviate her heart, which was so full of bitter grief.

And Andrés? What a role he played and what punishment he got for his indiscretion! At first he did not go beyond the doorway. From there he observed that everybody's curiosity was satisfied by what Sotileza was saying and doing and that no one was any longer concerned about him. As soon as the group in front turned around to chase Carpia up the street and everybody was looking in her direction, he was convinced that Sotileza was not running any physical risk. Then he left the doorway and slipped away stealthily down the street until he reached Hospital Hill, where he breathed more easily. Here he kicked the ground a couple of times in disgust, clenched his fists and walked faster, as if someone were pursuing him with steel hooks.

While going along the shore he saw Sidora going up Somorrostro Street with another woman. She stopped and gave one of those hearty laughs of hers, with her chest and stomach trembling. That laughter was like a whiplash on Andrés' face and a pair of pincers on his conscience. He started to walk faster and kept on going, without knowing exactly where until it was time to eat. Then he went home without daring to think about all the repercussions that episode might have. Even the details of the event, stamped in fire on his memory, made his face turn red with shame.

24   SOME RESULTS OF THAT SCANDAL

Did that scandal get noised about! It couldn't help but be under such circumstances, at that time of day, and Andrés being who he was and his accomplice so popular in High Street and other places, and the city so small! Everything, yes everything was learned and a great deal more added, because the imagination is very productive in making suppositions; and the frankness of the general public was calmly accrediting such suppositions with some pretext of truth, and "it was said," "and people said." Who is capable of knowing what was said, or how the snowball kept rolling and getting larger until even the blind could see it, and even the deaf could hear its crunchings?

Don Pedro Colindres frequented many places where there was the smell of tar. Nearly all the customers at such places were members of his seafaring profession. These people, perhaps with more enthusiasm than any other group, discussed and argued the facts and hearsay of what had happened on High Street. No one was so unwise as to tell the story with all its details to the father of the protagonist. But the captain was gradually accumulating fears and suspicions because so many conversations were cut short when he approached. These suspicions, increased by what his wife feared, were making him worry.

His wife's worries were almost unbearable for her because she knew the truth long before he did. Her friends had been less discreet than those of the captain, and had told her something, but not all, of what had happened on High Street. What little she needed to fill it all in could be seen in Andrés' excitement and his alarming irritability.

In the evening Andrés had entered the house in the same state as at noon. His parents had wondered what caused it. His father called him to his office where he had just had a long talk with Andrea. Andrés went to the office without even trying to hide his state of moral martyrdom. He went in like a brave convicted prisoner to his last church service, with agony in his soul, but not docile nor in despair.

Don Pedro Colindres, on seeing him thus, noticed that his own indignation changed to deep grief. He said to him:

"In all justice, Andrés, you cannot consider me a strict father. You cannot say that I have made you a slave to my implacable will, nor that I have not given you all the freedom you asked for, nor that I have not used everything in my possession to win your affection. This has not been with harshness, because I did not want you to be afraid of me but to respect me; and in everything that is compatible with your obligations, I wanted your confidence."

"That is all true," replied Andrés.

"Well, in testimony of the fact that you think that way, and that you are not ungrateful, you are going to tell me, right now, what is the matter with you and what happened to you this morning."

Andrés felt his body bathed in a cold sweat. He seemed to

lack the strength that he thought he had and slumped into a chair near which he was standing. His mother became frightened to see him so pale and came to his side in one jump from the chair in which she was seated. The captain approached him too, not in alarm, because he knew better than his wife the cause of Andrés' weakness.

"What's the matter with you, Andrés, my son!" exclaimed his mother, taking his head in her hands.

"Nothing," replied Andrés, straightening up and trying to smile by great effort of will.

"Sure, it's nothing," observed Don Pedro in order to calm his wife.

Then, bending his body to get between her and Andrés, he said to him, trying to soften as much as possible the natural harshness of his voice:

"I know that I am putting you in a tough spot with my demands, but what the devil! We men have been in worse storms—a little scared, perhaps, but always with a serene, calm face. So you see, you have to set an example. A little courage, boy, and you easily make the plunge. Do you have any objection to talking in front of your mother—about certain things that are mixed up in it all? Do you want her to leave? Do you have more confidence in her, and want me to leave? Frankly, man, tell us whatever you want, provided that you free us from these anxieties that are worrying us."

"I don't want anybody to leave," replied Andrés, "because I am not ashamed of anything that I have to say. Although what happened may have seemed a dishonor to some, actually in itself there was no dishonor."

"Well, we are listening," said his father, "so go ahead and talk, but please do not try to hide any of the truth from us."

Here Andrés began to tell the story with the greatest exactitude, and even some touches for more color and interest, with the intention that the iniquity of the Mocejón women should appear as large as possible.

His mother touched her eyes with her hands when he described the shouts of the quarreling women and the curiosity of the bystanders while he was locked in the house and when he came out behind Sotileza, who was so furious. Later he told how he had left there burning up the road, and flashing fire in his eyes.

"Holy heavens, what a shame for you—and for all of us, Andrés!" exclaimed his mother when he finished his story.

The captain let out a good loud sailor's oath, although half suppressed. He looked harshly at his son and said:

"That's not a bad story. I'm saying that because on hearing it from you I would have sworn that my face was being painted red. But the most interesting part of the story is missing, and I hope that you will tell it to us with the same exactness that you have told the rest."

"Well, there isn't anything more to tell," said Andrés with little sincerity.

"Sure there is," exclaimed his father. "Now you have to tell us why you went to that house on High Street."

"Well, I was going . . ." replied Andrés hesitatingly and confusedly, "I was going to pick up some fishing tackle that . . ."

"That's a lie, Andrés, just a lie," interrupted his father with angry tone and gestures. "For that, you could have gone any other time of the day or night without failing in your obligations at the office as you did this morning. Confess the truth to us, Andrés!"

"I already have told you."

"I repeat that you are lying."

"But, what do you want me to tell you?" asked Andrés with a tone in which were mingled opposition and poorly concealed anger.

"The truth, and nothing but the truth," insisted Don Pedro. "What intentions took you to that house at that time of day?"

"The same ones that have taken me there so many other times," replied Andrés unwillingly.

"I am beginning to suspect," the captain said with a terrible voice, "but, at least, on those other occasions there was someone else at home besides that girl. Then you weren't neglecting your duties and you could excuse the strength of your affections. But in this case there is nothing to excuse you, Andrés, nothing, nothing of what this all heaps on you. All of it condemns you. And if you keep quiet, what should we believe?"

Andrés remained a few moments with his head down, his glance indecisive. He was twisting one end of his mustache with a nervous hand. Then he got up from the chair and began to walk excitedly around the room. His mother never took her eager eyes from him. His father persisted with his question:

"What should we believe, Andrés?"

Seeing no other way out, Andrés replied harshly and brutally: "Whatever you want to."

"Don't you see, Pedro, don't you see? Don't you see that what I feared has happened?" exclaimed the mother at this point. "This is the first result of his evil companions. They are ruining us. Tell me now that I'm imagining things and that I am an impertinent mother."

"Leave me in peace with those devilish ideas, Andrea. This is not the time to talk about them," replied Don Pedro in a voice like a hurricane. Then turning to Andrés, he said to him, trembling with anger: "The only answer that would fit with what you just told me would be a slap on the mouth that would knock all your teeth out. You fool. But we'll skip all of that if you want it that way. I assure you . . . what are you trying to get with such answers, after all that has happened to you? Are you trying to kill your embarrassment, which comes from remembering what you have done, by trampling on the affection of your parents? Or are you trying to deceive us with the truth itself? You understand that I am taking you at your word, and I'll believe whatever I want to. But I think that will be the worst. You understand that well?"

"Yes, sir," replied Andrés, hard-hearted and gloomy.

"All right," added his father, clenching his fists and biting his lips in anger. "Now there is another matter to discuss with you here. It is of more importance than all the others put together."

Poor Andrea did not stop a minute from looking anxiously from her husband to her son.

"In what happened this morning you alone have not been the cause of this shame, nor are you the only one affected by all this gossip in half the city. Considering this—because you must have considered it well—what ideas are going through your head now? With what rigging are you going to face this storm?"

"With whatever is necessary," replied Andrés without hesitation.

"That is not saying enough."

"That's all I can answer just now."

"Don't test my patience any more, son."

"Well then have a little leniency with me."

Andrea then looked at her husband with an expression which recommended that he follow the desires of Andrés.

"Leniency!" replied the captain without paying any attention to his wife. "Are you having any with me? Don't you think that each reply of yours is like a dagger thrust for us? I'll not let you go even though you cry to high heaven, because the blows caused by your words hurt me much more. With your answers you have demonstrated to me that my question has touched you in the quick, and that's what I was shooting at, Andrés. This is all very serious. I can tell that by the way you are trembling, and by what you are not saying more than by what you do say. Speak, son, but straightforwardly, with no tricks and no beating around the bush. Your mother and I need to know the extent of these adventures and the course of your intentions. Notice that we fear that they may be bad, because you would have told us if they had been good."

To tell Andrés that his intentions were very bad was enough to drive the fiery young man out of his mind. It was wrong to suppose that he thought of saving Sotileza's honor by marrying her. The intention or thought that his father feared did not cross his mind, which was mature and seasoned at least. This thought did not cross his mind because Sotileza herself had scorned it during those moments that were so critical for the poor girl. But, in the supposition that this thought did exist, why was it so bad? Why shouldn't the honor of the orphan girl, capable of noble disinterest, be as worthy of respect as that of the proudest matron?

And these considerations, made in an instant by Andrés, disturbed him to such a degree that he used the words he did when he replied to the requests and warnings of his father.

The captain's wife had to interfere between them in order to prevent her husband from carrying out the threats that he had just made.

Don Pedro Colindres was not a man who was capable of holding in low esteem anyone's honor just because its owner had simple clothes. But because Andrés' answer was unconnected, disrespectful and confused made him believe that it was only a question of some boyish passing fancy, of a dangerous girl, of a surge of passion that it was necessary to extinguish at all cost and without loss of a single minute. And in case the suspicion did not have enough substance by itself, Mrs. Colindres, who was astonished by Andrés' declarations, reinforced it with these words:

"And after hearing this, Pedro, don't you realize all the rest? Don't you see that being locked inside of Mechelín's home and the scandal in the street has been just a trick by that rascally girl to trap this innocent boy?"

"That supposition is false," Andrés replied angrily, forgetting the respect due his mother because of the great injustice that she was committing against the respectable Sotileza.

"Even that, Andrés! Even that!" his father rebuked him, looking daggers at him. "You even step on your mother's affection and respect in order to get your own way. They have corrupted your heart even to that extent. You have been blind to that extent."

"I am not trampling on those things, Father," he replied, half choking, "but I am not made of stone, and certain blows hurt me greatly. Don't give me any more of them."

"And what about the ones that you are giving us now, my dear boy? Do you think they don't hurt us?" asked his mother crying.

"Bah!" exclaimed Don Pedro Colindres with ferocious irony. "What do these blows matter? I am already an old ship that has been cast adrift, and you are on the way to becoming one. He surely has done his duty toward us! What matters right now is that nothing unpleasant may happen to him and that the tattered young lady may not lose any sleep. Anger of God! This can't be tolerated and I am not reckoning with it, because neither your mother nor I deserve it, Andrés. Ungrateful son!"

"Father," Andrés murmured hoarsely, choked by the effect of these words, which fell on his heart like drops of molten lead.

"Pedro, for the love of God, calm down a little," said his wife, crying. "He will talk and will tell us what we want. Isn't that right, Andrés? Aren't you going to tell . . . what should be told . . . because up to now you have not told us anything calmly."

"After what he has confessed to us," interrupted the captain without any lessening of his anger, "he can tell me nothing that will not be some new folly, or some lie that I will not swallow."

"Now you listen," said Andrés to his mother. "I am not needed here, because if I am asked anything, I can't help but answer according to the way I feel."

"Well, for that reason," said the captain, reaching the limits of his exasperation, "and because I know the poor quality of your feelings, I do not wish to hear any more from you. For that reason you are no longer needed here, and I want you to get out of my sight. I do not wish to see you again until you come to me thinking otherwise. Do you understand, you fool? You ungrateful rascal?"

"I shall not forget it," answered Andrés gruffly. And he left the room quickly.

Some Results of That Scandal 259

Don Pedro Colindres remained in the room walking from one side to the other like a tiger in its cage. His wife followed him in his confused movements with tears in her eyes and some ideas in her mind which she did not express. Quite a while passed in this manner. Suddenly the captain said, without stopping his walk:

"Give me my hat, Andrea."

"Where do you want to go?"

"I'm going to High Street right now. It is necessary to study this matter on the scene itself and not squander a single instant nor any details that will conspire against this evil thing, cost what it may."

This seemed like a good idea to the captain's wife—almost as good as another one she had had ever since Andrés started to answer their questions.

Don Pedro Colindres had scarcely reached the door when his wife was putting on her shawl. A few minutes later she was walking toward the home of Don Venancio Liencres.

25 OTHER CONSEQUENCES

In a very few hours, how the appearance of the interior of Mechelín's home had changed! What a sad picture it represented at the time Don Pedro Colindres turned his steps in that direction! Silda was weak and tired from crying. Now there were no tears in her reddened eyes. She was seated on a stool, leaning against one side of a dresser opposite the bedroom door, the curtains of which were open. She gave no other signs of life except an occasional broken sigh which she tried to suppress but couldn't, or the sad glances which from time to time she directed through the doors to the bed where Mechelín was lying. Sidora, seated about halfway between them, was suffering from their grief as much as from her own. She ceased consoling

Sotileza only to try to cheer up her husband. And in the meantime, how the tears rolled, first one by one and then in a stream, down the cheeks of his noble old face.

Mechelín recognized his wife's feelings by her changed voice, even though the feeble candlelight did not show much of her facial expression. Then, trying to comfort her, he said from his bed:

" 'Tain't nothin', my dear, nothin', except when one's old hull is in such bad condition and so worn that when it hits a clam on the bottom it makes a hole. Just see how it was. I was coming back from a day at sea with a little laughter in my soul because I had some left from yesterday's accumulation, and I even thought I had enough to last me all this week. After that, God only knew, as I was movin' along that way I heard somethin' said here and somethin' else there in the street. I asked a question or two and things seemed to be gettin' worse. By the time I got home, I was nearly sunk. Here I find a sigh and there tears. And I was about ready to sink without bein' able to help it. 'Cause one ain't used to that, 'cause one is not made of stone! But I came to the surface again, and although there was some damage to the ship, or a bitter taste in my mouth, and this can change, time cures these wounds in one way or another, and we keep on rowin', Sidora. And this is the case, 'cause I'm not worse than yesterday, although it may seem so to you. A few of the trimmings are stripped off, which can be explained. The old body asked for a little rest and I am givin' it. And that's all there is to it."

"And that seems only a trifle to you, Mechelín? It seems only a little matter?" replied his wife.

"Just a trifle, Sidora," he said again; "and it would seem still less if that little angel there didn't grieve so much and would realize that she hasn't done nothing to be ashamed of, nor any blame for what has happened . . ."

"That's what I say, Mechelín; that's what I say; and she says what good does it do to tell the truth when no one believes it."

"God saw it all and He knows, daughter; God saw it all,"

exclaimed Mechelín from his bed, "and with such a witness on your side, what difference does it make if the whole world is against you?"

"But we don't have any enemy, Mechelín, because you have seen how the whole street came in here to console her in her trouble and to point the finger at those who caused it. But, holy heavens, of what stuff are these devilish souls made? Why are they so wicked? What pleasure do they get out of causing so much harm to other people who don't deserve it? How can they live even an hour with such rotten hearts?"

"Those women!" exclaimed Silda then, seemingly coming to because of vivid memories. "Those women have put a dagger here—right in the middle of my heart. Isn't there any justice in this world to punish them before God gives them what they deserve in the next?"

"We'll see about that too, daughter. We'll catch them any place we can, as is right," replied Sidora, "and if we are not strong enough to do it ourselves other stronger hands also interested in the matter will help us. I have already told you. You were not the only person offended."

"Right," said Mechelín.

"Yes, and when I think of that, my grief is twice as big," replied Silda, with a meaning that Sidora and Mechelín were far from grasping.

"The truth is," said Sidora, "in regard to that other detail, that this blotch could not have fallen on any cloth that we like more. That's the way things are, daughter. Evil never comes alone. But God is in heaven, and will not allow this person to be angry at those who were not to blame for the harm done to him. He came of his own accord. No one asked him to and the message he brought could have been done on an occasion of less risk. Am I saying risk? How could his generous heart have thought of any risk? And as for others of his family they will know that we do not repay them with insults for all their favors toward us. You'll see to that, won't you, daughter?"

Sotileza bit her lips and closed her eyes, pressing the lids down hard, as if inner sinister visions tormented her. Mechelín let out a complaint full of anguish and turned over on the bed.

"Do you want me to do something else, Mechelín?" Sidora asked him, going quickly to the head of the bed.

"Don't bother now," replied Mechelín, giving a big sigh. Then he added, putting his head close to his wife's ear: "Try to cheer Sotileza up, and don't pay any attention to me; with a rest I'll get along fine."

Consolations of that kind wounded Sotileza's pride, although she was grateful for them. She had heard so many since noon. Sidora recognized that. She kept still, and silence again reigned in the house.

This is the picture inside the house when knocks were heard at the door. Sidora went to open it after drying her eyes with her apron. She found Don Pedro Colindres there. His angry appearance frightened the poor woman. Fearing the worst, she would have gladly asked for a little consideration for their grief and sorrow, but she did not dare. Don Pedro, after a few sharp words, entered the room in front of Sidora. Sotileza, very surprised to see him, got up quickly. Mechelín sat up in bed when he heard the captain's voice. He walked to the door but had to hold on to it in order to keep from falling.

"What's the matter, Mechelín," Pedro asked him, surprised at the appearance of the poor old fisherman who was so pale, weak and dejected.

"Nothin' much, Don Pedro; nothin' much," replied Mechelín, trying to smile. "I wanted to receive you with the courtesy which you deserve, but my apparatus failed me. I couldn't make it."

As the poor fellow seemed to get weaker the longer he talked, the captain took him in his arms and put him back on the bed.

"I feel all right now, Don Pedro," Mechelín said a moment later. "Apparently that's all I needed—for the present."

When the captain went back to the living room where the two women were, he noticed that they were crying in silence. His heart, with an apparent tough covering, was—as is known—

soft and compassionate. It is not to be wondered then that Andrés' father, when it came time to unleash the tempests that were beating against his brain when he left his house did not know where to begin or how to state the reason for his presence in the midst of such a sad scene.

Finally, wishing to show that he was more vigorous than he seemed to be, he said to the distressed women:

"What the devil is going on around here? Let's see. Mechelín's sickness isn't severe enough for such bawling."

"Oh, sir!" replied Sidora between stifled sobs. "His illness, coming right after the other trouble . . ."

"And what is the other trouble, woman?"

"The other! Well, I thought that was why you came."

"Right!" said Mechelín from his bed.

All the memories of the recent interview with Andrés came to the captain's mind, and all the anger which this had produced in him made him say very excitedly:

"That is true, Sidora; that's exactly why I came. Do you think it motive enough for a call?"

"More than enough. Half that motive would be too much," replied the poor woman, intimidated.

Silda, who seemed unable to stand, sat down again in the same corner where we saw her before.

The captain faced her and said with a certain brusqueness:

"I need to learn from you what happened here this morning. Do you have a mind to tell it, without adding or subtracting anything from the truth?"

"Yes, sir," she replied courageously.

"Of course, Mechelín," said Don Pedro, turning toward the bedroom, "it is to be supposed that this account will not add to your illness. Although the matter is urgent, it is not that urgent. I can come back some other time."

"No, sir," Mechelín hastened to say. "There ain't no reason to bother you. As far as that is concerned, I grow fat on stories like this one. And don't you worry about it. The more I hear the better I understand and the less it hurts my heart. Go ahead and tell it, darlin', without any bashfulness at all, so that Don Pedro will know it well."

"And you may well believe Mechelín," added Sidora, "because by his own desire, he won't talk about anything else in this house during the whole blessed day."

With these manifestations, Silda very willingly began to relate the episode with the same details as Andrés had done at home.

"Exactly," said the captain as soon as Sotileza finished her story. "I knew all that right up to the point where you left off. But, after that, what more happened?"

"From the way it seems, and from what the neighbors all say who have been coming in here," said Sidora, "the miserable enemy who stirred things up so much really was sunk when she saw how other people pulled her around by the hair. 'Cause before this blessed girl got out of her prison, others had already been fightin' Carpia with insults and attacks, but she and her mother thrive on that. Then Carpia went upstairs and shut herself in the house with her mother, without even daring to open the doors to the balcony, 'cause all the neighbors had insulted them so much, and regardless of how bad they are it must weigh on their conscience—even out of fear. Then father and son came back from the sea. One might say day and night because the men are so different from the women. People say that there was quite a rumpus in the house because the father started in on 'em just with words 'cause it all seemed of little importance to him. But the boy was brokenhearted and hid his face in shame. I believe that he mistreated his sister and he almost came to blows with his mother. He has come down here I don't know how many times but ain't went beyond the street doorway, and there he is leanin' against the wall with his hands in his pockets, his eyes angry lookin' and his hair all messed up. He don't say nothin' regardless of how many people try to cheer him up by tellin' him that he ain't responsible for the sins of his household—and he don't change at all. There are some neighbors who say that witnesses could do all right against these she-devils for what they said and conspired against the ruination of this house. Such evil doings should not go unpunished. And that's all we can tell you, Don Pedro, from what they tell us about what happened to make us all so sad. As far as poor Mechelín is concerned, you can realize his situation; he is old and very sickly, and to find this when he got home—he who has always been bubblin' over with joy. He was almost overcome. So nobody is surprised when Sotileza and I cry once in a while. But the walls of this house have seen so few tears, Don Pedro!"

Don Pedro almost contributed a tear of his own by the time Sidora finished her story between sobs, because much of Andrés' character was like his father's. But he got out of the situation, resolved to complete his plan to examine the group carefully, since he could do it easily, without bothering them much. He continued his questioning as follows:

"That is not exactly what I was trying to find out, Sidora, although I am glad to know it."

"Say then what you do want, sir."

"I would like to know what impression this episode has caused."

"It is all very evident, sir."

"No, it isn't. Maybe I have not stated my question well. What plans do you have now after what happened? Whom do you blame?"

"Blame? Whom should we blame? The ones who are to blame, of course, those rascals upstairs. This misfortune states that very clearly."

"Yes, yes, I understand. But it usually happens, when things like this are examined in the family, some say that if it hadn't been for this, then something else would not have happened, and if you, and if I, and if something else . . . in short, you understand me. Then comes the reckoning of accounts, shall we say it that way, and then this and then that, and what should have happened . . . and what will happen . . . and what they hope . . . and what they are afraid will happen . . ."

"What is hoped! What is feared!" repeated the poor woman, looking at the captain from head to foot

"Say it, Sidora, say it. Now is the time," called Mechelín from his bed.

"And what is it that she should tell me?" asked Don Pedro Colindres, turning with a frown toward the bedroom.

"What she knows, and what is to the point now," replied the fisherman. "Come, Sidora, now that he is here. Have courage, woman, because he is good natured."

"Yes, man, yes, why shouldn't I say it?" answered Sidora. "It is not a mortal sin."

The captain was worried to death, and Sotileza was like a statue of ice in her corner by the dresser.

"May you know, Don Pedro," said Sidora, "that aside from the sorrow caused by the matter, the only thing that bothers us here is not knowin' what we can expect from Andrés."

"Let's see, let's see," murmured the captain, getting more comfortable in his chair to concentrate all of his attention.

If he had noticed Sotileza's face a little at that moment, what an icy smile he would have seen on her lips and what a spark in her eye!

"Andrés," continued Sidora, "was accustomed to come here like his own home, because we always had the door open wide for him. He deserved to have that done for him even in the best palaces in Spain. And because he did deserve it, there were only hearts that enjoyed seeing him so much a part of us and so good-hearted with people who was not even good enough to clean the soles of his shoes. You know well, sir, that if we have anything to eat here in this house, we owe it to his generosity and the kindness of his family. In order not to cause him any grief, or to anybody in his family, each one of us would have pulled out stones from the street with our teeth, if that's what needed to be done. But there are some souls of the devil, sir, who get sick because their neighbors are well—and you know this mornin's episode. The blow was against the honor of this

Other Consequences

unfortunate girl, but half of it was also against Andrés, who was in the house then, as anyone else could have been. By our own grief we want to try to lessen his grief and the annoyance to his whole family. It is just and natural that it be this way. But, for the love of God, Don Pedro, look at the matter coolly and take from us half the grief that is choking us by pardonin' what we say, without more of it than what the devil left for us."

"Right, Don Pedro. Right!" added Mechelín from his room. "That's what we ask. That's what we want—there is nothin' greater in the law of justice and good will."

"And that is all that is happening to us?" asked the captain, breathing more easily than before. "That is all you want as far as I am concerned—for all that this unfortunate matter may mean to me, for the share that has fallen to my son?"

"And do you think that this is a little part?" Sidora and Mechelín asked almost at the same time.

From the depths of his heart, the captain let out a big interjection motivated by certain qualms of conscience which he was beginning to feel when faced by the candid disinterest of that honest couple. In order to hide these feelings better, he said:

"That is understood, Sidora. In my house there is no one so inconsiderate that, regardless of how much he regrets the matter—and you may be sure that we all regret it greatly—who tries to make you responsible for any harm that you have not caused. But I had imagined that you might want, and it would be very natural if you should, something quite different—something, for example, like the punishment of those two scoundrels by human justice and that I should help you in this undertaking, since I could do more than you."

"Right, right," said the voice of Mechelín inside the bedroom.

"That has also been discussed some," said Sidora, encouraged by the captain's attitude. "But there were some pros and cons about it. Someone has said that it is better to leave things as they are, because these things that have to do with honor shouldn't be fiddled with very much. Someone else has thought that punishment of the culprits will merely put the truth more in evidence."

"Right, right."

"From appearances," said the captain, "you are in favor of carrying that out, Mechelín?"

"Yes, sir," he replied, "and with full sail!"

"And you, girl," asked Don Pedro of Sotileza, "how about you, the one most concerned?"

"Me too," replied Sotileza courageously.

"Well, if you think that this is best," added Sidora before she was asked, "don't stop on my account. I ain't revengeful, sir, but the truth is that you can't live with any peace where those foul women are. If they are triumphant with this evil, as they always have been, I do not know what might happen here tomorrow."

"Well, everything possible will be done to see that they get what they deserve this time," concluded the captain, who thought that any punishment of the Mocejón women would also relieve Andrés' situation as far as public opinion was concerned.

A little after this he got up to leave. Sotileza got up too, and said to him, overcoming with a visible effort of will the repugnancy which detained her:

"Don Pedro, you have not come to this house tonight just for what has been said so far."

"What do you mean, girl?" exclaimed the captain looking at her with surprise.

"That's the pure truth," replied Sotileza valiantly, "and 'cause it is the truth, I'm sayin' it without any idea of offendin' nobody with it. And 'cause I want you to leave here certain to get peacefully what you expected to get by war."

"Daughter!" exclaimed Sidora, frightened.

Mechelín sat up in bed and Don Pedro Colindres could not conceal to any great extent the floundering in which those precise affirmations of Sotileza placed him.

Other Consequences

She continued:

"I want you to know, and hear from my own lips, that I never allowed myself to be tempted by covetousness nor did any ideas of belongin' to the upper class ever make me giddy, and that I esteem Andrés for what he is, not for what he might be worth to me; and that if there was no other way to save my good reputation than by becomin' his wife, I would prefer to have my honor in doubt rather than take on such a heavy cross to bear."

"For the love of God," replied the captain, looking at the brave young lady with a gesture that was as bitter as it was sweet, "I do not know what you are driving at."

"And I thought that half of what I told you would be more than enough to make you understand."

"Well, just imagine that I have not understood one bit of your thoughts and that I want you to make it clear to me."

Sotileza continued: "I know Andrés very well 'cause I have had dealin's with him for so many years. For that reason, and for somethin' that he told me this mornin' on seein' me here in the agony of shame, and by the air that you had when you came into this house tonight, I could very well believe that he had repeated to his father somethin' that I do not want to leave without an adequate answer."

Don Pedro Colindres, interpreting her last words in a sense not very honorable for Andrés, was offended in his family pride, and replied harshly:

"Well, if he told you what I presume he told you, what more could you wish? Are we agreed on that now after so many demonstrations of humility?"

With this reply, it was Sotileza who felt wounded in her pride. In order to finish once and for all that matter which troubled her, she concluded as follows:

"I have not told you nothin' that is contrary to what I said before. I thought that it was more than enough to talk this way so that you alone would understand me, but now that I miscalculated, I'll tell you more clearly. I live on charity here, and with these few rags I am worth only the amount that people respect me. Dressed in silks and loaded with diamonds, I would be a ridiculous sight, and my feet would slip in shiny shoe soles. That would be bad for all who had to endure me, and worse for me, 'cause I would be out of place. I am made for this poverty and am all right in it without desirin' nothin' better. This is not virtue, sir. It is simply the way that I am. That's why I told Andrés what he knows well, and you have to know too, 'cause I do not want to answer any more for my misdeeds . . . and I don't want no one to get ahead of me in cases like the present. Regardless of how humble one may be, the blows always hurt that one gets for ideas never even thought about. With this, you are takin' away more than you come lookin' for, and I have one worry less. And now pardon the liberty that I have used to talk with you at least because everyone's grief requires it that way."

In truth Sotileza was giving Don Pedro Colindres much more than he had gone to her home to look for. But the captain could not confess that because he understood that such a confession would not greatly emphasize the quality of the thoughts which such a move implied. For that reason he said to Sotileza as his only comment to her statement:

"Although I applaud this honest modesty which is so becoming to you, I want you to know that this time you have been guilty of being a little tricky with me. Let's not talk any more about the matter, if it is all right with you. Forget everything. You can rely on me, as always, and now more than ever. Take care of yourself, Mechelín. Good-by, Sidora, good-by, girl."

And Don Pedro Colindres went out, well convinced that if the tail of this well-known scandal continued wagging in this house, it would not be because of Mechelín's family. This greatly simplified the conflict that had made him leave his home that evening. And because he did believe it this way he returned to his wife much more calm than when he left.

In the meantime, Silda, by using the charm which her voice seemed to have on Sidora and Mechelín, said whatever she took a notion to, by giving to the words she said to the captain an interpretation far from their real meaning.

Were the old folks taken in? It seemed that they were, although it should not be taken as an indication to the contrary, the fact that Mechelín got worse as soon as the women left him alone. Neither could the strange look on Sidora's face be taken as an indication to the contrary. With the emotions resulting from this unexpected scene both things could be explained, without considering them as any new worry.

26 ✎ FURTHER CONSEQUENCES

Andrés left his home because he needed air and the noise and movement of the street in order not to choke in the narrow confines of his room and not to go mad with the unsteady battle within himself. Furthermore, his father had thrown him out and told him not to come back to see him while he had those same thoughts which had produced such a storm in the family. Because Andrés was now tasting the first bitterness of the obstacles of life, he was taking these events in the value of their entire application. And he did not find strength of will to start a new direction of his ideas, nor sufficient impudence in his youthful enthusiasm to calm his father's anger by means of a lie. He left his house, then, to get a change of air and scenery, in order to get away from what seemed to be pursuing him closely and to seek at random, in the noise of the crowds and the mysteries of the night, a peace which the solitude of his room could not give him. The walls of his room had seemed to press in on him, because they were heated by the anger of his family.

For that reason he walked and walked with no fixed course. Even nature seemed opposed to him. He had relied on the cool of the evening to refresh the hot oven of his brain, but there was no breeze and the night was dark and muggy. The warm atmosphere was heavy. Even from the street lights the wandering boy got more torture from the heat which burned the blood in his veins, and he longed for some Arctic cold and the noise of a storm.

He left the streets in the center of the city, because they were too stuffy, and directed his steps to the outskirts.

When he reached the big sycamore trees along Becedo Street, he remembered that Padre Apolinar lived only a few steps from there. He was tempted to go to his house and tell him all that had happened. But what would he gain from that? What would the poor priest know about the things that were happening to him? What was his prestige, compared to that of a man like Don Pedro Colindres, to calm his fury or to reduce him to reason? To reason! But did Andrés himself know where he ought to start in the defense of his dispute, or whether this dispute was defendable, or whether it was even a dispute? In short, just what was it? Was it a supposition which he was trying to impose on his family because of his sense of honor, and a tenacious resistance on the part of his father to recognize it as such? Was there room for serious mediators in such a quarrel? And even if there were, would anybody try to sustain the case of a son against the authority of angry parents? And even if they did, how were his parents going to consider themselves vanquished if the mere statement of such defeat was humiliation and loss of prestige of their inalienable rights as parents?

Furthermore, when his present situation was considered, it did not come about as a result of this discord, but from the bickering which it produced. That was partly due to his own stubbornness in not stating what his father claimed, and to the harshness with which his father reproached him for his unaccustomed defiance. This was the case, then. And for the

Further Consequences

definite solution he saw nothing but time, whose fatal, unalterable march erases the big impressions from the mind, calms struggles in the brain, changes the appearance of things and puts human discords in order. For the present, the poor young man could only feel sorry and suffer.

After walking back and forth beneath these trees he was tired and sat down on a bench off to one side in the shadows. But there the memories of High Street assaulted him with implacable fury. What could have happened there since he had gone down the street after that big scandal? What effect had this caused on the old folks, when each of them had returned from his work? What would they think about him? What had Silda told them? Her words in reply to his manly offer were so disdainful, so crude, when they both were in the worst part of the conflict!

With this memory, he was stringing together all that had happened since then. The consideration of what was happening to him stirred up the tempest in his head more and more. He believed that he would go mad under the din of that struggle of such incongruous ideas and despairing conclusions. Then he got up, nervous and excited, and started to walk back and forth. He walked and walked again without knowing where, until after fully an hour had passed, he noticed that he was at the other side of the city and within a couple of steps of the Zanguina Bar. The sailors from the Lower Town were teeming around it. Therefore he tried to go away from it. People who knew him frightened him now. But where was he going? He looked at his watch and saw that it was ten thirty. By ten o'clock he was accustomed to be at home. His mother was probably missing him, and perhaps dying with anguish when she remembered how he had left the house. But he would not go back home in his present state of mind, and go before his father who had thrown him out of there and told him not to come back while he was thinking the way he was! And the next day would be the same old thing over again. Furthermore, he would have to return to that jail of an office, where they already knew everything that had happened. What an infernal complication of obstacles for such a fiery, deluded young man!

While these thoughts were going through his brain and it seemed that the least logical ones would be followed, he felt a slap on his back and heard a voice say:

"Your boat is beached and you are in trouble, Andrés."

He turned around, surprised, thinking that someone was having fun by trying to read his thoughts, if he had not been thinking them out loud. It was Reñales, one of the most serious and capable fishing boat captains of the Lower Town.

"Why do you say that to me?" Andrés asked him.

"Don't you see how the poor people walk around here like a flock of sheep seeing a wolf?"

"And why is that?"

"I thought that you knew, Andrés. It's all because of the navy draft."

"That was to be expected. And how is it?"

"Well, boy, almost a clean sweep. I don't remember a bigger one. This afternoon they have been notified by the Port Naval Office. There's hardly a young man left in the two guilds. Of those of the Lower Town, there are four who are being drafted for the second time, because there weren't enough others. So you can imagine . . ."

"That's too bad, Reñales, but it's an obligation of a sailor's occupation."

"That occupation is certainly a good one, Andrés. We haven't gone to sea for two days."

"Why not?"

"Haven't you noticed how the weather looks?"

"It seems calm enough right now."

"Yes, but it is a treacherous calm. Who can trust it, Andrés?"

"It's been like this for three days, and nothing has happened."

"I see that now. We know that because it is past."

"The wind from the south is not bad now. This is the season for it."

"We know that. And somewhat for that reason, and a great

Further Consequences

deal because of necessity, we intend to go out tomorrow. These poor people will surely be in good spirits with this stormy blast from the government."

Andrés was thoughtful for a few minutes, and then asked the captain:

"Did you say that boats will be going out tomorrow?"

"If God wills it, and the tempest does not get worse."

"For what are you going out, Reñales?"

"Hake."

"I am glad of that, because I want to go with you."

"You?"

"Yes, me. What's unusual about that?"

"Nothing unusual about it. You are more than qualified for it, and the ocean knows that well."

"Well then . . . ?"

"I was saying that because you could wait for a better occasion."

"What better occasion than this?"

"There are better, Andrés, much better, whenever the weather is from the northeast."

"Well, I prefer the weather from the south when it is in season, like now."

"Everyone has his own likes, Andrés. Although you will not find a single fisherman who has an opinion like yours. In that regard, I was simply telling you what I think."

"And I thank you for your good wishes, so there is nothing more to be said."

"Of course you will want someone to go to your house to call you?"

"By no means. There is no need to arouse the neighborhood. I'll be here, or on the ramp, at the agreed time. And if I am not, go without me. In the meantime, this is just between us, and don't tell anyone a word about what I plan to do. I might not go, and there is no need to blame that on something else."

"Ha ha! Come! That means that you are not sure about the last minute."

"Exactly. I might not be so brave then."
"And you think that they might think you are afraid?"
"That's it."
"Well, no one would believe that who knows you, Andrés."
"Maybe. But just in case, don't tell anybody."
"I don't know how to tell secrets."
"Until tomorrow, Reñales."
"If God wills it."

Andrés had not calculated wrong when he had given himself more or less to mere chance or fate in order to be free to get out of the mess he was in. It was this destiny that had taken him to the Zanguina Bar and to Reñales at the critical moment of solving this serious conflict of what to do. Reñales already knew of his desire to go to sea on a fishing boat. The offer to take him along tomorrow did away with all of Andrés' ideas of doubt and mistrust. He could forget today's troubles in a new adventure tomorrow.

Why return home, after being thrown out by his father with no motive or reason? Let him suffer; let him suffer a while for his harshness! That would teach him not to be so unjust or so violent the next time. As far as his mother was concerned . . . but what had she done to defend her afflicted boy? Hadn't she added her bit of fuel to the fire of his father's anger by slandering the generous intentions of the innocent Silda? Well, let her suffer a little, too . . . because he himself was also suffering a great deal. But even if he tried to prevent this grief by deciding to return that night to his abandoned home, what would this solve? The discord would still exist and would break out again the next day, perhaps mingled with the pleas of unbearable mediators. Nothing doing. They would be stone deaf to the voices from his heart. . . . So, on with his new project! This would solve everything for him at once. One bad night would soon pass. On the other hand, the next day there would be no unbearable faces, no impertinent words, no mocking glances. Instead of the crowded streets, the smell of the

Further Consequences

crowds and the torment of conversation, there would be the immensity of space, the greatness of the sea, the salt air, the motion of the waves and the land forgotten . . . the land which was infected with men. In the meantime, the hours would be passing and opinions would be changing. And gradually everything might change. . . . In this way Andrés was affirming in his mind the resolution inspired by his chance meeting with Reñales, and even believing in good faith that what had seemed a happenstance was really Providence. When, as a matter of fact, he had really seized that chance as he might have grabbed at the wings of a fly at the moment of trying to decide whether to return home—as was logical and convenient—or to declare himself in open rebellion against all his obligations, which was scatterbrained. But we already know what these pressures are like in an adolescent head like that of Andrés, and it is not to be wondered that he chose the worst when faced with the necessity of choosing between two things which seemed to him absolutely bad.

He thus became very firm in his sudden resolve. As soon as he took leave of Reñales, he left the vicinity of the Zanguina Bar in order to think at his leisure, without arousing anybody's curiosity. He did not want to run the risk of failure in his plans because there was still one more interesting point to figure out. Where and how was he going to spend the hours until dawn? He couldn't think of inns or hotels where the least of the risks was being well known to all the proprietors. He couldn't go to the home of any friend either. To spend so many hours walking in the streets, besides being very tiresome, would attract attention to him more than necessary. With no hesitation he decided on the Zanguina Bar.

Inside the Zanguina, before too long, there would not be a solitary sailor, although many of them were used to sleeping there. This usually happened in the most difficult part of the fishing runs. He would arrive about the time that the doors would be closed, and the last customers had left. He didn't want to get there much before that time, because someone from his home might go there looking for him. He would tell the bartender, whom he knew very well, only what was necessary to keep him from being too shocked at his wanting to spend the night there, stretched out on a bench, until time to go to sea on Reñales' boat. And he began to put his plan into action before it cooled off too much.

With great precautions, because the place was one of the most frequented in the city, he observed, at the greatest possible distance, how the most persistent customers of the famous establishment were leaving one by one. As soon as he saw that the doors were going to be closed, he approached and explained his plans to the bartender. These did not shock him to any great extent because he knew how fond Captain Bitadura's son was of the customs of the seafaring people.

"But don't tell me, Andrés, that you are going to spend the night here on top of these hard benches? I'll fix up something soft for you from my own bed."

"Nothing of the kind," replied Andrés. "If I'm going to sleep on something soft, I'll not wake up when I need to."

"But in any case, I have to open up the place before the men go to sea."

"That doesn't matter. I understand what I am doing. Let me have the table of the last booth over there, with a piece of cheese and some bread, and a glass of wine and a candle, and don't worry about me, except to wake me up tomorrow in time, if I am not already awake."

The bartender began to do what Andrés asked by lighting a candle for him. Later, he put it in a tin candlestick and went with him to the booth that Andrés had indicated. While walking in that direction, Andrés noticed a form on the floor of one of the first booths. He heard frightful snores.

"Who is sleeping there?" asked Andrés.

"It is Muergo," replied the bartender. "We understand that he nearly went wild with rage when he learned that the draft was taking him. He swore that he would jump into the ocean before he would consent to being taken into the service. Then he got dead drunk and went to sleep where you see him. Aside from the fact that he has a soul, he is really a beast."

At that moment Andrés envied even Muergo's luck!

Minutes later, in a dark corner of the Zanguina Bar, the reckless young man was trying to restore his physical strength with rest. The hardness of the dirty bench was softened somewhat by the things that the barkeeper had provided for him. While breathing this vile atmosphere, he felt in his head the noise of the battle that his uncontrolled ideas were having there.

Later on, tired from thinking and fear, he stretched out his legs on the bench where he was sitting, leaned his back against the wall, crossed his arms on his chest and tried to get some sleep, which he needed badly. But about all that he accomplished was to be alone in the darkness with his rash thoughts.

27   ANOTHER RESULT THAT WAS TO BE EXPECTED

By a rare chance Don Venancio Liencres was at home when Mrs. Colindres came to look for him. He already had his hat on to go to the Círculo de Recreo where friends of his would be waiting to hear his opinion on various matters. However, he received her with no visible sign of displeasure.

When they were alone, Andrea started to cry as if in the secret of the confessional. She told Don Venancio all that was happening to her son. She feared by the answers he had given to his father that he was involved in the idea of marriage to that High Street woman. And this couldn't be, for it would be his ruination, the shame of the whole family and the greatest scandal of the city. Her husband was already taking the necessary steps to find out more about the magnitude of the danger, but that was not enough. It was necessary for Don Venancio himself, who had so many qualifications to deserve the respect of this foolish young man, to talk to him in a heart-to-heart way, to admonish him, to demand respect from him, and if necessary to invoke the love of God . . . and the saints. And then there were more tears and more sobs. Don Venancio did not get over his surprise except to consider how much his word must be worth when the captain's wife continued coming to him in every serious conflict of her life. It goes without saying that he calmed her with his talk, promising her that everything would be arranged as well as possible. Mrs. Colindres reached home before her husband did, and Don Venancio Liencres went to the club, satisfied that he had a great problem to solve.

When he came back for dinner, surrounded by his family, his wife could not resist a single minute more the curiosity of knowing why Mrs. Colindres had come to their house at that time the way she did. Nor could he control the desire to clear up everything in that solemn moment, with the saintly purpose of showing what happens to thoughtless young men like Andrés without men of mature judgment and genuine authority to bring them back to the straight and narrow path of duty.

And it so happened that just when he was telling the most serious part of the adventure on High Street, Luisa dropped her fork on her plate and said that she didn't want to eat any more. The story continued with comments by the narrator himself, gestures and monosyllables of disgust on the part of his wife and excitement on the part of Tolín. Luisa's lack of appetite continued. A change of look on her face showed a violent nervous agitation. She broke two plates with one blow of her fist. Then she withdrew to her room. Before she left, she stated that if such improper stories were told at the table, everybody's nerves would be upset and they would all lose any desire to eat.

Her venerable mother agreed that it was not a good thing

Another Result That Was to Be Expected

to talk about such sickening matters in front of such important ladies. Then she ordered a cup of something for Luisa to calm her nerves.

In her room, after taking a couple of sips of the concoction, she told her mother that she now felt all right, and that the only thing she longed for was rest in bed.

Don Venancio was glad to hear this. As he orated quite a while to Tolín, who didn't get over being surprised at the episode, he considered the matter well discussed by that time. Don Venancio yawned. His wife put away the dessert that was left. Everyone said the usual good nights and each one went to his room.

Tolín was taking off his dressing gown after having feasted his eyes by looking at the pictures on the wall, when he heard a slight knock on his door and heard his sister say in a gentle voice:

"May I come in?"

Tolín hastened to open the door and Luisa came in on tiptoes with an unlighted candle in one hand and the index finger of the other over her lips. She was very pale, with rings under her eyes. Her hands and voice were trembling considerably. She closed the door carefully and said to her brother, who was looking at her in astonishment, pointing to a chair near the table on which was a folder stuffed with drawings and water colors:

"Sit down there."

"But what's the matter, woman?" asked the bewildered Tolín, putting his dressing gown on again.

"You'll find out," she replied in a whisper. "But don't raise your voice and don't make any noise, because there's no need for anybody to know that I have made this visit to your room."

Tolín sat down and Luisa remained standing in front of him, refusing to take the chair that Tolín insistently offered her.

"I don't want to sit down," she said. "I talk better like this, like we are now. If we were face to face, maybe I wouldn't be as brave with you as I need to be now. In short, man, let's cut out these trifles . . . Oh, my goodness! . . . See here, Tolín, if

I have to go to bed with this ache that I feel here inside me, and if I do not succeed in unburdening myself with you a little here, I think that I'll have an attack of some sort tonight . . . that I'll die . . . just like I'm telling you . . . just like that . . . Tolín!"

More and more consumed by the curiosity of knowing what was the matter with his sister, Tolín insisted again that she explain herself.

"I'm getting to that," she said with more desire than courage to say it. "You heard the story that father told at the table?"

"Sure, I heard it."

"You heard it?"

"Yes, I repeat that I did."

"I'm glad, Tolín. I'm glad that you heard it well. And what do you think of it?"

"Well, what a turn this conversation has taken," exclaimed Tolín, very provoked.

"Well, what should I be saying to you?" his sister asked frankly.

"Of course, your own ideas, by gosh."

"Well, you fool, that's where mine begin!"

Tolín shrugged his shoulders and turned his head for a moment in another direction.

"As always, Luisa, as always," he added a moment later, "I'm darned if I can make any sense of your ravings. Tell me what you want; we'll see how it comes out."

Luisa looked at her brother with a grimace which was a compliment to his wisdom and said:

"I want to know what you think of that indecent story."

"It seems rather bad to me, Luisa, rather bad. Just as indecent as you think it is. Do you want it any plainer than that?"

"That's what I wanted to know, Tolín, just that, precisely that."

"Then you have your answer."

"To think that a man who dresses like a gentleman, who is the son of good parents, who works in father's office, who is a good friend of ours, would mess up his wealth that way. He even ate in this house as a friend many times. A man like that, locked up in a house with a fish-selling hussy, had to leave there in shame amid the derision of those vulgar women and the drunks on the street! And furthermore when he is pressed a little, he tells his mother and father that he wants to marry that girl! Have you ever seen anything like that anywhere, Tolín? Have you even read the likes in any book, regardless of how shameless or filthy it was? Come, man, tell me frankly."

"No, Luisa, no . . . I have never seen anything like it. So what?"

"It should not go on this way!"

"You heard that father is going to take a hand in it."

"It is not enough for father to do that. You have to take a hand too."

"Me?"

"Yes, you, and the first thing tomorrow, Tolín."

"But what the devil does it matter to me?"

"What does it matter to you? Aren't you his friend; his childhood friend, Tolín, which is about as much a friend as anyone can be? Doesn't he work in the same office with you? Aren't the two of you destined to be partners and owners of this business one of these days?"

"I have heard you say the same thing at least twenty times about some of Andrés' trifling faults."

"But this is a big fault, a very big one. I'm telling you again, because this time it is really serious."

"Let it go, then. The matter is in capable hands when father says that he will see about it."

"But I want you to take it in your hands."

"And how do you know whether I'll be able to handle it or not?"

"What you don't know, you learn, and when the situation demands it . . . and right now it does, urgently."

"But, you devilish chatterbox . . . why, anybody listening to you and seeing you so demanding and so nervous about a matter which after all, doesn't matter one whit to you . . . would think . . . are you an attorney to defend Andrés, or what?"

"It's nobody's business what I am, Tolín. But I don't want a dirty trick like that to happen, and it won't happen, you understand?"

"And if it should happen? So what?"

"Holy heavens! You shouldn't say that even as a joke, Tolín."

At this point Luisa's pale lips trembled, and Tolín looked at her with an expression never before seen on his face.

"Do you know, Luisa," he said without ceasing to look at her, "that what I am hearing from you, and recalling what else you have said in the same vein, is making me have some funny ideas?"

"Ideas about what, Tolín?" asked Luisa, ready not only to hear everything that her brother might tell her about his notions, but also to make him talk as soon as possible. "Come, tell me frankly."

"Ideas," continued Tolín, "that something more than friendship is making you so interested in behalf of Andrés."

"Well, it took you a long time to figure that one out, you innocent thing," she exclaimed with such anxiety that she seemed to be unburdening herself of a great weight.

"And you are confessing it so brazenly, Luisa!" said Tolín, greatly surprised.

"And why shouldn't I confess it, Tolín? Whom do I offend by that? Is there anything wrong about Andrés that doesn't deserve these bad moments I am enduring for him? Isn't he a pearl? Isn't he as good as gold? Isn't he strong and brave? Doesn't he have as good a position as any of these other whippersnappers that come around trying to court me, to your great delight? Haven't we known him and liked him all our lives? And if all that is true, why shouldn't I . . . why shouldn't I love him, yes, sir, love him as I have for so many years?"

"But, Luisa, is it possible that you, who treat all men so coldly, and are so hardhearted with all who even look at you

... that you are capable of loving anyone with such a passion?"

"Underneath snow-capped mountains there are volcanos, Tolín. I don't know who said that, but it was somebody like me. But whoever it was, he stated a great truth as shown by what is happening to me now."

"When you caught fire, you certainly did a fine job of it!"

"Why do you say that, Tolín?"

"It is quite evident, Luisa. You caught fire for someone who hadn't even noticed you."

"Well, he will now."

"Now?"

"Yes, now . . . because it didn't matter up to now."

"Luisa, are you in your right mind? You are in love with a man who has been amusing himself sinfully with a crude fish seller?"

"There has been no such amusement, if everything they say is the truth."

"And he even wants to marry her! You yourself were afraid of that. . . ."

"Well, I told you, just to hear what you would say. But even if that is the truth, and also even if he has amused himself sinfully, for that very reason it is necessary to open his eyes for him, so that he can see what he never dared to look at before, because he is humble . . . timid."

"Would you be capable of trying that, Luisa . . . of losing your head completely?"

"I do not know, Tolín, what I would be capable of doing in the present situation. But in any case, I am not the one to take that step. It's you!"

"Me? I am going to offer my own sister?"

"Offer nothing! What the deuce, man! Calling things that way makes no decency possible anywhere. But if you go to him, with the confidence he has in you, and you begin to condemn what he has done, and is thinking of doing . . . and you talk to him about his true worth . . . and about the consideration which he owes his family and his friends . . . about what a good idea it would be for him to have a sweetheart from one of the best families in town . . . and little by little, quite gradually, he starts to understand what you mean . . . and without telling him what I think, you make him understand that he could think the same . . . or anything else that comes to your mind."

"Luisa! What the devil! But even if you esteem yourself so poorly . . . what do you take me for?"

"You cruel wretch! That's about what I expected from you! But what did you take me for when you wheedled me into singing these same tunes to my friend Angustias on your behalf? Then the rôle you were giving me was most honorable! A sister looking out for the welfare of her brother; that breaks my heart with pure delight. 'Do it furtively and diplomatically, so she knows what good judgment I have, of how efficient I am in the office . . . of how good-hearted I am . . . how crazy I am about a certain young lady . . . that I spend my evenings sighing.'"

"Luisa, you parrot!" said Tolín, turning around in his seat as if someone had jabbed him with a pin.

But Luisa didn't pay the slightest attention to the interruption. She seemed to enjoy the anxiety of her brother, and continued mimicking him as follows:

"'But since I am so bashful by nature, I would rather die of grief than to say the slightest thing to her.' And I hope you rot!"

"Luisa!"

"And certainly, you big wretch, right away I carried out your wishes successfully, and prepared the ground for you . . . and then it wasn't very hard for you to get as far along as you are now. Very little is lacking for you to get what you want, because even her harsh old father is sweet with you. And now it turns out that I was playing a very ugly rôle, and . . . and that . . ."

"For the love of God, Luisa, let me speak or I'll kick you out into the corridor . . . and I'll holler for everybody to hear us."

"That would be the last straw, you big selfish brute! Ungrateful brother! And what can you say to what I have been telling you?"

"That even though all of it were true . . ."

"And even truer than a lot more that I haven't wanted to tell you!"

"That even though all that and all that you haven't said were true, the cases are very different."

"Different! Where? How?"

"Because you are a girl."

"Exactly. And you are every inch a gentleman. And just because women are obliged to keep up appearances by remaining quiet about what they feel toward a man . . . and can't even make him understand by a sly glance . . . it is very shameful for you to help your own sister get out of the pinch she is in by mentioning a few words about it to a man who is furthermore one of your most intimate friends. Bah! But a gentleman has an obligation, because he is a man, to be brave and dashing and to make all calculations by himself and then ask a young lady to arrange a matter like this for him . . . then, there is nothing unusual about it. It is a splendid deed, and even an act of mercy . . . what do you think of such a scrupulous character? Gosh! I don't know what I would tell you now, if I could shout all I wanted to!"

"All right, all right. Let's consider it all shouted. Now leave me in peace."

"That's it, boy, that's it. That's the way to get out of the whole thing. And that's why we have brothers, and that's why we are crazy about them . . . and . . . holy heavens!"

Here, Luisa started to cry as if her heart would break. Tolín tried to console her as best as he could. But that crying was more powerful than her words, and had more effect on Tolín than all her vague remarks. Suddenly Luisa stopped crying and said resolutely to her brother:

"Understand me then, that if you don't do what I ask, I am going to do it myself . . . I . . . myself! I shall even be capable

of confessing it to his father and mother . . . and to the priest
. . . if you put the pressure on me. And even Don Silverio
Trigueras' daughter will know how you repay a foolish sister
for what she did for you."

Tolín was badly worried. He believed his sister capable of
carrying out what she threatened, but at the same time he was
frightened by the ticklish undertaking she had entrusted to him.
Her desires were not bad, but his lack of resolve made him
fearful. He talked to her again in this way, begging her to let
him find the way and the occasion to his liking, because everything would be worked out in time.

"No, no," she insisted, "there is not a moment to lose. Tomorrow morning you are going to take the first step. . . ."

"But listen to reason. . . ."

"Do it this way: As soon as he comes to the office, you call
him to one side and, when the two of you are alone, you begin
to talk to him, and then . . . gosh! If it were me, I could soon
tell him certain things that ought to be said. . . ."

"And although everything comes out the way you want it,
you devilish crackpot, do you know what mother will think
about it?"

"That's my business, Tolín. As if she could disapprove it.
It is such a wonderful match for me! Don't you worry about that
part of it. You take care of the other."

"All right, then," said the weary young man, perhaps to be
freed from such a tenacious attack. "I'll do everything I can
to please you."

"It has to be done," insisted Luisa without yielding a point.
"Not only what is possible, but everything that is necessary. And
if that is done or left undone, I'll know it by tomorrow night
when Andrés comes here . . . because you will in some discreet
way have him come tomorrow night without fail . . . you
understand that well? Without fail!"

There was no escape for Tolín, because he knew very well
that whenever his sister got an idea in her head, her character
was such that any outburst was possible. He understood that

the best way to avoid more violent outbursts was to carry out zealously her wild demands. Consequently he promised her to carry them out.

When she was convinced that Tolín's promise was not just a vain recourse to get out of the present jam, her abuses changed into lullabies. She lighted her candle, gave him a fervent good night, opened the door carefully and went out on tiptoe. Then, sliding along rather than walking, she reached her room and locked herself in. If she were not free of worries, at least she had a calmer mind after unburdening her rage. On the other hand, Tolín, who had got up from the table with many thoughts going through his head, couldn't get to sleep till nearly dawn. That devilish girl!

28 ✎ THE MOST SERIOUS CONSEQUENCES OF ALL

On Front Street there still resounded the shouts of *apuyaaaa* with which the call boys were arousing the sailors by yelling in front of the houses where they lived. Even the most diligent of them had not yet arrived at the Zanguina Bar to take his light breakfast of alcohol or a big cup of ground cocoa-bean husks when Andrés, aching in his bones and rather dejected in spirit, was already leaving. He crossed the street in front and went to the docks by using the Long Ramp. It was scarcely five o'clock. There was no other light than the tenuous clearness of the horizon, forerunner of the dawn. There was no other noise than that made by his own footsteps, or that of the occasional shouting of some cabin boy, or that of the oars which other cabin boys were moving on top of benches on board. The dark silhouette of the bored night watchman who was going to his home, his unpleasant work finished, or the obscure profile of a discouraged day laborer, drawn from his miserable bed by the hard necessity of earning a meager breakfast, were the only objects seen on the whole extent of the dock.

For Andrés' purposes that early dawn offered a better aspect than the night before. The atmosphere was less rarefied, one could breathe cool air, and in the cloudy sky, over the line of the horizon where the sun would appear, certain reddish tints were noticed. This detail, by itself, had very little importance.

Of this same opinion was Reñales, in whose boat Andrés was already waiting very impatiently, because in each form that he could see on the dock he thought he was seeing an emissary who was coming from his home to look for him. It should be noted, although it may not be necessary, that his short sleep on the bench in the bar was an endless nightmare in which he saw, with all the details of reality, the anguish of his mother, who was calling for him and waiting for him without a moment's peace; the restlessness, the misgivings and even the anger of his father, who was walking from street to street, from door to door looking for him in vain; and finally the conjectures, the consolations, the bitter reproaches . . . and even the tears of both his mother and father. This picture which he dreamed did not disappear from his imagination after waking up. His spirit was tormenting him and was sapping strength from his body; but his plan was made; it was suitable and had to be carried out at all cost.

Finally, the sound of harsh voices and heavy steps was heard on the dock. A crowd of fishermen appeared carrying their tackle, their food, their waterproof slickers and many of them with a good share of the equipment of the boat. Andrés was very pleased to see that Reñales' boat was rigged and had a full crew.

They mounted their oars, the captain took his, and stood in the stern to steer; the longboat started away; it received the first shove from its fourteen oarsmen; it started toward the open ocean and its slender keel began to cut the wide, quiet surface of the bay. But regardless of how swiftly it went, others were ahead of it, some from the Lower Town and some from the Upper Town, and when it was opposite the San Martín Hill it passed Mocejón's boat in which Andrés saw Cleto, whose sad glance, given only as a greeting, stirred in his mind the unstifled memories of the event of the day before, the cause of that absurd adventure of his.

The light of dawn was beginning to sketch the profiles of all the landmarks of what had previously been, on the starboard, a confused blotch, a black prolonged mass, from Quintres Point to the Cabarga Hill. One could appreciate the reflection of the coast of San Martín in the glassy surface of the waters through which the slender craft moved swiftly. In the meadows and fields nearby there was appearing again the orderly movement of country life, the most distinct of this world's struggles. To the right, the red of the dawn was reflected on the shining sands of Craggy Hill Beach. The green top of Craggy Hill seemed to be held high by these sands, while the sea, its treacherous accomplice, kissed its feet with gentle, caressing waves. These two seemed like tigers gamboling while waiting for a victim for their insatiable voracity.

I do not know whether Andrés, seated in the stern with the owner, although he was looking silently in every direction, saw and appreciated in this same way all the details of the panorama that was unfolding before him. But there is no doubt about it that he did not look at these sights without feeling the bitter wounds in his heart and the increasing battle of his thoughts.

For that reason he wished to get away as soon as possible from those well-known shores and from those places which reminded him of so many happy hours without any bitterness in his soul or pangs in his conscience; and therefore he saw with great joy that they were unfurling the sails in order to take advantage of an off-shore breeze which was beginning to blow and thus give an added impulse to the speed of the boat.

He sat with his head between his hands and his eyes closed,

his ear listening to the dull rumble of the ship's wake. They soon reached Harbor Point and entered the overcast narrows formed by Mouro Island and the coast of this side. Without changing his position, Andrés gave thanks to God from the bottom of his heart when Reñales, taking off his hat, ordered a prayer with a very fervent plea, because right there was beginning the tremendous region full of black mysteries, among which there is no safe moment and only when the rocking and pitching of the boat made him understand that they were out beyond the sand bar did he stand up straight, open his eyes and dare to look, not toward the land where the roots of his troubles were, but toward the limitless horizon, to this immense watery waste on whose restless surface glistened the first rays of the sun, which was rising from the depths in an extensive reddish halo. There, in that direction, he was going to the imposing solitude and silence of the great marvels of God and to the absolute oblivion of the miserable quarrels ashore, and he wanted to get there quickly and even wished that the breeze which was filling the sails would suddenly change into an uncontrolled hurricane.

But the boat, disdaining the fiery young man, went on its way peacefully, going as fast as necessary to arrive on time at the place where its owner was steering it. Suddenly he attracted Andrés' attention to say to him:

"Look; what a school of sardines!"

And he pointed toward an extensive dark blotch over which wheeled a cloud of gulls. By these signs the school was recognized. Later he added:

"Good business today for the boats that come out for sardines. But the next time I come out for sardines, the hake will probably jump into my boat. That's just a man's luck."

And the longboat continued advancing into the sea, while the greater part of its leisurely crew members were sleeping on the floor boards. When Andrés decided to look toward the coast, he could not recognize a single landmark because his inexperienced eyes could see nothing more than a narrow brownish strip over which was raised a whitish grotesque figure, which was the Cabo Mayor Lighthouse, according to what the skipper told him.

And still the longboat kept going farther away toward the northwest without the slightest surprise on the part of Andrés, who, although he had never yet been out to sea this far, knew full well that for hake fishing the boats usually go fifteen or eighteen miles from port, and when it is tuna they are after, even twelve to fourteen leagues, and that for such trips they are equipped with compasses to find their way back.

As the slender, fragile longboat advanced on its course, Andrés was gradually scattering the misty haze from his imagination and was becoming more talkative. Few were the words that he had exchanged with the skipper since their leaving the Long Ramp dock; but as soon as he was so far from land, he didn't keep quiet a moment. He asked questions not only about the things that he wanted to know, but also about things that he had once known and had forgotten; about places, tackle, about other years and about the profits and the risk involved. In addition, he found out how many and which of the crew members had been called by the military draft. There were three of these, one of them his friend Cole, who was one of the ones sleeping idly now. He lamented the luck of those sailors, and discussed extensively whether this burden which weighed over the group was more or less just, and whether one could or could not impose other conditions less severe, and even pointed out a few as examples.

And with Andrés talking, talking about everything imaginable, the owner ordered sails lowered and the longboat stopped.

While the sailing tackle and rigging were being arranged, the fishing gear was made ready and the spindles were tied to the gunwales. Andrés looked around him and fixed his attention for a long time on what was left behind. All that extensive space was sprinkled with little black points, which appeared and disappeared momentarily on the crests or troughs of the waves. Those nearest to the coast were the smaller boats that never got more than three or four miles from shore.

"Those other boats," Reñales was saying to him in response to one of his questions, and tracing in the air at the same time a wide arc with his arm, "are after sea bream. These first ones over there are at Mieley, those farther on at Betun, and the closest ones at Laurel. You know that these are the best sand banks or places for fishing for sea bream."

One of the hake boats, almost as far out as Reñales' boat, was the least distant from the coast. Andrés' eyes could hardly make it out; but Reñales' eyes, and those of all the other crew members, could have seen a gull fly on Cabo Menor.

On seeing the lines go over both sides of the boat, with the fine wire hooks well baited, Andrés sat with his elbows resting on the starboard gunwale with his eyes fixed on the nearest line, which one fisherman was holding in his hand after having put it on the smooth, rounded surface of the spindle, in order that the line would not rub against the rough gunwale when it was pulled in with a hooked fish. After quite a while, without the slightest pull being noticed on any of the lines, suddenly Cole shouted from the bow: "Praise be to God!"

That was the sign of the first bite. Immediately, Cole hauled in his line, quickly bringing in half a fathom with each haul, but not without real physical effort. He pulled into the boat a hake, which seemed like an unusually large shark to Andrés, who had never seen one caught before. The impressionable boy applauded with enthusiasm. Moments later he saw another one landed and then another and right away a couple more, and he became so ardent about the sight that he asked to have a line to try his luck with it. And he had good luck because he felt a fish biting on his hook in about half a minute. But landing it was something different! He would have sworn that colossal whales were pulling on his line from the bottom of the ocean, and that they wished to sink him and the launch and all that were in it.

The Most Serious Consequence of All

"It's getting away from me—and it's taking me along," shouted the deluded fellow, pulling and pulling on the line.

Seeing him in such a fix, the others began to laugh: a sailor came to him and placing the tackle as it should be, showed him in a practical way that, knowing how to haul in, one could haul in a young whale, or at least a medium-sized hake like that one.

"Well, now we'll see," said Andrés, nervous with emotion as he threw out his line again. He did not remember the unfortunate adventures which had brought him on this fishing trip. Doubtless he was well endowed by nature with exceptional aptitudes for that trade and everything related to it. After he had tossed out his line the second time, none of his companions in the launch surpassed him in ability to haul in a hake quickly.

The worst of it was that soon the fish got the idea of not taking the bait offered them in the tranquil depths or they went some other place to maraud something more to their liking, and the remaining hours of the morning were lost in useless attempts and exploring.

In view of that, they talked about going out farther, or as the fishermen say in their lingo, "Levy another tax."

"Things ain't too good today," said Reñales, looking around the horizon. "Let's eat now in peace and the grace of God."

Then Andrés realized that when he left the Zanguina Bar he had not remembered to provide himself with even a crust of bread. Happily he was not very hungry, and with the few things that the fishermen gave him from their baskets and a good drink of water from the keg which was on board, he took care of the needs of his stomach.

The breeze, in the meantime, was gradually lessening. On the horizon toward the north there extended a stubborn black cloud, which broke up into large, irregular strips of bright blue in the southeast, against a bright, orange-colored background. Over the Peaks of Europe enormous banks of clouds were piling up, and the sun, at its zenith, warmed somewhat more than usual whenever it broke through the clouds. The lookouts on the boats farthest out to sea had given the precaution signal by an oar straight up in front of them, but no flag was waving on any of them, indicating the signal to pick up and go home.

Reñales was paying as much attention to the clouds and the signals from other boats as he was to the morsels that he put in his mouth from time to time with his right hand. His companions, although they had not lost sight of them, seemed not to give them as much importance as he did.

Andrés asked him what he thought of it. He answered: "I don't like it much when I am far from shore." Then suddenly pointing toward Cabo Mayor he said as he got to his feet: "Look, fellows, what Falagan is telling us."

Then Andrés, looking fixedly at what the fishermen close to him pointed out, saw three puffs of smoke that were rising over the cape. It was a sign that the south wind was getting stronger in the bay. Two puffs of smoke would have meant that the sea there was becoming quite rough.

A strong south wind is bad for sailboats to take, but it is more terrible than that because of what it may bring along unexpectedly: the northwest wind, that is, a sudden shift of the wind in that direction.

Reñales tried to get away from risks of that kind by turning back to the harbor at once. Looking toward the port he could see that smaller boats were already going in and that the sea bream fishing boats were trying to do the same. Without losing a moment he ordered the sails hauled up and the men to row, because there wasn't much favorable wind. All the boats in the area imitated his example.

Andrés was not apprehensive in critical moments like this, and because he wasn't, he wondered not a little on realizing that he was now as glad to be approaching shore as he had been to get away from it earlier, and he noticed, too, that no longer did those soul torments that had driven him from his home and made him spend a devilish night in one corner of the Zanguina Bar seem as large, as terrible, as unsurmountable as previously. However, in his reflections, he thought that he could well have been a little less stubborn with his father, and with that alone he could have saved himself the bad night's sleep in the Zanguina Bar and all that followed, including this present adventure in which he found himself, an adventure which although it had delighted him greatly, left him with the bitterness of the motive. Finally, he was quite concerned about the relatively slow speed of the boat. Observing all this, wondering at it and not taking his gaze from the gloomy face of Reñales except to watch the none-too-happy faces of his companions, or toward the rocks on the coast, now more and more visible, he did not get the idea that all that behavior was the result of an unconscious desire to save their own hides, now threatened by a great danger. This was seen clearly in the suspicious attitude of those men who were so accustomed to the perils of the sea.

Thus more than an hour passed without hearing any other noises in the boat than the creaking of the oar straps, the rhythmic falling of the oars into the water and the heavy breathing of the men who, with their toil, were helping the half-filled sails. At times the wind was stronger and then the rowing men could rest a little. No change of any importance was noticed in the cloud formations. Off the prow and astern, boats could be seen taking the same course as Reñales' craft.

Everything then was going as well as possible and thus continued for another half hour. Andrés, without any help from anyone, could make out some landmarks on the coast line.

Suddenly his ears perceived a frightful distant noise, as if gigantic artillery convoys were rolling on hollow roads. He felt on his face the impression of a cold, wet blast, and observed that the sun was growing dark and that over the ocean big greenish-black spots were approaching from the northwest. Just then Reñales shouted: "Lower all sails!" and Andrés, frozen with fright, saw those very brave men drop their oars and rush, pale and speedily, to carry out the orders of the skipper. One single instant of delay in this maneuver would have caused the dreaded disaster, for scarcely had the mainsail been lowered when a furious gust of wind, full of rain, broke against the rigging and, with its push, enveloped the boat in roaring whirlwinds. A very dense mist covered the horizon, and one could guess, rather than see, where the coast line was by the crash of the heavy waves that beat against it, and the boiling of the foam which attacked it with all its fury.

All that his eyes could take in around him then was a frightful series of waves which followed each other in a confusing race, and whipped each other with their white crests shaken by the wind. To run before such unbridled fury without being assaulted by it was the only means of saving oneself or even trying to save oneself. But the attempt was not easy, because only the sail could give the necessary impulse, and the boat could scarcely resist, without foundering, even the impulse of the very small sail that it carried in the center.

Andrés knew that very well, and observing how the mast creaked on its base, and swayed like a willow rod, and the way the sail was crackling, the way the boat was diving into the waves headfirst, and then leaning over dangerously on one side and the sea hammering it on all sides, he didn't even ask why the captain had ordered the dogvane raised, or why they were preparing in the little cabin on the bow the small bit of canvas called "extreme unction."

Even more terrifying than what this maneuver meant in such an agonizing moment was the horrible name of that narrow piece of cloth unfurled at half mast from a rather short pole. This name seemed to freeze the blood in Andrés' heart. Extreme unction! That is to say, between life and death.

Fortunately, the boat took the storm better than the weather sock, and with its help, the boat flew along between the dashing waves. But these got larger as the hurricane whipped them up, and the danger that they would break over the weak craft was growing with each passing moment. In order to avoid it, all human means were exhausted. The fish livers which were on deck were thrown over the stern. Something was gained, but very little, with these last resources . . . move, move on ahead . . . this alone, or submit to death!

The boat continued climbing onto the foamy crests, falling

into the troughs, straightening out again courageously only to fall again into a deeper chasm, but always going ahead, and trying in its flight not to expose its side to the raging seas.

From time to time the fishermen shouted fervently: "Virgin of the sea, forward! Forward, Virgin of the sea!"

To Andrés the minutes passed in that frightful peril seemed like centuries. The experience was new to him. He began to be disturbed and bewildered by all that deafening clamor, by the whiteness and mobility of the mass of water which dazzled him, by the fury of the wind which whipped his face with handfuls of heavy rain, by the dizzy lurchings of the boat and by the sight of a possible grave in the folds of that limitless watery mass. His clothing was soaked by the rain and by the salty spray which came down on him when waves splashed against the boat's side; his dripping hair waved in the air, and he was beginning to shiver from the cold. He did not open his lips to ask a single question. Why do anything so useless? Weren't the roars of the hurricane filling everything and replying thus to all that a miserable human voice could ask?

Thus he spent a long while watching mechanically how his companions, at times with the anguish of despair, and other times with the serenity of dauntless hearts, bailed out with anything available the water that some dashing waves splashed into the boat, or how they moved the rigging at a signal from the captain during a moment's respite from bailing.

The very excess of horror, stopping the courage of Andrés, was gradually predisposing his reasoning to the regularized activity and the coordination of his ideas, although in an orbit somewhat strange to the conditions of a spirit like his. For example, he didn't think about the probabilities which he had of being saved. For him, death was a nondebatable, certain thing. But he did worry a great deal about the kind of death that awaited him, and he analyzed the fatal event moment by moment and detail by detail. From this minute analysis he deduced that his own body, thrown suddenly into that roaring hell, would represent much less than a speck of dust which falls into the gullet of a tiger in proportion to the air that he draws in during a yawn. But was it possible to imagine a more frightful helplessness or loneliness, a mournfulness surrounding a man about to die? At once there passed through his memory, in a rather sad parade, all the martyrs he could remember from the infinite legion of heroes, among whom surely belonged the unfortunate men who surrounded him, men destined perhaps to disappear at any time into that horrible cemetery. And he saw them, one by one, struggling for brief moments with the strength of desperation against the immense power of unchained elements, sinking into the abyss, reappearing with fear in their eyes and death in their hearts, and again being submerged, not to appear again except as shapeless debris of a disaster, floating between the folds of the waves, dragged along at the whim of the storm.

And seeing them all thus in his mind's eye, he also saw the drowned Mullet, and on seeing Mullet he remembered his daughter, and by remembering his daughter, by a logical association of ideas, he began to think about everything that had happened to him and what was the reason for being in such a fix. Then, by the light which human eyes can see only on the brink of death, he judged all those happenings in their real importance. And he felt ashamed of his deviltries, of his stupidity, of his ingratitudes, of his last craziness, the cause no doubt of the despair of his parents. Then his mortal being reclaimed again its rights; and he loved life, and again he was frightened by the dangers he was in at that time; and he feared that God might have planned for him to die in that way as punishment for his sin. He was trembling with horror, and each creak of the mournful rigging, each shudder of the boat, each dashing wave that overtook it, seemed to Andrés the sign of disaster. As the limit of anguish, he suddenly saw an oar floating near the side of the boat in the foam, and then two more. The saddened fishermen also saw them. And they saw more in just a few moments. They saw a black mass bobbing up and down among the waves. It was a lost boat. But whose? And its men? Andrés

The Most Serious Consequence of All

read these questions on the livid faces of his companions. He noticed that all of them got on their knees and, looking to the heavens, made a promise to go the next day barefoot, carrying their oars and sails, to hear a mass dedicated to the Holy Virgin if God would work the miracle of saving their lives from that terrible danger. Andrés raised to heaven the same promise from the bottom of his Christian heart.

As a result of this new moral effect, another thought assailed him, a thought which filled his generous soul with bitterness. If he got out of this alive, it was within his power not to expose himself again to such dangers, but the unfortunate fellows who were with him, even though they were saved with him this time, wouldn't they feel their joy at being saved somewhat embittered by the fears of dying some other time in another upheaval of the sea as terrible and as sudden as this one?

Unhappy occupation that held such dangers! And he noticed all the fishermen in the boat one by one. There were all kinds of men there from a beardless youth to a gray-haired old man, and they all seemed more resigned than he; and nevertheless each one of those lives was more necessary to the world than his own. This consideration, wounding his conceitedness, infused some warmth in his dejected spirits.

The tempest continued unchecked, and the now half-submerged boat was moving ahead of it madly. On one side, very near the gunwales, was an object which was rocking between two waves, with heavy mats of bristly hair floating on the water.

"Muergo!" shouted Reñales, desiring at the same time to grasp the cadaver with his hand. Again Andrés felt that the coldness of death was filling his heart, that life was going to fail him and only something that might happen there in that same instant could revive his crushed courage.

And so it happened that Reñales, trying to make his movements coincide with a heavy lurch of the boat, lost his balance and fell on his right side, striking his head against the gunwale. The boat, now with no rudder, lay momentarily stationary on the ocean; then the mast snapped, broken into splinters and the wind carried away the dogvane. Then Andrés, understanding the seriousness of the new danger, shouted, "To the oars!" to the terrified fishermen. At the same time he hurled himself at the rudder, abandoned by Reñales when he fell. Thus he was able to place the boat on a good course again, with an expertness and ability that was surely fortunate for all.

By this time they were passing in front of Cabo Menor, over whose small rocky heights the seas were crashing and then running down the other side in a roaring cascade. From there, or rather from Cabo Mayor to the mouth of the port and following along by the small Mouro Island as far as Quintres Point, the whole coast was just one strip of roaring foam which boiled and rose up and grasped hold of the slopes, only to fall down and try the assault again, shoved on by the inconceivable force of those mountains of water which were breaking furiously without any letup against the immovable barriers.

"Forward, Virgin of the Sea!" the oarsmen were repeating with a firm voice in rhythm with their toil.

Andrés was grasping the steering oar. He had his feet practically fastened to, not just standing on, the catwalk on the floor of the boat. Thus struggling and seeing his brave companions struggle with superhuman efforts against the death that was threatening them on all sides, he began to sense the sublimeness of so many horrors together, and gave thanks to God for such a frightening testimony of His greatness.

During all this time, Reñales did not move a hand or a foot. Cole had been bailing water ceaselessly with another man. At a signal from Andrés, who had his eye on everything, Cole suspended this very important work and went to raise the captain, who had been stunned by the blow and was bleeding freely from the wound on his head. Cole took as good care of him as he could under the trying circumstances. Reñales revived little by little and even tried to return to his post at the moment that the boat was going like lightning in front of Sardinero Beach. At this particular place, whoever was steering the boat needed nerve, intelligence and unusual strength.

Reñales realized that he did not possess all these qualifications just now, while Andrés possessed them abundantly.

"Forward, then, and may God's will be done," the captain said to him as he curled up on the catwalk floor, because his aching head could not endure the lashings of the storm.

Forward! That meant to make port, or in other words, gamble life itself in the last and most imposing chance by trying to enter the harbor which was closed by a wall of enormous waves. On reaching this narrow harbor entrance and being compressed there, a part of each wave assaulted and enveloped the uninhabited Mouro Island, and the crest of the wave hurled itself at the dark gullet of the harbor entrance. At the same time each wave seemed to expand and raise its colossal shoulders in order to fit into it better. At its passing the granite rock shuddered. But how could one flee from the harbor? Where else could one direct his course in search of refuge? Wasn't each instant that passed without the boat foundering on that horrible course that it was following a miracle?

The best part of the whole situation was that it would soon be decided. This conviction could be read clearly in the faces of the crew, with their eyes fixed on Andrés' face. Momentarily they were motionless, as if all of them had suddenly been petrified by the same thought. Reñales now was sitting up and said to Andrés: "You already know, Andrés, by lining up the prow between the two highest peaks, the sand bar at the harbor entrance is exactly halfway between them?"

"Surely," answered Andrés bitterly, without taking his eyes from the harbor entrance nor his hands from the oar with which he was steering. "But when you can't see either the Codío de Solares or the Rubayo Heights, as is the case right now, what do you do, Reñales?"

"Put yourself in God's hands and go in wherever you can," replied the owner after a brief pause during which his eyes devoured the horribly critical place which was less than a quarter of a mile away.

Up to this time everything that had been done to run before

the storm was to draw nearer to safety, but from now on the rapid advance could be as dangerous as stopping; because the boat now was between the hurricane which impelled it forward and the mouth of the harbor which it had to assault during an opportune moment when the seas were not breaking in it.

Andrés, who knew all this, seemed like a statue of stone with eyes of fire; the oarsmen moved like a machine that moved at a command from his glance. Reñales was a man who scarcely dared to breathe.

On San Martín Hill there was a multitude of people looking with fear at the terrible situation of the boat.

Fortunately for everybody in the boat, Andrés did not look up then. He was giving all his attention to the inspection of the horrible field in which the decisive battle was to be engaged.

Suddenly he shouted to his oarsmen: "Now! Row! Row! More!"

Seemingly getting miraculous strength from their long toil, they raised up rigidly in the air, holding onto the benches with their feet and hanging from the oars with their hands.

An enormous wave just then came rushing into the harbor entrance, swollen, shining, roaring, and on the crest of it the boat was riding with all the might of its oars.

The crest of the wave stretched from one side to the other of the harbor's mouth. More than the crest of a wave it seemed like the coil of a gigantic reptile which was unrolling from head to foot. That huge coil continued advancing inside the harbor entrance toward the Quebrantas Sand Bar on whose sands it would crash with a roar. It passed underneath the keel of the boat, which began to slide aft, like the curtain of a waterfall, into the bottom of the chasm which the fleeing wave had left behind. There the boat was running the risk of being becalmed, but Andrés was thinking about everything and asked his oarsmen for another heroic effort. They responded, and while they were rowing hard to overcome the ebb of the big wave, another bigger one was coming in without breaking at the harbor entrance. The boat was raised on the back of this giant wave and shoved along toward the port. The height this time was frightening and Andrés even felt dizzy because of it, but he did not become terrified nor did his body lose any of its self-assurance in that unusual position.

"More! More! Harder!" he shouted to the enfeebled oarsmen, because the decisive moment had arrived.

The oars creaked, the men panted and the boat kept on climbing, but making headway. When the stern reached the peak of that roaring mountain of a wave, and the frail craft was about to receive from it the last favorable shove, Andrés vigorously brought the prow of the boat directly into the wind and shouted with great emotion, putting into his words all the vigor that remained in his soul: "Dear Jesus, help us make port safely!" The wave passed too without breaking toward the Quebrantas, and the boat began to slide down the slope of a new chasm. But that chasm was the salvation of all because the boat had gotten around the point (on Magdalena Peninsula) and was now in safe harbor.

At that same time, when Andrés, full of emotion and anxiety, shoved his hair back and wiped away the water that was running down his face, a voice, whose tone could not be described, shouted from the top of the point, "Son! My son!"

Andrés trembled and raised his head. In front of a stupefied crowd he saw his father with his open arms extended, his hat in one hand and his hair blown about by the wind of the storm.

That supreme emotion put an end to the strength of his spirit. The chastized youth leaned over the stern and, hiding his face in his trembling hands, began to cry like a child, while the boat rocked back and forth among the bubbles of the backwash, and the tired oarsmen gave some necessary rest to their panting lungs.

At the same time, in the midst of the haze in front, there was a wretched abandoned patache with its deck awash and its sails torn and unraveled ropes snapping in the wind. With frightful tumbles and wild pitchings it made one last lurch and the rigging came tumbling down on the gunwales. The anchor chains snapped in desperate anguish, and a heavy wave broke against the exposed keel, hurling the mutilated hull into the middle of the fury of the dashing waves, whose foam in the same action, spat out the splinters of its shattered framework.

Those gloomy floating fragments were all that remained of the *Joven Antonito de Ribadeo.*

29   IN WHICH EVERYTHING COMES TO AN END

The very kind reader who has followed me thus far with Christian patience does not deserve to be tormented again by an account of the events of little importance at the point where we are with the principal theme—if there is any principal theme in this book.

Let us assume, therefore, that the following events take place: many hours pass after the unhappy ones described in the preceding chapter and bitter tears warm the cheeks of the afflicted. Other tears, somewhat sweeter, roll because of joyful embraces by people whose hearts feel no grief. The pious vows to God, made during moments of great danger are fulfilled and Andrés and the fervent sailors, barefooted, wearing clothes still wet from the storm, with oars and sails on their shoulders, go to church and come out from it with the respect and consideration of the people of the city. Many more days pass and the zest for new events deadens in the public voracity the concern for the past, regardless of how sad or sensational it may have been. The lessons learned are taken to heart by some in order to pardon, by others to correct their ways and Andrés regulates his life to the new course to which he was attracted by a sudden and hearty aversion to his previous levities and entertainments . . . as well as a certain interview with his friend

In Which Everything Comes to an End

Tolín, requested by the latter and held in the most secret and isolated part of the office of Don Venancio Liencres. As an indication of his intentions to carry out his plans, and how deep-rooted were his aversions to the old way, he burns his ships behind him; that is to say, he sells his *Zephyr* and fishing tackle and gives the money to Pa'e 'Polinar to give to old Mechelín, because Andrés is not allowed to set foot in Mechelín's house again. This deserving family rejoices in the belief that its prayers, and a votive candle lighted before the image of Saint Peter when it was learned that Andrés was at sea in the hurricane, had contributed powerfully to his salvation. Andrés calls Cleto and swears, with the same solemnity as he had done once before, but with greater confidence in his efforts to do so, all that the generous son of Mocejón needs to believe that his love is reciprocated, except for the shame of being the son of such a mother, which is no slight burden. Two more days pass and Cleto is dressed in the uniform of a sailor on the king's ships on the eve of being taken to the nearest naval base. Human justice has locked up in jail the two females of the fifth floor of the house on High Street, for the purpose of starting a lawsuit against them as defamers of character and scandalmongers.

And now, let's take a last look at the home of Mechelín on the ground floor of the house on High Street. Padre Apolinar is there, and while Sidora and Sotileza come and go sadly and silently, he is walking back and forth in the room talking with Mechelín, who is seated in a chair warming himself in the rays of the sun which come in through the window. He no longer cares to smoke his pipe, and his sad eyes are looking at everything without any curiosity whatever, because yesterday he was on the verge of death and had already confessed to the priest, who had administered the last rites of the Church. But today he feels a little better.

He counted on getting well enough to return to his fishing tasks. These are things of sickly old men, as well as children, who seem like the "four o'clock flower" which droops and then comes to life again quickly. Except that in sickly old men each time that sickness makes a swat with its paw, it takes away a good slice of the man in its claws. The doctor, sent by the Upper Town Council, gave encouragement to his hopes. But I believe that the doctor had another opinion about it.

The morning had been a hard one for the poor old man. As he could not leave the house, all the fishermen called by the draft, except Cleto, had been to see him to say good-by. Cole had come with Pachuca. That poor girl cried so much that she almost went to pieces. Everyone in the house tried to console her, but the more consolation they tried to give her, the more full of anguish were her cries. At the same time the street seemed a sea of tears, and each time that Sidora and Sotileza went out to the doorway to cry with those that were crying there, Mechelín heard these sounds and also felt the need to cry a little himself. In addition to the grief of all those who were crying, he had the fear of never seeing again those companions who were going away.

But in short, this had passed, and the people on the ground floor in High Street had talked a great deal about it. When we enter that house again to find out what is going on there, they are already talking about another matter about which Pa'e 'Polinar is saying:

"That should not surprise you, Mechelín. After what happened in this house, there could be no other conduct for a decent man. Just consider the circumstances, Mechelín, just consider the circumstances."

"Well, don't you see how I'm doin' that, Pa'e 'Polinar?" replied the sailor. "And because I do, I'm not surprised at nothin'. But it's one thing not to be surprised, and another matter the way you feel about a person. He's doin' well in not comin' back here for appearances' sake and for his own sake. But we were so used to seein' him here an' grew so fond of him. And I haven't been able even to shake his hand once since God rescued him alive from that storm in which so many unfortunates died. Of course I did shake his father's hand and would you

In Which Everything Comes to an End

believe it, Pa'e 'Polinar, you who know what kind of a man Captain Colindres is . . . well he was cryin' like a child! He is a good man. Ever since what happened here, he has been to see us many times . . . he is lookin' out for me . . . he is lookin' out for my family . . . he has consolation for everybody . . . he don't want me to lack nothin' . . . not even a chicken for the pot. Could any one ask for more? All that in addition to that money his son gave you to bring to me . . . it is there, in that chest, 'cause I don't know what to do with it, 'cause durin' the last few days, there ain't been no possibilities. The captain give me everythin' . . . a double blanket, and new undershirts; and his wife sent us some chocolate . . . well, they do not seem to tire, and I, from what I see, can't understand why God is givin' me such a pampered old age. Who am I to end up this way with so many benefits? But gettin' back to that matter, I can't help but confess that it is hard for me to get used to not never seein' Andrés around here. He's as good as gold. That's what I feel about him way inside of me and can't help it. And the two women in my family feel just about the same as I do. Real affection, man, real affection."

"All right, Mechelín, all right," replied Pa'e 'Polinar, walking in front of this affable sailor. "All this is the pure truth, and with it one does not violate any law of God, who wants grateful hearts and tongues with no venom. That's a foregone conclusion. But there is another matter, Mechelín, that can't be left as it is now. It's something that is of great importance to you and all those of your house . . . darn important . . . and it has to be settled today . . . right now . . . because before long it will be too late. And, see here, Mechelín, thinking about it and not relying to any great extent on my own strength, which can't always struggle against human stubbornness, I have already talked with Don Pedro Colindres and he promised to drop around this way to help me with what I want to do . . . which up to a certain point is a work of charity, and a big one, by thunder! The worst part of it is Don Pedro is late, and if the other man gets away before . . . you know it well, Mechelín . . . a young man may die but an old man can't live forever . . . and if anything should happen to you! And then to your wife right away! Eh? What do you think?"

"I have already taken that into consideration, Pa'e 'Polinar, and you know well what I think about it, but her decision is not as clear as it should be, and that's the bad part."

"Well, her decision must be cleared up, Mechelín, and without any delay, and in the way it ought to be, because now this house is free from fears. Now one can come in here in full daylight and not have to sneak in because that corrupt flesh from upstairs is in its rotting place. Certainly there are three years in between here in which that lucky fellow carries out his military obligations, and in that length of time those horrible women might get out of jail if they are not sent to the house of correction, as many believe will happen. But even if they don't go, or the punishment doesn't kill them, and they come back to their house here, and the chastisement doesn't do them any good, what difference does it make to us, by gosh? We have good protectors, and if need be you could move from the neighborhood or even change towns, if that is necessary. The plan will have to be carried out, Mechelín, and let the chips fall where they may. That fellow is a good boy and she is surely not going to be a nun . . . gee, there is no other road . . . Silda! Silda, come here, and you too, Sidora!"

And both of these women came without any delay from the kitchen.

In Sotileza could be seen traces of her recent sufferings. It was more a case of rings under the eyes than paleness. But with all that, her natural beauty stood out. Padre Apolinar urged her strongly to solve the matter in question right then and there, and explained what the reasons were that the solution be in agreement with the desires of her loving protectors.

"Do you have," the priest asked her, "any plan in your head that is opposed to this project?"

"No, sir," replied Silda with great serenity.

"Do you find in Cleto anything repugnant to you except the vile make-up of his whole family?"

"No, sir. Cleto, as far as he himself is concerned, is all that any poor girl like me could want. That's the truth. He is good, and decent . . . and I think even that he has a higher opinion of me than I deserve."

"All right, then, by gosh! What more do you want? What are you waiting for after what he has told you? At times, by gosh, it seems that you are persisting in trying to repay with sorrow all that these poor old people are doing to show their love for you."

"We'll never think that, daughter," shouted both of them almost at the same time. The priest was not daunted by this, and added at once:

"Well, I'll think that all by myself then . . . and so would anyone else who has his full senses."

Silda remained silent for a few moments, and then as if the observation of Padre Apolinar had grieved her or as if she were prepared to take a heroic resolution, she asked with a certain haughtiness, but with great firmness: "Do you believe that what they desire is really what suits everybody best?"

And all replied in one voice that they did. "Well, that's what it will be then," concluded Silda solemnly.

"But not that you should be hurt, daughter!"

"But not that it should be a Calvary for you, you sweet thing!"

To these emotional exclamations on the part of the two old people, Sotileza replied: "No burden is heavy when carried willingly."

Just then Don Pedro Colindres came into the house. Padre Apolinar told him what had just happened and the captain said:

"I am very glad. In fact I was just coming to help with any advice I could give, knowing that time is hastening on. My congratulations, young lady. And now that you won't believe that I am offering it as bait in order to have you make up your mind, I am offering to be best man at your wedding, and I want it understood that I will be responsible for Cleto's being the owner of his own boat the very next day after that. And if you don't like that occupation for him, he won't lack either a shop or the tools for any other trade that you like better. Do you know what that means coming from a man like me?"

"That's a real man! This is the finest kind of offer!" exclaimed Padre Apolinar, squirming three times inside of his clothes. "Don't you see, Silda? Don't you see, Mechelín? Don't you see, Sidora? Don't you see that God is in His heaven and has something for all who deserve it?"

But neither Silda nor Mechelín nor Sidora were in any mood to answer. Silda wasn't because she fell into a kind of stupor difficult to define, and the others because they began to cry. Then the captain added:

"All that isn't worth two cents, Padre Apolinar; but even though it were, they deserve it here; and you more than anyone else, girl . . . because I know what I am doing. So cheer up, you are still young and three years soon pass."

"Virgin of the Sea! Give me life only to see all that!" exclaimed Mechelín between sobs, almost at the same time that his wife said:

"Praised be the Lord Who gives His help on all occasions."

Just then Cleto came in. He was dressed in a white shirt with a wide white collar over his shoulders; on the back of his head he wore a blue cap with long ribbons hanging down and in his arm he was carrying a bundle, which was all his gear. Really he was handsome. He came in with a resolute air, and going straight to Sotileza without paying much attention to the others with her, spoke to her as follows:

"I got only a few minutes left, Sotileza. To take advantage of 'em I come to find out whether your answer is yes or no, 'cause I ain't leavin' Santander without no answer even if they have to drag me away . . . and look at me well 'fore answerin'. If you say yes, there'll be no work there in the navy that'll worry me. If the answer is no, then I'm goin' away never to return no more. And that's as sure as God's daylight."

In Which Everything Comes to an End

In Cleto's action there was a certain crude greatness that suited him very well. Sotileza answered him, giving with her sweet words a beautiful glance of consolation.

"I want to say yes to you, because you deserve it well, and even greater than my own feelings about it has been your insistence in wantin' it." Afterwards she put her hands around her white, well-formed neck, underneath her scarf, and removed a little chain, from which was hanging a small silver medallion of the Virgin, and added as she gave it to him: "Take this so that the road back will be easier for you. And whenever any evil thoughts keep you awake, just ask that Lady whether I'm the kind of a girl who fails to keep her promises."

Cleto rushed impetuously to the warm medal and covered it with kisses, made the sign of the cross with it, and then kissed it some more. Then he held it over his heart and finally hung it around his neck. In the meantime, big tears came to his eyes as he said hurriedly and convulsively:

"Blessed be the goodness of God Who has so much pity for me. This is more than I expected. Let any hardships come. I've got a helper now. Does anyone want to know what Cleto is capable of doin'? Well, then let him ask me to surrender my ideals or to abandon them . . . Mechelín . . . Sidora . . . Don Pedro . . . Pa'e 'Polinar . . . I have only one regret about leavin' . . . the way my dad is now! I left him stretched out on the mattress. I don't know whether he got that way from sadness or from drink, because for the last couple of days his stomach ain't had no bottom when he drinks rum. What is goin' to become of him in his loneliness? I ain't been home much, and now less than ever, but the law is the law, and it has no favorites. But at least for charity's sake, please don't let him die in want! I well know that my family ain't done nothin' to deserve no help, but he's my father, and he's old and he's alone. Once in a while, gosh, make him take somethin' warm to eat. Come on, forget the offense, for God's sake!"

Everybody tried to calm Cleto by promising him to look out for his father. Right away the good-bys started. When it was Mechelín's turn he asked Cleto to embrace him. While doing so, he said in Cleto's ear:

"I'll probably not see you again, Cleto. That's why I want to tell you now what I can't tell you later on. You're gettin' a wife that no man alive deserves. If you make her happy, even the king and queen in the royal palace will envy you, but if you kill her with grief, God'll never pardon you."

For his only reply, Cleto hugged the old man harder in his arms. Not being in any mood now for much ceremony, he let go of Mechelín and walked quickly out of the house. Padre Apolinar put on his hat and went out running after him.

"Wait, man!" he shouted to him. "I'm going down to the dock to say good-by to all of you fellows. That would be the last straw, by gosh, to have you embark without God's blessing from this sinful hand."

And while Don Pedro Colindres remained for a while in the house encouraging Mechelín to smoke a pipeful of tobacco and discussed in passing Mocejón's being alone, Pa'e 'Polinar overtook Cleto, who was now the last one of those called by the draft not on board the launch.

Public curiosity makes everything important. For that reason all the balconies on the last third of the street were full of spectators when Padre Apolinar and Cleto passed by there going toward the dock, which was also full of sailors and their families from all over the city as well as a lot of curious onlookers of all kinds.

If Padre Apolinar had been observant and had known what was going on, perhaps he would have given some malicious importance to the friendliness with which Luisa and Andrés were chatting on one of the balconies of the home of Don Venancio Liencres. They were not paying any attention to what was happening in the street nor to the facial expressions of Tolín and his mother, who were near them.

But by not noticing, this saintly man didn't even see Mrs. Pedro Colindres, gorgeously attired, standing on the sidewalk and looking askance at the balcony, her face bathed in satis-

In Which Everything Comes to an End

faction, perhaps because she saw that devilish boy so well entertained.

About what happened on the dock on the occasion of the departure of the sailors for service to their country, I shall say, to say something, so that the affair will not be without due honors, that it was as imposing as it was simple: it was just two launches crowded with men leaving the bay and the arms of men waving good-by.

And as there is nothing else to say about events of this book, let's leave it here, merciful and patient reader, because it is time for us to leave it; but not without declaring to you that, on giving rest to my tired hand, I feel in my heart the grief produced by a very profound misgiving that I have not fulfilled my duty in this large undertaking of singing, in the midst of other disbelieving and colorless generations, the noble virtues, the wretched life, the great frailties, the incorruptible faith and the epic labors of the brave, valiant, picturesque sailor of Santander.